Understanding
Macbeth

The Greenwood Press "Literature in Context" Series

Understanding *To Kill a Mockingbird:* A Student Casebook to Issues, Sources, and Historic Documents
Claudia Durst Johnson

Understanding *The Scarlet Letter:* A Student Casebook to Issues, Sources, and Historical Documents
Claudia Durst Johnson

Understanding *Adventures of Huckleberry Finn:* A Student Casebook to Issues, Sources, and Historical Documents
Claudia Durst Johnson

UNDERSTANDING
Macbeth

A STUDENT CASEBOOK TO ISSUES, SOURCES, AND HISTORICAL DOCUMENTS

Faith Nostbakken

The Greenwood Press
"Literature in Context" Series
Claudia Durst Johnson, Series Editor

GREENWOOD PRESS
Westport, Connecticut • London

Library of Congress Cataloging-in-Publication Data

Nostbakken, Faith, 1964–
    Understanding Macbeth : a student casebook to issues, sources, and historical documents / Faith Nostbakken.
        p.   cm.—(The Greenwood Press "Literature in context" series, ISSN 1074–598X)
    Includes bibliographical references (p.   ) and index.
    ISBN 0–313–29630–8 (alk. paper)
    1. Shakespeare, William, 1564–1616. Macbeth. 2. Macbeth, King of Scotland, 11th cent.—In literature. 3. Politics and literature—Sources. 4. Literature and history—Sources. 5. Tragedy.
    I. Shakespeare, William, 1564–1616. II. Title. III. Series.
PR2823.N63   1997
822.3'3—DC20   96–35013

British Library Cataloguing in Publication Data is available.

Library of Congress Catalog Card Number: 96–35013
ISBN: 0–313–29630–8
ISSN: 1074–598X

First published in 1997

Greenwood Press, 88 Post Road West, Westport, CT 06881
An imprint of Greenwood Publishing Group, Inc.

Printed in the United States of America

∞™

The paper used in this book complies with the Permanent Paper Standard issued by the National Information Standards Organization (Z39.48–1984).

10 9 8 7 6 5 4 3 2 1

For my father, whose many years of teaching *Macbeth*
—though never formally directed at me—
must have mysteriously seeped into my pores

Contents

Preface

Understanding Macbeth could not have evolved to its final present form without the good will and assistance of other people. I extend my heartfelt thanks to Linda Woodbridge for providing me the initial opportunity and inspiration to write this book. I gratefully acknowledge Rick Bowers for the enthusiasm and critical eye with which he responded to each chapter, bringing his share of gentle encouragement to the work-in-progress. I owe an immeasurable debt to Heather Holtslander, who generously proffered her time and skills to transcribe a large portion of the manuscript from my tape-recorded muttering when tendinitis crippled both my arms during virtually the entire duration of this project. Without her help and resourcefulness, someone else would likely have authored this book.

Others deserve recognition for their kind offerings, from research access across the globe and through the Internet, to patient ears and inspirational ideas. I thank especially Carol Everest, Maxine Hancock, Kim McLean-Fiander, and Arlette Zinck. To these friends and many more, I can say that they play a large part in my continued efforts to cope and achieve through debilitating injuries and prolonged illness.

I also acknowledge and thank my parents for unknowingly providing me—among countless other gifts—my earliest introduction to *Macbeth*. During the years my father taught high school English and my mother typed some of his assignments, copies would find an occasional brief resting place on the kitchen table. Shortly after learning to read, I remember studying a few questions from these assignments and formulating in my mind some vague notion that Shakespeare was the guy who wrote *Hamlet*, and Macbeth was the guy who wrote something else, though I couldn't quite figure out what. From such humble beginnings I had much to learn, and I hope now that students and teachers who use this book can share some part of my ongoing adventure discovering who this guy Macbeth really is, what the play is all about, and why, 400 years after Shakespeare wrote it, we continue to read it, talk about it, and watch others re-create it on stage.

Introduction

Macbeth is one of Shakespeare's most well-known tragedies. The frequency with which it is read in the classroom and performed on stage attests to its popularity and perhaps its accessibility. An unusually short play, it follows the simple plot of Macbeth's rise and fall through a series of murders beginning with that of Duncan, King of Scotland, and ending with Macbeth's. It is a drama charged with energy generated by the intensity of Macbeth's ambition and played out in conflicts at personal, political, and cosmic levels. The main plot follows a pattern typical of Shakespearean tragedy: A figure of great magnitude falls to destruction, but a promise of social order restores harmony in the last scene. *Macbeth* also deviates from convention, however, for the central character is somehow both hero and villain, a combination that unsettles the tragic tone and that continues to challenge readers, audiences, and performers who are drawn to the play as much for its ambiguity as for its energy and simplicity.

In spite of its enduring appeal in the twentieth century, *Macbeth* is also one of Shakespeare's most topical plays, including many direct and indirect references to contemporary issues in the early seventeenth century. In 1603 Scotland's King James VI succeeded Elizabeth I as England's new monarch. His ascent to the throne sparked renewed interest in the rights and duties of kingship, as

well as concerns about the union between Scotland and England
created by his dual kingship over both countries. James's reputation as an intellectual with theories about kingship and witchcraft
suggests an obvious influence on Shakespeare's decision to write
a tragedy in 1606 based on Scottish history and incorporating the
supernatural powers of witchcraft. The Gunpowder Plot of 1605,
a Catholic conspiracy that almost destroyed King James and all his
government members, fostered both relief and anxiety as English
subjects celebrated James's dramatic victory but feared another attack. The high-profile trials of the conspirators following this
aborted plot became one of England's leading news stories during
the months in which Shakespeare was likely composing *Macbeth*,
and the play's themes of treason, violence, and deception share
clear connections with this captivating, horrifying national event.

The period between these relevant seventeenth-century concerns and *Macbeth*'s popularity today unfolds a dynamic history of
the play's performance and interpretation that reflects changing
attitudes and expectations about acting styles, political viewpoints,
and social values. These diverse influences turn *Macbeth*'s journey
from 1606 to the present into a cultural adventure that extends far
beyond Shakespeare's words on the page. Furthermore, understanding *Macbeth* in relation to these many literary and historical
concerns invites even broader consideration of issues, events, and
stories that share similar patterns and themes. Modern stage productions experiment with these connections, but the classroom
provides a similar opportunity to experience *Macbeth*'s rich possibilities by engaging the powers of both intellect and imagination.

"Context" is a term that can unite these many perspectives on
Macbeth, for each offers a different answer to the question, "What
does it mean to study literature in context?" Conditions of time
and place are complex and varied. The following study is directed
toward an understanding of *Macbeth* that examines some of its
many contexts: literary, theatrical, critical, social, historical, and political. Several underlying questions guide this exploration. How
do specific aspects of a given culture illuminate the play or influence approaches to it? How do *Macbeth*'s many transformations
and adaptations over the centuries reflect and respond to historical
change? Conversely, what aspects of the drama seem to transcend
history by capturing human qualities or behavior that appear somehow universal? In other words, can human experience itself pro-

vide a context that defies the boundaries of time and place? All these questions point toward the issue of relevance by addressing ways in which both the past and the present contribute to *Macbeth*'s appeal and accessibility.

Numerous documents throughout this study function as resources to provide a more direct approach to *Macbeth*'s context, encouraging students to read widely and think broadly in their exploration of the play. The following list samples the diverse range of materials included:

political tracts and treatises

a speech from the throne

recorded court proceedings

a prisoner's confession

history book narratives

gentlemen's letters

an actor's journal

dramatic criticism

newspaper articles

editorials

movie and stage reviews

excerpts from other plays

an excerpted short story

performance photographs

a royal portrait

Questions and suggested readings at the end of each section are designed to serve a variety of purposes. Some questions directly address the excerpted documents as a guide for reading and understanding them. Others encourage students to relate the documents to *Macbeth*, drawing parallels, making comparisons, analyzing drama in light of history or history in light of drama, considering the connection between fact and fiction, and assessing the merit of different theatrical productions and critical approaches to the play. Some questions call for individual responses—sentences, paragraphs, essays, or oral reports. Others recommend group work, such as class projects or debates. Some are brief exercises, whereas others require research into various sources beyond this book, including but not limited to the suggested readings at the end of each chapter. Some assignments are reportorial or informative; others are imaginative, involving media such as the visual arts, video cameras, music, journal writing, and court-room drama as creative approaches to *Macbeth*. Many questions are general enough to be adapted for various classroom purposes, and the range of projects and assignments should challenge the most capable, enthusiastic students while providing opportunity for others to grow in their knowledge and appreciation of the play.

Beyond the most immediate goal of breathing life into *Macbeth* for those who may or may not be experiencing it for the first time, this book strives secondarily to inspire interdisciplinary thinking that challenges easy generalizations about history, literature, and their relationship to each other. Historically, for example, Shakespeare's England held more than one view about issues such as kingship and witchcraft; as a result, *Macbeth* emerges from the ferment of debate rather than merely reflecting a unified cultural perspective. From a literary, dramatic standpoint, because interpretation draws together an objective text and subjective impressions of readers, viewers, and performers, understanding *Macbeth* becomes a plural rather than a singular pursuit in which diverse ideas coexist, their legitimacy emerging out of the tension between them. This pursuit engages scholars with years of training, but it can begin with an introduction to Shakespeare that presents his drama as an experience in education, philosophy, politics, psychology, and history that constantly resists the move through interpretation to simplistic conclusions, and that encourages creative connections within and beyond the text.

NOTE

All quotations from *Macbeth* in chapter 1 and throughout the book are from the Arden edition: William Shakespeare, *Macbeth*, ed. Kenneth Muir (1951; London: Routledge, 1984).

1

Dramatic Analysis

This first chapter examines *Macbeth*'s dramatic elements from several different perspectives, considering the play's critical and theatrical heritage, its historically based plot, its textual development, and its poetic and literary patterns. In haste to label Shakespeare a genius, some might overlook the numerous influences that contributed directly or indirectly to his artistry. Elements that may seem unique to *Macbeth*—its plot, structure, character, and theme—reflect conventions and stories that Shakespeare shared with contemporary dramatists, historians, critics, and their predecessors. Seeing the play in this context does not deny Shakespeare his craft and creativity but gives these qualities meaning within a specific time and place and within a larger literary tradition. By narrowing the focus gradually from a historical perspective to a closer study of the play, the following discussion aims to explore the many ways *Macbeth* integrates poetry and action into a unified dramatic experience.

TRAGEDY

Although few would question *Macbeth*'s status as a tragedy, the more challenging task is to identify the play's specific tragic elements according to a clear definition of the genre. Students may be confident to sketch out general patterns, suggesting that tragedy ends with death, that the main character experiences suffering, that misfortune is a prevailing theme. In *Macbeth*, all these observations hold true. But the play also exists in a dramatic tradition that includes echoes of classical Greek and Roman theater, as well as early medieval English plays. These influences illuminate *Macbeth*'s tragic development and address problems raised by a central character who demonstrates a capacity for both heroism and villainy.

Aristotle

Greek philosopher Aristotle's definition of tragedy (c. 330 B.C.) became influential among Renaissance dramatists and literary critics and has continued to guide and shape an understanding of tragedy as a literary form. His theory concentrates on dramatic structure: (1) identifying plot as the most important element, (2) describing the central character as one who is neither wholly good nor wholly evil and whose fall results from an error in judgment, (3) suggesting that the hero eventually realizes his error and its consequences when it is too late to change, and (4) indicating that the audience responds with a combination of fear and pity to a story about a character who elicits their sympathy. The following excerpt develops some of these ideas by distinguishing tragic form from other plots and indicating how the differences affect an audience's involvement.

ARISTOTLE, *THE POETICS* IN *ARISTOTLE'S THEORY OF POETRY
AND FINE ART*, TRANS. S. H. BUTCHER
(London: Macmillan, 1907)

[Tragedy] should . . . imitate actions which excite pity and fear, this being the distinctive mark of tragic imitation. It follows plainly, in the first place, that the change of fortune presented must not be the spectacle of a virtuous man brought from prosperity to adversity: for this moves neither pity nor fear; it merely shocks us. Nor, again, that of a bad man passing from adversity to prosperity: for nothing can be more alien to the spirit of Tragedy; it possesses no single tragic quality; it neither satisfies the moral sense nor calls forth pity or fear. Nor, again, should the downfall of the utter villain be exhibited. A plot of this kind would, doubtless, satisfy the moral sense, but it would inspire neither pity nor fear; for pity is aroused by unmerited misfortune, fear by the misfortune of a man like ourselves. Such an event, therefore, will be neither pitiful nor terrible. There remains, then, the character between these two extremes—that of a man who is not eminently good and just, yet whose misfortune is brought about not by vice or depravity, but by some error or frailty. (45)

As a skilled artist writing in his own age, Shakespeare did not simply impose Aristotle's earlier classical form on his tragedies, each of which develops its own vision of human devastation. Some aspects of *Macbeth* even run contrary to Aristotle's ideals. As a psychological tragedy, it emphasizes the interior activity of the mind as much as the outward physical action of plot. It also shifts some attention away from the central hero by including Lady Macbeth as a partner in crime.

Nevertheless, Aristotle's classical theory provides one standard from which to consider Macbeth as a tragic hero. If tragedy cannot rely on a bad man descending into misfortune, then Macbeth must exhibit redeeming qualities, some of which others express on his behalf and some of which he articulates himself in his wrenching struggle between crime and conscience. Although he is blinded by a conviction that the end can justify the means and that good can come of his many evil deeds, eventually he does realize his own folly and the irreversible, devastating consequences of his choices. Finally, too, if tragedy necessitates a response of fear and pity, then Macbeth and Lady Macbeth must generate some sympathy; otherwise the play's ending merely becomes a triumph of good over evil, a celebration that verges on comedy. Simplistic or melodramatic interpretations may encourage this understanding, but Shakespeare invites a much more complex reaction, one that sees in the Macbeths' profoundly dark ambitions—as Aristotle suggests—something of ourselves.

Seneca

Roman writer Seneca (4 B.C.–A.D. 65) also influenced dramatic form in the Renaissance. His Latin plays were studied in Elizabethan schools, were revived on stage, and served as models for many English playwrights. Some Senecan elements that are particularly relevant to *Macbeth* include (1) violence and sensationalism,

(2) the role of the supernatural, especially its darker forces, (3) the presence of ghosts, often associated with a theme of revenge, (4) powerful female characters, and (5) a hero who is morally free to make his own choices, who demonstrates introspection or thoughtful reflection, and who manifests stoicism or courage and a strong will in the face of adversity.

These aspects are reflected in *Macbeth*. Blood and violence pervade the play in vivid imagery and in murders on and off stage. The supernatural maintains a sinister presence through the witches, Banquo's ghost, and even Lady Macbeth's invocation,

> Come, you Spirits
> That tend on mortal thoughts, unsex me here,
> And fill me, from the crown to the toe, top-full
> Of direst cruelty! (1.5.40–43)

Her violence and ambition resemble qualities of Senecan women characters, such as Medea and Clytemnestra. Macbeth is an introspective hero who thinks deeply, whose imagination shapes his goals, and whose conscience condemns him. He is also courageous, "bloody, bold, and resolute" (4.1.79), willing to fight to the death rather than cower before his enemies. Revenge or retribution characterizes the play's conclusion as Macduff slays the murderer of his own children, freeing Scotland from tyranny's cruel yoke. These parallels reflect direct or indirect Senecan influences, indicating Shakespeare's debt to an earlier dramatic tradition.

English Medieval Drama

A third legacy that can be traced in Shakespeare's tragedy comes from England's early religious drama, the morality plays and miracle plays popular in the fourteenth and fifteenth centuries. Morality plays are allegories enacting the struggle of human pride against divine will, a struggle that threatens despair and eternal damnation but that also provides opportunity for repentance and redemption. The main character is a representative of humanity with a name such as Everyman or Mankind, whereas the other characters who either tempt or sustain him bear the names of moral abstractions, such as Avarice or Death, Fellowship or Good

Hope. This early drama strives for moral instruction and celebrates trust and faith in a providential universe.

Secular drama in the Renaissance period reflects this same moral impulse. A clear example is Christopher Marlowe's *Dr. Faustus* with its good and evil angels advising Faustus as he lives out the consequences of a contract made with the devil. The connections are not as apparent in *Macbeth*, but many scholars see it as one of Shakespeare's most moral tragedies. Few of his other characters sink to Macbeth's depths of evil, and references to devils and angels appear frequently throughout the play. Good ultimately triumphs, instructing audiences about the consequences of ambition and tyranny and comforting them with a view of benevolent, providential power.

English miracle plays, contemporary with the moralities, also preceded and influenced secular Renaissance drama. Medieval communities celebrated Christian salvation history in cycles or series of miniplays that focused on biblical characters. Shakespeare's *Macbeth* borrows from one of these plays. In Act 2.3 just after Duncan's murder, the drunken Porter responds to the sound of knocking at the castle door by pretending to be the gatekeeper of hell, greeting the eternally damned. His satiric antics allude to a miracle play about the harrowing of hell in which Christ enters hell-gate to conquer Satan and death. If Shakespeare intended pure allegory, Macduff's imminent appearance would parallel Christ's entrance in the earlier play. However, Shakespeare's Porter abandons this game of make-believe before admitting Macduff, saying, "But this place is too cold for Hell. I'll devil-porter it no further" (2.3.16–18).

At one level, the Porter's monologue simply provides a necessary dramatic interlude while Macbeth changes his clothes and washes his hands before reappearing. But the deliberate dramatic allusion also creates strong moral overtones in this scene. Macbeth's castle becomes identified with Hell as the sin of his bloody and horrible "deed without a name" hangs in the air, awaiting discovery and precipitating evil's destructive energy. Shakespeare's play is neither allegory nor religious drama, but it confronts crime and suffering at a moral as well as political and personal level, reflecting connections with earlier English drama.

Typically, Shakespearean tragedy involves misfortune, suffering, and death. Exploring these patterns in *Macbeth* draws attention to dramatic structure, character development, moral vision, and audience response that together demonstrate not only Shakespeare's poetic inspiration and understanding of the human condition but also his dramatic tradition, including earlier classical and medieval influences and the thriving secular theater of his own time.

HISTORY REWRITTEN

Although tragedy is central to *Macbeth*, the play shares common ground with another genre that became popular in the secular theaters of Elizabethan England, the history play. Shakespeare wrote ten English history plays that individually dramatize different reigns of medieval or Tudor kings and together explore England's growing sense of national identity through the struggles of civil and international war. In 1603 the crowning of England's new king, James VI of Scotland, also raised public interest in Scotland's past. Shakespeare appealed to this interest, finding the primary material for *Macbeth*'s plot in the same history books that provided sources for the English plays. Although several possible historical influences exist, Raphael Holinshed's *Chronicles of England, Scotland and Ireland* (1587) is the main source. Relevant sections not only give historical background to *Macbeth* but also indicate how Shakespeare exercised artistic license, compressing a rambling narrative into a two- or three-hour performance by combining some events, omitting others, breathing life into flat characters, and unifying the plot according to common themes and images.

Macbeth brings together two periods of Scotland's history, the reigns of King Duff (A.D. 952–967) and King Duncan (A.D 1034–1040). Both monarchs were murdered by one of their nobles—Duncan by Macbeth and Duff by a loyal and trustworthy noble named Donwald. Shakespeare conflates the two incidents, primarily drawing details from King Duff's assassination. Donwald becomes angry with King Duff for slaying traitors who are his kinsmen. When Donwald shares his frustrations with his wife, she persuades him to kill the king, and together the couple devise a plot, making the chamberlains drunk and sending servants to the king's chambers to commit the murder. King Duff's reign also includes an incident of witchcraft (see Chapter 2), but Shakespeare relies more directly on Holinshed's account of Macbeth and Banquo's encounter with the witches during Duncan's reign. Other details in the play follow parts of Macbeth's history quite closely, from Macdonwald's rebellion, through Macbeth's cruel tyranny, to his beheading by Macduff.

Shakespeare's departures from his source are as interesting as the parallels. His revisions sharpen the contrasts between Duncan and Macbeth. Historically, Scotland's laws of succession gave Macbeth a legitimate claim to the throne, as well as reason to be troubled when Duncan named Malcolm as heir. Moreover, Holinshed's Duncan was a younger, weaker king whose leadership created problems for Scotland; and Macbeth, once king, reigned successfully for many years before his demise. Shakespeare's changes dramatically emphasize Macbeth's guilt and ambition. Perhaps in the interest of developing these qualities even further, he adds the banqueting scene with Banquo's ghost and invents Lady Macbeth's sleepwalking scene and suicide.

Several other alterations indicate contemporary political concerns. Banquo, as King James's ancestor, appears much more favorably in *Macbeth* than in Holinshed's *Chronicles*, where he is as ambitious and aggressive as Macbeth. Also, the battle recounted in Act 1 deliberately omits Norway's ally, Denmark, quite possibly to avoid defaming King James's father-in-law, King Christian of Denmark. In short, Shakespeare's choices reflect both artistic motivations and political motivations.

The following excerpts from Holinshed include several sections particularly relevant to *Macbeth*. The first [i] describes Donwald's murder of King Duff. The succeeding portions record [ii] the contrast between Duncan and Macbeth, [iii] Macbeth's plan to kill Banquo, and [iv] his own execution. Comparing the history book and the play shows that Shakespeare not only borrowed from a nondramatic source but shaped and adapted it. Spelling has been modernized and regularized throughout.

RAPHAEL HOLINSHED, *CHRONICLES OF ENGLAND, SCOTLAND AND IRELAND* [1587], VOL. 5
(London: 1808; New York: AMS Press, 1965)

[i] For the king being in that country, was accustomed to lie most commonly within the same castle, having a special trust in Donwald, as a man whom he never suspected.

But Donwald, not forgetting the reproach which his lineage had sustained by execution of those his kinsmen, whom the king for a spectacle to the people had caused to be hanged, could not but show manifest tokens of grief at home amongst his family: which his wife perceiving, ceased not to travail with him, till she understood what the cause was of displeasure. Which at length when she had learned by his own relation, she as one that bare no less malice in her heart toward the king, for the like cause on her behalf, than her husband did for his friends, counseled him . . . to make him away, and showed him the means whereby he might soonest accomplish it.

Donwald thus being more kindled in wrath by the words of his wife, determined to follow her advice in the execution of so heinous an act. Whereupon devising with himself for awhile, which way he might best accomplish his cursed intent, at length gat opportunity, and sped his purpose as followeth. It chanced that the king upon the day before he purposed to depart forth of the castle, was long in his oratory at his prayers, and there continued till it was late in the night. At the last, coming forth, he called such afore him as had faithfully served him in pursuit and apprehension of the rebels, and giving them hearty thanks, he bestowed sundry honorable gifts amongst them, of the which number Donwald was one, as he that had been ever accounted a most faithful servant to the king.

At length, having talked with them a long time, he got him into his privy chamber, only with two of his chamberlains, who having brought him to bed, came forth again, and then fell to banqueting with Donwald and his wife, who had prepared diverse delicate dishes, and sundry sorts of drinks for their rear supper or collation, whereat they sat up so long, till they had charged their stomachs with such full gorges, that their heads were no sooner got to the pillow, but asleep they were so fast, that a man might have removed the chamber over them, sooner than to have awaked them out of their drunken sleep.

Then Donwald, though he abhorred the act greatly in heart, yet through instigation of his wife he called four of his servants unto him (whom he had made privy to his wicked intent before, and framed to his purpose with large gifts) and now declaring unto them, after what sort they should work the feat, they gladly obeyed his instructions, & speedily going about the murder, they enter the chamber (in which the king lay) a little before cocks' crow, where they secretly cut his throat as he lay sleeping, without any buskling at all: and immediately by a postern gate they carried forth the dead body to the fields. (234–235)

[ii] Macbeth [was] a valiant gentleman, and one that if he had not been somewhat cruel of nature, might have been thought most worthy the

government of a realm. On the other part, Duncan was so soft and gentle of nature, that the people wished the inclinations and manners of these two cousins to have been so tempered and interchangeably bestowed betwixt them, that where the one had too much of clemency, and the other of cruelty, the mean virtue betwixt these two extremities might have reigned by indifferent partition in them both, so should Duncan have proved a worthy king, and Macbeth an excellent captain. The beginning of Duncan's reign was very quiet and peaceable, without any notable trouble; but after it was perceived how negligent he was in punishing offenders, many misruled persons took occasion thereof to trouble the peace and quiet state of the commonwealth, by seditious commotions which first had their beginnings in this wise. (264–265)

[iii]Shortly after, [Macbeth] began to show what he was, instead of equity practicing cruelty. For the prick of conscience (as it chanced ever in tyrants, and such as attain to any estate by unrighteous means) caused him ever to fear, least he should be served of the same cup, as he had ministered to his predecessor. The words also of the three weird sisters, would not out of his mind, which as they promised him the kingdom, so likewise did they promise it at the same time unto the posterity of Banquo. He willed therefore the same Banquo with his son named Fleance, to come to a supper that he had prepared for them, which was indeed, as he had devised, present death at the hands of certain murderers, whom he had hired to execute that deed. (271)

[iv] Then cutting his head from his shoulders, [Macduff] set it upon a pole, and brought it unto Malcolm. This was the end of Macbeth, after he had reigned 17 years over Scotishmen. In the beginning of his reign he accomplished many worthy acts, very profitable to the commonwealth . . . , but afterward by illusion of the devil, he defamed the same with most terrible cruelty. (277)

QUESTIONS FOR WRITTEN AND ORAL DISCUSSION

1. Review Aristotle's plot and character descriptions and discuss how Macbeth conforms to the tragic model. Could you argue instead that Macbeth is simply a "bad man" or a "villain"? If so, how does that challenge your understanding or view of *Macbeth* as a tragic play? Perhaps hold a class debate, arguing the two positions.

2. Discuss how and to what extent *Macbeth* inspires fear and pity for you. Find specific examples in scenes and characters that contribute to these responses. Does one of these reactions appear more common or frequent than the other?

3. Discuss whether you see Macbeth and Lady Macbeth as sympathetic characters. For Aristotle, "misfortune" defines the experience of the tragic hero, who nevertheless contributes in some way to his own suffering. Sympathy arises from the tension between suffering and deserving. Consider how these principles apply to *Macbeth*. What part do the witches play?

4. Write a character sketch of either Macbeth or Lady Macbeth, considering both their admirable or redeeming qualities and their flaws or weaknesses. Discuss the balance of virtues and vices and offer some conclusions about how that balance shapes the tragic dimension of the play.

5. Aristotle suggests that a tragic hero resembles each of us in some way. Although perhaps you cannot imagine committing crimes as appalling as the deeds of Macbeth and Lady Macbeth, can you recognize in their hopes, dreams, and actions qualities that you share or with which you can identify? Compose an account of some personal temptation or aspiration—imagined or real—and the consequences of acting on it. Consider whether this exercise makes Macbeth's and Lady Macbeth's crimes seem more or less horrific.

6. Aristotle's understanding of tragedy emphasizes the central character's ultimate awareness of his frailty or error in judgment. Discuss whether you think Macbeth and Lady Macbeth eventually realize the devastating consequences of their mistakes after the damage is irreversible. Can you find a specific speech or action in Act 5 that demonstrates this self-discovery for each character, or does the process seem more gradual?

7. Choose one of the five Senecan elements of tragedy listed in this chapter and write a paragraph or prepare a short oral presentation explaining how this element functions in *Macbeth*.

8. If you are interested in classical mythology, find and read stories of

Medea and/or Clytemnestra and write an essay that discusses parallels you see between these mythical characters and Lady Macbeth.

9. Discuss the role of revenge in *Macbeth*. Who are the revengers and how do they achieve their goals?

10. Whereas courage is demonstrated in outward action, introspection is the inward reflection that examines actions and consequences. Discuss how Macbeth demonstrates both of these qualities and how each contributes to your understanding of his status as a tragic character. Does one quality seem more significant than the other? Does Lady Macbeth also demonstrate courage and introspection? How does her display of these traits compare with Macbeth's?

11. Classical Senecan and Aristotelian ideas of tragedy share with early medieval religious drama an emphasis on morality. Referring to these traditions, establish a definition of morality and then discuss how it applies to *Macbeth*. How is the battle between good and evil developed and resolved? Which characters most strongly represent the voices of good and evil? Debate the play's moral vision, with one group arguing that evil is the most prominent and compelling force while the other group contends that good is more powerful and victorious.

12. Consider the importance of religion in *Macbeth*. Find evidence that supports the power and presence of providence or God in the play and discuss to what extent *Macbeth* is a Christian drama.

13. Shakespeare's dramatization of Duncan's murder resembles Holinshed's historical narrative of King Duff's murder. Read Holinshed's excerpted account and create parallel lists of similarities between the two, following with a second set of comparisons that balances the differences. Share your lists with several classmates and then discuss possible reasons for the differences. How might the adaptation of history to the stage explain some of the changes? How do the variations affect Macbeth's characterization?

14. Have one group act out King Duff's murder as recorded in Holinshed's *Chronicles* and another group enact the murder scene from *Macbeth*. Hold a class discussion about the relationship between the two.

15. Examining Holinshed's brief contrast between Duncan and Macbeth, discuss how Shakespeare revises this picture and how these changes affect both the tragic vision of the play and the development of Macbeth's central role. Perhaps work in pairs, with one student studying the two Duncans, the other comparing the two Macbeths, and then collaborate to draw conclusions about Shakespeare's revisions. What

would happen, for example, if the play emphasized Duncan's weaknesses? Why does it matter that Shakespeare's Duncan is old whereas Holinshed's is young?

16. Holinshed refers to the "prick of conscience," which Shakespeare develops into a major theme. Write an essay about the role of conscience in *Macbeth*, considering how it influences action and contributes to the development of the two main characters.

17. Historically, Macbeth reigned for seventeen years, resorting to cruelty only near the end. Discuss why Shakespeare might have changed the focus and how the variations affect the balance between history and tragedy. Is it wrong or dishonest to adapt the "facts" of history in this way? Why or why not?

18. If military and political history interests you, research Scotland's medieval past and prepare a report that explains the national conflicts during the tenth and eleventh centuries. Enhance your presentation with visual aids such as maps or sketches of military armor and weapons used in battle.

SUGGESTED READINGS

Bratchell, D. F. ed. *Shakespearean Tragedy*. New York: Routledge, 1990.
Bullough, Geoffrey, ed. *Narrative and Dramatic Sources of Shakespeare*. Vol. 7. London: Routledge, 1973.
Cunliffe, John W. *The Influence of Seneca on Elizabethan Tragedy*. Hamden CT: Archon Books, 1965.
Leech, Clifford. *Tragedy*. London: Methuen, 1969.
Margeson, J.M.R. *The Origins of English Tragedy*. Oxford: Clarendon Press, 1967.

THE TEXT

Modern readers may assume a much closer relationship between author and text than existed in the seventeenth century. They may be surprised to learn that although Shakespeare enjoyed considerable popularity in his own time, *Macbeth* did not appear in print until 1623, seven years after Shakespeare's death and likely seventeen years after the play's original composition. Shakespeare, however, appears to have been more interested in performance than text. Moreover, publishing activity was burdened by the labor-intensive, time-consuming processes of writing and printing. Many hands contributed to the final text, and consequently inaccuracies often occurred, creating problems for scholars later attempting to recover and restore Shakespeare's "authentic" works.

Although *Macbeth* presents fewer difficulties than other Shakespearean plays existing in several inconsistent versions, its textual history also raises some questions. First, *Macbeth* is one of Shakespeare's shortest plays and, especially in comparison with the other nine tragedies, its brevity is both surprising and puzzling. Second, evidence within the play indicates that a writer other than Shakespeare contributed some lines, raising doubts about the relationship between the printed version of *Macbeth* and Shakespeare's original manuscript. Without completely resolving these concerns, knowledge about early printing practices and theater activity can help to explain why and how they may have occurred.

The First Folio, printed in 1623, included thirty-six plays representing the first collection of Shakespeare's complete works. Unlike eighteen of those plays, *Macbeth* did not exist in an earlier individual or quarto edition. Folio scribes likely reproduced it not from an original manuscript but from a theater copy, known as a prompt-book, used for performances. This source may explain *Macbeth*'s brevity because typically Shakespeare's plays were shortened for performance. Another influence may have been the government's policy of actively censoring politically sensitive material before it reached the public stage. The original manuscript may, therefore, have been longer than the published version. However, *Macbeth*'s single, focused plot may also partly explain its length. No digressions or subplots expand or detract from the main storyline, and despite its shortness, the play's action does not appear disjointed because of obvious omissions or deletions.

Performance practices illuminate other textual inconsistencies. The two scenes that include Hecate among the other witches (3.5 and 4.1) are not entirely Shakespeare's. The style of language changes, and Hecate's sudden appearance is neither necessary to the plot nor consistent with previous witch scenes in Act 1. Furthermore, full versions of the songs mentioned in these two scenes—"Come Away, Come Away" and "Black Spirits"—appear in a later play, *The Witch*, written by Thomas Middleton possibly ten years or more after *Macbeth*. Whether or not Middleton also composed the dialogue added to Shakespeare's play, the songs indicate a clear connection between the two. Most likely at some point in *Macbeth*'s long run on the public stage, performers chose to revise the original play, possibly replacing earlier lines with these new ones and incorporating Middleton's songs for no other reason than to take advantage of their popularity and to satisfy an ongoing public fascination with witchcraft.

Other less significant problems in *Macbeth* have also generated some debate. One apparent inconsistency exists between Act 3.6 and Act 4.1. The Lord speaking to Lennox in Act 3.6 indicates that Macbeth knows of Macduff's retreat to England, but later in Act 4.1 Macbeth responds with surprise to Lennox's report, asking, "Fled to England?" (4.1.142). The contradiction suggests a textual inaccuracy; perhaps the two scenes originally appeared in reverse order and the witchcraft additions simply contributed to the problem. Similar but less glaring details provoke questions, too. Why, for example, does a third murderer appear in Act 3.3 after Macbeth recruits only two men to kill Banquo? Such concerns do not expose serious gaps in the play's development, and for all we know, the seemingly puzzling details may have originated with Shakespeare himself. Many of these mysteries may never be solved, but knowing about *Macbeth*'s evolution from the stage to the page can at least raise awareness about the existence of textual problems and increase appreciation of the many contributors—performers, government officials, scribes, typesetters, and publishers—who played a part in preserving a text of the play for modern readers and actors.

POETIC AND DRAMATIC PATTERNS

Shakespeare's language is considered to be early Modern English, but it can present difficulties for twentieth-century readers because word meanings and speech patterns constantly change as language evolves through time. Simple, informative glossaries included in most editions of Shakespeare's plays benefit readers, although, surprisingly, audiences often find that the barriers of understanding easily break down in performance as actors bring the words to life through gesture and expression. At a literary level, however, the lines on the page open up many possibilities of meaning that expand and challenge the simple connections between words and definitions. Shakespeare is a poet as well as a dramatist, and the complex intellectual and emotional experience of *Macbeth* resonates in associations and tensions between words and images, and between those images and the characters who articulate, embody, and unfold the play's themes. Time spent reading and exploring *Macbeth*'s language, therefore, can only increase the power of its drama and poetry.

Blank Verse

Shakespeare writes in blank verse, unrhymed lines composed in iambic pentameter. "Iambic" refers to the pattern of stresses with an accented syllable following an unaccented syllable. "Pentameter" identifies the number of syllables in the line: five stressed syllables alternating with five unstressed syllables. Although blank verse adheres to a strict poetic pattern, the resulting rhythm approximates natural speech in such a way that poetry and prose appear to be blended. Shakespeare develops this natural rhythm even further by frequently varying the iambic pattern to avoid monotony and predictability. Scenes often end with a couplet, two rhyming lines of iambic pentameter that contribute to a sense of completion or closure.

Typically, Shakespeare reserves blank verse for nobility and adopts prose for his common or low-class characters. In *Macbeth* blank verse dominates because most characters belong to noble or royal classes who engage in serious interaction. But the Porter, a commoner, speaks in prose and the witches use short lines of verse, incorporating rhyme into their chants and spells. Shakespeare occasionally adapts these speech conventions, one notable exception being Lady Macbeth's shift into prose during her sleepwalking scene to reveal her distressed, unsound mental state. Such examples of variations in style and rhythm indicate that Shakespeare uses poetic technique not simply as a mechanical structure but as a means to develop character, theme, and mood.

Imagery

Figurative language also adds to this development. Some prominent techniques in *Macbeth* include imagery, metaphor, simile, personification, antithesis, and irony. All these techniques help to expand meaning beyond the literal level, connecting characters and actions to much larger cosmic and philosophical issues. Many passages, for example, rely on images crafted into similes and metaphors that develop the theme of deception by articulating contrasts between appearance and reality. Lady Macbeth warns Macbeth before Duncan's murder:

> Your face, my Thane, is a book, where men
> May read strange matters. To beguile the time,
> Look like the time; bear welcome in your eye,
> Your hand, your tongue: look like th'innocent flower,
> But be the serpent under't. (1.5.62–66)

Her references to books, serpents, and time convey the necessity for false appearances.

Other metaphors help to express the mental struggles underlying this conflict between outward actions and inward intent. Lady Macbeth attempts to overcome Macbeth's reservations about murder by invoking the image of a soldier screwing the cord of his crossbow for war: "But screw your courage to the sticking-place, / And we'll not fail" (1.7.61–62). Later Macbeth articulates his anguish and insecurity about Banquo by adapting the serpent metaphor:

> We have scotch'd the snake, not kill'd it:
> She'll close, and be herself; whilst our poor malice
> Remains in danger of her former tooth. (3.2.13–15)

Animal images and personification appear frequently throughout the play to intensify the darkness, violence, uncertainty, and inhumanity surrounding the crimes of the two main characters. These and other figures of speech add richness and texture to the relentless, linear action of plot.

Antithesis and Irony

Antithesis and irony perform similar functions. Antithesis, a rhetorically balanced contrast, effectively expresses the play's central struggle between good and evil. Just after conquering the traitors and before meeting the witches for the first time, Macbeth voices a paradoxical truth that echoes again and again as the plot develops: "So fair and foul a day I have not seen" (1.3.38). The witches themselves most clearly embody evil and express this theme of moral discord in confusing, antithetical terms, promising Banquo, for example, that he will be "Lesser than Macbeth, and greater. / Not so happy, yet much happier" (1.3.65–66). Banquo recognizes the slippery logic of these prophecies, warning Macbeth,

> And oftentimes, to win us to our harm,
> The instruments of Darkness tell us truths;
> Win us with honest trifles to betray's
> In deepest consequence. (1.3.123–126)

His balanced sentence structure, opposing "honest trifles" with "deepest consequence" and "Win us" with "betray's," reinforces the thematic contrast, as do words and phrases joined to signify opposites and opposition throughout the play.

Irony involves the audience more directly in this dramatic conflict by supplying viewers at times with more information than some characters enjoy. When Duncan and Banquo approach Inverness and praise the pleasant air surrounding Macbeth's castle, the audience already knows that Macbeth and his wife are plotting murder at that very place and the atmosphere there is decidedly unpleasant. When Macduff arrives to rouse the king the next morning, viewers watch the scene unfold, having already seen the host and hostess stained with Duncan's blood and knowing that the king will never again awake. These examples of dramatic irony intensify suspense, guilt, and horror by positioning audience members and readers almost as Macbeth's accomplices, as knowing partners in crime.

Later Lennox adopts verbal irony, cataloguing Macbeth's wrongs in words that portray the tyrant as noble and just when the opposite is intended (3.6). One can imagine his tone to be sarcastic, inviting the audience to share his condemnation of Macbeth and therefore helping to free them from their earlier identification with Macbeth so they can participate wholly in the victory of his overthrow in Act 5. As these examples suggest, verbal and dramatic irony demands the audience's participation but can influence the audience's involvement in different ways depending on the context.

Stage Conventions

Attention to language leads naturally into discussions about character and theme because the three elements are so closely interconnected. In the absence of a narrative voice, all language in drama issues from the mouths of characters. Their speech conforms to dramatic or stage conventions based on several forms of discourse: dialogue, asides, and soliloquies. Dialogue occurs between two or more characters; an aside happens when one character addresses the audience or when several characters share words that others on stage do not hear; and a soliloquy takes place when a single character speaks alone to the audience.

These different forms of communication are called conventions because although they may not seem completely realistic, actors and viewers accept them as part of the play's dramatic illusion. How often do people actually think aloud before a crowd of attentive listeners, or does one person speak clearly while another nearby seems completely deaf and oblivious? In *Macbeth*, however, these conventions are common and serve to reveal characters' motives and fears, to create and explain the conflict between them, to drive the plot forward, and to give the audience a much more complex understanding of the play than any single character experiences. Macbeth's asides and soliloquies provide a glimpse into his heart and soul, but viewers also see him through the eyes of others; the tragic vision becomes possible precisely because the audience knows more than anyone else yet cannot change the consequences.

Character

Just as language creates patterns in the exchange of dialogue and use of imagery, these conventions and techniques also help to develop larger character patterns through the balance and contrast of roles and actions. Characters who share common ground invite consideration of their similarities and differences. (1) The proliferation of kings raises an obvious point of comparison. How do Duncan and Macbeth differ, and how do those differences help to define them? What part do other kingly figures play: Malcolm, King Edward the Confessor (4.3), the apparition of Banquo's royal successors? (2) Both Macbeth and his predecessor, the former Thane of Cawdor, are traitors. How are they alike? (3) Both Banquo and Macbeth see the witches. How do their reactions compare? (4) Macbeth and Lady Macbeth are partners in crime. What distinguishes their contributions and reactions? (5) Macbeth and Macduff become archenemies. How does that conflict unfold and resolve? (6) Lady Macbeth and Lady Macduff have similar titles and functions as women and wives. What differentiates their roles? (7) Lady Macbeth and the witches both invoke evil powers. How are their supplications alike?

Similar patterns exist even among minor characters. (8) Who are the fathers and sons in *Macbeth*, and how do their relationships compare? (9) Who are the loyal and disloyal nobles, and what do their responses contribute to conflicts within the state? If dialogue and action move the play forward in a linear fashion, all these other patterns add another dimension through weblike connections that do for character what imagery does for words, expanding the possibilities of meaning and rewarding dramatic analysis to strengthen theatrical performance and enrich interpretation of the text.

Theme

Language studies lead to character analysis, which develops further into themes. Themes are more than single words—"murder" or "evil"—and *Macbeth*, like most literary works, advances more than one theme. Key words, however, can help to identify the central ideas or motifs that expand into thematic statements. To say that *Macbeth* is a play about evil is to state the obvious; to say that the play presents evil as a social and a psychological force that dehumanizes all who come into its contact is to argue a theme that merits further consideration and analysis. Many words and image patterns suggest other motifs: babies, magic, the supernatural, reason, madness, ambition, power, blood, order, morality, guilt, conscience, equivocation, sleep, disease, security, fertility, sterility, time, animals. Themes emerge when these words and images are examined in relationship to one another. Considering what the play means, then, becomes a broad exploration into a vast range of ideas rather than a narrow quest for a few simple solutions.

Conclusion

Dramatic analysis combines literary and theatrical concerns; interpretation grows out of the ability to see patterns within and between the many elements that shape the play. Characters, themes, images, stage conventions, setting, mood, action, and tension are woven together to create the overall experience of reading or watching *Macbeth*. Theatrical tradition and narrative sources play their part; the relationship between publishing and performance reveals mechanical and technical aspects, as well as elements of human error and artistic license, that also contribute to the play's production. To approach *Macbeth* as drama in this context invites consideration of words such as "tragedy," "history," "text," "imagery," and "illusion," which are generalized in conception and rich in interpretive possibility. Fruitful discussion, therefore, must begin with clear definition and focus that can be expanded to offer the opportunity for instructive and engaging debate.

QUESTIONS FOR WRITTEN AND ORAL DISCUSSION

1. Research the printing practices of the sixteenth and seventeenth centuries. Write an informative report or a fictional narrative (written perhaps by an English typesetter) that suggests how *Macbeth* was first published. Discover, for example, what "quarto" and "folio" mean, what skills were required in the printing business, and who made the profits.

2. Pretend that as director of *Macbeth* at the Globe, you have the authority to change the script as you see fit. Someone has presented you with the idea of adding new scenes around a few popular songs recently heard in performances of Middleton's *The Witch*. At first you are reluctant, but eventually you decide the adaptations might improve the play. Write a journal entry relating your decision and the reasons for it. To make the account more dramatic, perhaps include an encounter with Shakespeare himself. How did he respond to your choices?

3. Write another scene for *Macbeth* that explains the appearance of the Third Murderer just before Banquo's assassination. Why do you suppose Macbeth recruited him?

4. *Macbeth*'s energy derives from the conflict between opposites, particularly between good and evil. Find examples of antithesis, statements or phrases that balance and contrast opposing ideas or forces. Discuss how these examples contribute to the play's tension, ambiguity, and suspense.

5. Write an essay about animals, babies, blood, clothing, *or* sleep in *Macbeth*. How many examples of one of these image patterns can you find, and how many functions does it serve? Does one character use an image pattern more than others? If so, why?

6. Choose one of the following assignments that addresses the function of color in *Macbeth*. (1) Write a short essay that discusses how the use of color contributes to theme. (2) As a producer write stage notes indicating how you would use color references in *Macbeth* to create specific sets or costumes. (3) Design abstract, symbolic, or realistic cover pages for several scenes or acts, paying particular attention to color and including brief explanations for each design.

7. Closely analyze one of Macbeth's soliloquies (1.7.1–28, 2.1.33–64, 3.1.47–71), identifying the figures of speech (metaphors, similes, antithesis, and personification), discussing their contribution to mood, and considering what Macbeth reveals about himself. Why is it important that the audience (and only the audience) hear his thoughts?

Alternatively, take the same approach to one of Lady Macbeth's soliloquies (1.51–30, 1.5.37–54).

8. Discuss the use of asides in 1.3 or 3.4. Guided by basic plot questions
   (what, when, where, and why), consider how this stage convention
   adds to the drama. How much does the audience know that other
   characters do not? Alternatively, assign parts and read through one
   of these scenes, discussing in advance how to indicate the illusion of
   separation between characters who speak and those who do not hear.

9. Discuss what the audience learns about Macbeth before he first appears (1.3.38) and how that information about his character is presented. Why might Shakespeare choose to introduce Macbeth in this
   way and how does this opening develop his character?

10. Under the heading "Character," this chapter poses a number of ques-
    tions about the relationships between different groups of characters.
    Write an essay that addresses one of these questions about the fol-
    lowing groups: kings, fathers and sons, traitors, Macbeth and Lady
    Macbeth, Macbeth and Banquo, Lady Macbeth and Lady Macduff,
    Lady Macbeth and the witches, loyal and disloyal subjects. How does
    comparing and contrasting these characters help to reveal who they
    are and why they act the way they do?

11. Discovering *Macbeth*'s themes involves turning key words into state-
    ments that the play supports and develops. Choose three or four of
    the following words and compose several themes that you see in
    Macbeth: the supernatural, madness, reason, ambition, power, order,
    evil, morality, guilt, conscience, deception, equivocation, disease,
    fear, security, fertility, sterility, time. After you have written your own
    statements, discuss them with several other students, paying partic-
    ular attention to words that may have generated different responses
    and then selecting one word as a group and trying to discover how
    many new themes you can generate from it.

SUGGESTED READINGS

Bradley, A. C. *Shakespearean Tragedy*. London: Macmillan, 1904.
Brooke, Nicholas. Critical Introduction. *Macbeth*. Oxford: Clarendon
    Press, 1990.
Muir, Kenneth. Critical Introduction. *Macbeth*. London: Routledge, 1984.

NOTE

Related questions and suggested readings appear at the end of chapter
3, "Currents of Criticism," which explores some of the common literary,
historical, and dramatic approaches to *Macbeth* in this century.

2

Historical Context

MONARCHY AND TYRANNY: THE BOUNDARIES OF KINGSHIP

Macbeth is a political play. It dramatizes a story about power and authority, about order and disorder, about the violence of civil war and the final restoration of peace. At the center of all these concerns lies the issue of kingship in its legitimate and illegitimate forms, including succession, the rightful transition of authority from one ruler to the next; regicide, the killing of the king; usurpation, the wrongful seizure of the crown; and tyranny, the cruel abuse of power by a state ruler. Questions about the proper exercise of power directly involve everyone on stage. In the course of the play, no less than three Scottish kings wear the crown: Duncan, Macbeth, and Malcolm. The English king Edward the Confessor is also mentioned with approval, and Banquo receives the politically confusing promise that he will father many kings. All the other characters, even the witches and Lady Macbeth, act either to make a king, to support and protect him, or to destroy him. There are no subplots and few digressions from this focus. Perhaps the simplicity of the plot contributes to its appeal. Many have gone so far as to say that the world vision in *Macbeth* is black and white because the conflict between good and evil is clearly defined.

Certainly, the struggle Shakespeare dramatizes between political leaders has a timeless quality that is recognized in national and international conflicts throughout history. But the political issues in the play have a specific as well as timeless context. Behind the apparent simplicity of the plot lie concerns that are particular to Shakespeare's England in the early 1600s. Some of those issues will be addressed in this chapter: (1) the effects of adapting legend or history for play, that is, for court and public entertainment rather than textbook instruction; (2) the peaceful transition of power between Queen Elizabeth of England and King James of Scotland; (3) the question of England's relationship to Scotland once James becomes king of both countries; and (4) the tension between official doctrine about monarchy and other contending political theories. Understanding this history can help to broaden and even challenge our modern perception and appreciation of the play.

Attention to political theories and national history in this chapter is designed to provide guidelines for a more informed exploration of kingship in *Macbeth*. Documents and summaries have been included to suggest the dynamic relationship between political beliefs and actual experience. Today, for example, it would be simplistic and misleading to say that democracy is the universally accepted form of government in the United States without taking into account vast regional differences and clashes between liberal and conservative interpretations of the role of government. Likewise, it would be misleading to assume that monarchy was the established form of government in Shakespeare's England without considering some of the debates and tensions that arose from the increasing power of the state, from continental influences, and from the political union of Scotland and England.

Much of that debate revolved around questions of legitimacy and whether or not political legitimacy derived from God, the law, the people, heredity, or a combination of them all. When was rebellion justified—ever or never? What were the rules of succession? Should a king be guided solely by Christian morality or by political practicality or both? What was the best balance of power to ensure national peace? What constituted tyranny, and what was the best solution to the problem? For every question there was always more than one answer.

These answers helped to shape the country's ideology or system of political beliefs. Ideology, however, sometimes denies, distorts, or seeks to change reality rather than simply represent it. King James upheld an ideology of divine right, as did his son and successor, Charles I, but by 1649 Charles was beheaded in the English Civil War, which temporarily overthrew the monarchical system. In other words, proclaiming something to be true does not necessarily make it so. Sometimes contradictory claims seem equally valid. The political truths or beliefs that are dramatized in *Macbeth* revolve around king making, king killing, and the assertion of kingly power. The crown is the symbolic center. Yet even as we applaud the ultimate triumph of good over evil, we may well ask whether the political battle is clearly defined or whether, instead, the complexity and unresolved ambiguity give *Macbeth* its ongoing appeal.

Dramatic Context

From a dramatic perspective, kingship was a popular and compelling topic on stage. With classical training, Elizabethans and Jacobeans believed that tragedy was high drama in which only highly placed people—kings and queens—were appropriate characters. By the time Shakespeare composed *Macbeth*, he had already written most of his famous tragedies such as *Julius Caesar*, *Hamlet*, and *King Lear* that portrayed the rise and fall of great public figures. He had also composed nine history plays, which receive less attention today partly because the portrayal of England's early history has less immediate appeal now than it did in the sixteenth and seventeenth centuries. Yet Shakespeare's contemporaries returned to their past as we do today to explore and celebrate their national identity.

Macbeth combines both the tragic genre and the historic genre by depicting the rise and fall of kings whose stories appeared in the history books. Today we recognize the Renaissance account of Scotland's ancient past as legend or pseudohistory because we know more about the inaccuracies of some of the "facts." We know that history writers fabricated many of the details to instill a feeling of national pride, sometimes by deliberately portraying past kings as either villains or heroes. Most Jacobeans, however, did not question the accuracy of their history. They accepted it as true and relied on the stories of past kings not only to explore their own identity but also to provide present rulers with good and bad examples of effective and acceptable kingship. King James was among the many who accepted history as a source of political legitimacy.

Although the representation of history or legend on the stage responded to and expressed the political mood of the time, play-houses functioned essentially as venues for public entertainment, as movie theaters do today. Because playwrights such as Shake-speare wrote to attract the masses, they concentrated on what they thought would be popular: good storylines with action and emo-tion. History plays and tragedies were appealing because battle-grounds provided exciting fields of action, and kingly processions offered an opportunity for lavish spectacles. To put it simply, play-houses did not serve merely as substitute classrooms to teach his-tory.

Nevertheless, the expectations and limitations of theater enter-tainment were different than we might now expect. From one an-gle, theaters were under attack because they were considered to be subversive places that encouraged idleness and contempt for authority. Consequently, government officials actively practiced censorship. It was unacceptable, for example, to portray contem-porary kings on stage because such portrayals were thought to undermine the monarch's dignity or to criticize his or her political performance. Thus, one play in 1605 was immediately suppressed for dramatizing a recent attack on King James's life in the Gowrie Conspiracy. Playwrights had to choose their topics carefully, and some, therefore, relied on historical topics and parallels to com-ment on contemporary political issues. Elizabeth I was once furi-ous when she interpreted herself as the tragic king in a performance of Shakespeare's *Richard II*. James I, on the other hand, likely felt flattered by allusions to his Stuart ancestry through Banquo in *Macbeth*. For dramatists, politics was both a popular and a potentially dangerous subject.

Those who supported the theaters against the attacks of critics often appealed to the instructive role of drama and claimed that plays about kings taught the public and the court about good gov-ernment by example. There was a strong tradition that literature, both drama and poetry, served a didactic purpose to educate, not strictly to entertain. An example in *Macbeth* that illustrates the con-nection between drama and philosophical or political debate is the lengthy discussion between Malcolm and Macduff about kingship in Act 4.3. Often that scene is left out of modern productions partly because it is all talk and no action, but also because it is a topic that likely held more interest and relevance in Shakespeare's time than it does now. We are removed from the historical context and have less patience with performance as means of debate or instruction. The best we can do almost four hundred years after the original performance of the play is to be conscious of some of the conflicting views about the impact and purpose of the theater.

In summary, several points are worth remembering. First, dramatized history or legend often reflected contemporary concerns that might involve flattery, debate, instruction, or even veiled criticism. Second, kings and commoners alike attended dramatic performances and so the topics had to meet the interests of both. Third, the stage was a place recognized for its instructive and its subversive roles, but it was also a place where people went simply to be entertained. These purposes may not seem consistent, but they nevertheless all contributed to what happened on stage and how audiences responded. An awareness of these conflicting attitudes can illuminate the relationship between kingship in *Macbeth* and some of the political views being expressed outside the theaters.

Political Succession from the Tudors to the Stuarts

Queen Elizabeth was the reigning monarch for most of Shakespeare's life. A member of the Tudor royal family, she was the third child of Henry VIII to sit on England's throne following Edward VI and Mary I. Governing from 1558 to 1603, Elizabeth boasted one of the longest reigns in England's turbulent history. Her era was not without its troubles, including attempts against her life, international conflicts culminating with the unsuccessful attack of the Spanish Armada in 1588, disease and plagues, economic troubles, and religious tensions between Catholics and Protestants. But the very longevity of her reign fostered a degree of stability and peace that England had not experienced for some time.

Her rule also created the problem of succession. Because she was the last of the Tudors and never married, there were no children to take over the throne when she died. Furthermore, she never openly proclaimed her choice of successor. Initially her advisors assumed that they would find an acceptable husband for her, but as she grew older and remained unmarried, her subjects simply hoped for a peaceful transition to a new monarch when she died. It was rumored that on her deathbed she chose James VI, King of Scotland, as her heir, and it had already become apparent that he was the obvious successor because of his royal birth and his Tudor connections through the sister of Henry VIII.

King James, for his part, spent his years as Scotland's king nurturing hopes that he would assume the English throne. When he came to England in 1603, most of his new English subjects were delighted that after years of speculation and concern, the succession from one monarch to the next appeared to be free of conflict and that peace would continue. Many also had high hopes for their new king after having grown restless and disillusioned with Elizabeth in her declining years. Before long his English subjects became disappointed with James's performance, too, but initially they welcomed him in style, and he became the first monarch of the new Stuart line as James VI of Scotland and James I of England. He had been on the throne for several years by the time Shakespeare wrote *Macbeth*.

Ancestry and Union

The Scottish theme of *Macbeth* obviously responded to interest in the heritage of the Stuart monarch who not only became England's king but also assumed official patronage or support of the acting company to which Shakespeare belonged, newly named the King's Men. Two issues in *Macbeth* appeal directly to James's concern for royal rights and ambitions: the Banquo ancestry and the union of Scotland and England. James traced his royal descent back to Banquo, a mythical figure whom Scottish chroniclers had actually invented to reinforce the legitimacy and longevity of the Stuart line. James himself accepted the lineage as true history rather than legend or myth. One sixteenth-century historian designed a genealogical family tree called "The Banquo Tree," which illustrated the succession of eight kings beginning at the root with Banquo and ending with James VI at the top.

Shakespeare honors this version of royal legend by making Banquo a more attractive figure in *Macbeth* than he was in the history books and by portraying him as the father of kings. The apparitions presented to Macbeth by the witches in Act 4.1 also refer to King James by showcasing the kings that precede him in the Stuart line and promising more to come. Stage directions indicate that Banquo appears as the last in this "show of eight Kings," and Macbeth complains,

> I'll see no more:—
> And yet the eighth appears, who bears a glass,
> Which shows me many more; and some I see,
> That two-fold balls and treble sceptres carry. (4.1.119–121)

This image no doubt flattered King James by reflecting the glory of his Scottish past and the hope he held for England's future.

Macbeth's description of the ball and scepter probably alludes to King James's two coronations. In Scotland, one scepter was used for the ceremony; in England, two (Muir 114–115, note 121, *Macbeth*). This vision captures another of James's ambitions to unite the two countries. By becoming England's king, he joined the nations politically, but early after his arrival he took steps to bring about a greater economic and religious union as well. The English resisted the plan, however. Many held strong anti-Scottish sentiments, and Parliament refused to pass a law of union. In 1606 the king nevertheless still harbored strong ambitions for such an alliance and certainly believed that his own successors would rule England and Scotland for generations to come.

One topical reference in the play that may have indirectly helped to celebrate the hope James initially embodied for England's future is the discussion of the medieval king Edward the Confessor in Act 4.3. While in England at Edward's court, Malcolm explains Edward's miraculous power to cure his subjects of a physical disease known as the King's Evil or scrofula. King James also practiced this healing ritual by laying hands on his subjects and praying for their recovery. Malcolm's speech could therefore easily have drawn attention to James, and this example of the benevolent healing art of good kingship would have placed not only Edward the Confessor but James himself in stark contrast to Macbeth, whose tyranny acted like a disease in Scotland.

The issues of succession and union reflected in *Macbeth* also associate it with another contemporary drama, a short Latin playlet written and performed for King James in Oxford on August 27, 1605. Dr. Gwinn's *Tres Sibyllae*, translated as "Three Sibyls," praises James's royal heritage as three sibyls or prophetic women greet and exult him by proclaiming his royal titles, his ancestral connection to Banquo, and his goal for peace and national unity. Shakespeare may well have seen the play. Alternatively, he may have heard about it afterward, for such royal performances would have received widespread publicity. At any rate, the three sibyls anticipate *Macbeth*'s three witches. The honors that the sibyls shower upon James echo in the "all hails" addressed to Macbeth, and the glory of Banquo is expressed in both performances. The plots are not completely parallel and the dramatic styles are quite different, but the similarities indicate some of the royal themes that were current shortly after Scotland's James VI became England's king (Bullough 429–430; Paul 163–164).

In the excerpt from *Tres Sibyllae* included here in translation, notice how the sibyls' greeting resembles the witches' prophecies in Act 1.1 of *Macbeth*, and watch for specific connections even in the language used to celebrate the king.

DR. GWINN, *TRES SIBYLLAE* (1605)

1. There is a story, O renowned King, that once in the olden time the fateful sisters foretold to thy descendants an endless empire. . . . Famed Lochabria acknowledged Banquo as its Thane; not for thee O Banquo, but for thine immortal descendants . . . did these sooth-saying women predict immortal sceptres . . . as thou didst withdraw from the court to the country for rest. We three sisters in like manner foretell the same fates for thee and thine, whilst along with thy family thou dost return from the country to the city, and we salute thee:
   Hail thou who rulest Scotland.
2. Hail thou who rulest England.
3. Hail thou who rulest Ireland.
1. Hail thou to whom France gives titles whilst the others give lands.
2. Hail thou whom Britain, now united though formerly divided, cherishes.
3. Hail thou supreme British, Irish, Gallic Monarch.

From Henry Paul, *The Royal Play of Macbeth* (New York: Macmillan, 1950) 163–164

Kingship in Medieval Scotland

The beliefs and practices of kingship in medieval Scotland differed substantially from those in the reign of Elizabeth or James, and because Shakespeare adapts history for the stage, bringing the perspective of his own time to the past, the differences are worth noting. In Macbeth's eleventh-century Scotland, monarchy did not have a long and stable tradition, and the crown did not automatically pass from one king to his son in hereditary succession. Instead, there was a complicated system based on both heredity and election. The king was chosen alternately from several different branches of the same family so that often a nephew rather than a son succeeded to the throne. If the heir appeared incompetent or too young, the nobility reserved the right to elect a more suitable king. Although several kings prior to Duncan had attempted to legislate lineal succession, they had been unsuccessful, and the resulting conflict and confusion frequently led to regicide and civil unrest. Not until Malcolm assumed the throne did hereditary succession become accepted, gradually leading to the Banquo line from which King James claimed descent (Bullough 431–432; Paul 165–168).

This evolution of kingship provides interesting background to *Macbeth* because it indicates that historically when Duncan named Malcolm as Prince of Cumberland and therefore as heir, he was not following the normal practice and tradition. Macbeth, as a cousin in the royal family, would have had some legitimate right to the throne. Shakespeare omits this detail and instead emphasizes Macbeth's personal ambition, allowing the play to reflect ideas about kingship current in seventeenth-century England rather than in eleventh-century Scotland.

At the same time Shakespeare incorporates some of the values of feudalism, a system that actually began after the period of Macbeth and Malcolm. Feudalism was a decentralized system of government in which lords and nobles had significant power. The balance of rights and duties between a king and his lords was based on strong personal ties of loyalty and rewards for honor. The feudal system is reflected in *Macbeth* in the lavish castles of the nobles that provide the setting, in the emphasis on loyalty, and in the arguments of conscience Macbeth struggles against as he contemplates the murder of his host and king.

English Theories of Kingship and Tyranny

Many of the ideas about kingship and tyranny dramatized and debated in *Macbeth* can be understood in light of the theories developed in England in the sixteenth century after Henry VIII became king and gave the role of kingship more power by breaking free from the pope's authority in Rome. Britain's constitutional monarchy was based on lineal succession from father to son, on a providential belief that kings were appointed and protected by God, and on a parliamentary system in which a legislative assembly worked with the king to pass laws. The divine right of kings and the absolute obedience of subjects are two beliefs associated with that period of English history. In simple terms, just kingship was valued and praised, and any behavior that resembled tyranny or rebellion was boldly denounced. The turmoil in England prior to the establishment of the Tudor monarchy had increased anxiety about succession and stability in the state, for no one wanted another century of civil war. Thus, the official ideology or system of beliefs strongly advocated values that would help to maintain order.

There was not, however, one single, universal view of kingship, and the differences stemmed partly from two facts: first, that not everyone agreed entirely on what balance of power should exist among king, subjects, and Parliament and, second, that some theorists were satisfied to present an ideal picture of how things ought to be, whereas others were more interested in what practical steps to take when reality did not measure up to that ideal. Examining some of the metaphors and analogies used in the ideology supporting kingship and government will help to put the debate into perspective.

The Chain of Being. One of the most common sixteenth-century views of order is referred to today as the Elizabethan World Picture. It is based on a metaphor of a vertical chain that links everything in the universe according to a hierarchy from the greatest to the least, descending from God at the top, to angels, to people, to animals, to plants, to the lowest inanimate objects including minerals and soil. The degree or order represented in this chain is divinely ordained and allows for harmony and unity when all parts perform their proper function. The metaphor also permits comparisons to be made from one level to the next because at all levels the highest or noblest member controls the others. For example, as God is greatest among the angels, so is the sun among the stars, the king among men, the head among the other body parts, and reason among the human faculties (Tillyard 30–31). The state or commonwealth is a miniature version of the universe, and man is yet a smaller version or microcosm of the state.

The importance of this metaphor in the political belief system concerns its emphasis on the power and greatness of the king, comparing him to God on a smaller scale. It also reinforces the providential or God-ordained appointment of the monarch and therefore impresses upon all subjects the necessity and virtue of obedience. According to this view of cosmic order, when any part of the chain does not perform its proper function in the hierarchy, it causes disorder or disease throughout the whole system. The higher in the chain the damage, the more devastating is the overall chaos. Thus a king who acts as a tyrant upsets not only his state but the cosmic balance as well, and subjects who respond with rebellion produce a similar effect.

Some of these beliefs about order and disorder appear in *Macbeth*. Notice, for example, what is happening in the natural world during Macbeth's regicide and tyranny, what the weather is like, and how the characters explain the ominous and unsettled conditions. Shakespeare's drama reflects the metaphor of cosmic order, which was widely accepted as a desirable ideal in a society where peace and stability were tenuous at best. (This section summarizes a portion of E.M.W. Tillyard's *The Elizabethan World Picture*.)

The following passage from one of Shakespeare's plays, *Troilus and Cressida*, is often appealed to as the clearest expression of the Elizabethan World Picture. This speech by the character Ulysses emphasizes the importance of "degree" or hierarchical order in the universe by describing the cosmic connections between all created things and the cosmic chaos that results when degree or order is shaken at any level. Notice particularly the close relationships of providence, the state, and the natural world that are also reflected in the disorder in *Macbeth*.

WILLIAM SHAKESPEARE, *TROILUS AND CRESSIDA*, *THE RIVERSIDE SHAKESPEARE*, ED. G. BLAKEMORE EVANS ET AL.
(Boston: Houghton, 1974) 1.3.85–110

Ulysses:
    The heavens themselves, the planets, and this centre

Observe degree, priority, and place,
Insisture, course, proportion, season, form,
Office, and custom, in all line of order;
And therefore is the glorious planet Sol
In noble eminence enthron'd and spher'd
Amidst the other; whose med'cinable eye
Corrects the [ill aspects] of [planets evil],
And posts like the commandment of a king,
Sans check, to good and bad. But when the planets
In evil mixture to disorder wander,
What plagues and what portents, what mutiny!
What raging of the sea, shaking of earth!
Commotion in the winds! frights, changes, horrors
Divert and crack, rend and deracinate
The unity and married calm of states
Quite from their fixture! O, when degree is shak'd,
Which is the ladder of all high designs,
The enterprise is sick. How could communities,
Degrees in schools, and brotherhoods in cities,
Peaceful commerce from dividable shores,
The primogenity and due of birth,
Prerogative of age, crowns, sceptres, laurels,
But by degree stand in authentic place?
Take but degree away, untune that string,
And hark what discord follows.

The King's Two Bodies. The power and dignity of the king depicted in the Chain-of-Being metaphor also found expression in another related metaphor that focused specifically on kingship itself. A theory that evolved from the Middle Ages described the king as having two bodies: a body politic and a body natural. The body politic involved his role as head of state. Whoever was king assumed the political position with all the power and duties it entailed. The body natural represented the king's personal body, his human side, which, when joined with his body politic, bestowed on him the divine appointment to govern by God's will and election. This theory echoes still today in the expression "The king is dead; long live the king." When one monarch dies, his natural body goes to the grave, but the body politic is immortalized in succession as the crown is passed on to a new heir. The chain is not broken; the king never dies; the social system is not destroyed.

In its early version this theory of the two bodies gave some control to the king's subjects, who were seen as part of the corporate body politic. As kingship gained power in the sixteenth and seventeenth centuries, the idea of the two bodies developed into a strong claim for the divine right of kings governing as miniature gods in the commonwealth and accountable for their actions not to subjects or Parliament but to God alone. In Scotland King James became a main proponent of divine right and had published his views about it even before he came to England. In England in Elizabeth's time, the attitude about divine right fostered a doctrine of nonresistance or absolute obedience, which held that subjects had no right to rebel regardless of the king's injustice. They were expected only to obey, for even tyrants were presumed to be God's agents, sent to punish the nation or to cleanse and rebuild it. This belief became a popular topic in church sermons.

Particularly in the Stuart era of King James, divine right became the manifesto of the monarch and his supporters. Needless to say, not everyone accepted the extreme position, however, and some critics even published support for tyrannicide, the subjects' right to overthrow an unjust king.

The theory of divine right, or absolutism, raises interest in the relationship between kings and subjects in *Macbeth*. Macbeth's succession is initially sanctioned by the majority after Duncan's sons have fled the country, but eventually his subjects rebel against him. The play may seem to portray a world order that is black and white, but the debate about kingship outside the theater raises questions about some of the assumptions that Shakespeare dramatizes, such as the clash between absolute obedience and the legitimacy of rebellion, the role of providence in succession, and the absolute authority of the body politic. What is the balance between a king's rights and his duties? How can Macbeth be both tyrant and king? The issue of legitimacy is complex because until Macbeth's crime of murder can be proven, he assumes the body politic when he wears the crown and theoretically deserves obedience.

A passage included here from an Elizabethan document, *The Commentaries*, explains how political legitimacy is defined by the metaphor of two bodies. The author, a lawyer and constitutional expert, Edmund Plowden, describes the mortal and immortal qualities that combine to give the monarch his power and that allow for a peaceful succession from one king to the next. This theory of the two bodies provided support for kings against those who might question or challenge their authority.

EDMUND PLOWDEN, *COMMENTARIES OR REPORTS*
(1571; London, 1816)

The King has two Capacities, for he has two Bodies, the one whereof is a Body natural, consisting of natural Members as every other Man has, and in this he is subject to Passions and Death as other Men are; the other is a Body politic, and the Members thereof are his Subjects, and he and his Subjects together compose the Corporation, as Southcote said, and he is incorporated with them, and they with him, and he is the Head, and they are the Members, and he has the sole Government of them; and this Body is not subject to Passions as the other is, nor to Death, for as to this Body the King never dies, and his natural Death is not called in our Law (as Harper said), the Death of the King, but the Demise of the King, not signifying by the Word (*Demise*) that the Body politic of the King is dead, but that there is a Separation of the two Bodies, and that the Body politic is transferred and conveyed over from the Body natural now dead, or now removed from the Dignity royal, to another Body natural. So that it signifies a Removal of the Body politic of the King of this Realm from one Body natural to another. (233a)

From Ernst Kantorowicz, *The King's Two Bodies* (Princeton, NJ: Princeton UP, 1957) 13

A Mirror for Magistrates. Another long tradition reflecting attitudes about kingship is expressed in the analogy of a mirror or looking glass. Again, this concept originated in the Middle Ages but became especially popular in Elizabeth I's reign with a collection of moral stories published about kings and nobles, titled *A Mirror for Magistrates* (1559). These poetic stories provided examples from history about tragedies that resulted when magistrates or rulers acted unjustly and when subjects rebelled. As the title suggests, the stories intended history as a mirror in which the current reigning monarchs could see their own actions reflected and learn from the contrast of good and bad government how to rule well and responsibly. William Baldwin describes this purpose in his introduction to the collection of tragedies. He says of magistrates:

What a foul shame were it for any now to take upon them the name and office of God, and in their doings to show themselves devils? ... How he [God] hath dealt with some of our countrymen your ancestors, for sundry vices not yet wept, this book named *A Mirror for Magistrates*, can show: which therefore I humbly offer unto your honours beseeching you to accept it favourably. For here as in a looking glass, you shall see (if any vice be in you) how the like hath been punished in other heretofore, whereby admonished, I trust it will be a good occasion to move you to the sooner amendment. This is the chiefest end why it is set forth, which God grant it may attain.

From *A Mirror for Magistrates*, ed. Lily Campbell (1559; Cambridge UP, 1938) 65–66

This popular story collection greatly influenced the development of history plays and tragedies on stage with their focus on the rise and fall of kings emphasizing the effects of pride, providence, and fate. *Macbeth* exists within this political, moral tradition as it contrasts various rulers, reflecting both good and bad examples of just, effective kingship and celebrating the restoration of peace when Malcolm ascends to the throne as legitimate heir.

The Lion and the Fox. Most Tudor and Stuart doctrines about kingship relied on an ideal vision of what good government ought to be, and those views were presented primarily in the form of instruction through political guidebooks for princes or sermons for common subjects. By the time James became England's king, however, another political influence had reached the island from the Continent through the writing of the Italian Niccolò Machiavelli. Machiavelli based his theory of good government on a pragmatic rather than ideal view of the world, on the way things were rather than the way they ought to be. He saw politics and religion as completely separate. Writing for the unstable Italian city-states of the sixteenth century, Machiavelli stressed the importance of power and the need to achieve and maintain it even if that meant using force, inspiring fear, and relying on false appearances. The analogies of state closely associated with him compare political leaders not to God, as the English did, but to beasts. A prince, Machiavelli felt, should have the strength of a lion and the cunning of a fox.

In general his theories were received with horror and hostility in England. Many critics relied on his negative reputation rather than his writing itself, and most condemned his separation of politics and religion as anti-Christian and immoral. Theaters became popular sites for reflecting a negative attitude toward Machiavelli. Characters that were monstrous villains or atheists began to be known as "stage machiavels," and to this day the adjective "machiavellian" retains notions of deceptive politics and double-dealing. Whereas such characters exaggerated the worst misinterpretation of Machiavelli's ideas, some political thinkers in England recognized practical value in his advice, and support for his ideas grew stronger in the 1600s. In spite of obvious anti-Machiavellian sentiments, therefore, he inspired a mixed reaction in England.

Given this varied response, studying *Macbeth* for expressions of Machiavellian philosophy is challenging but worthwhile. One of the best places to direct that study is to begin in Act 4.3 where in dialogue Malcolm tests the loyalty of Macduff on legitimate and illegitimate forms of kingship. Reading that scene in light of the play's action and in connection with the excerpts from political documents throughout this chapter can help to address questions about Shakespeare's vision of kingship. Is Macbeth machiavellian in the worst sense of the word, or is Malcolm machiavellian in his astute political decisions? Do the words and actions of the characters reflect an ideal or practical kingship? Do images of God or beast predominate? How do tyrants differ from good kings?

Following a chronology of relevant dates and events, excerpts from Machiavelli are included in the remainder of this section, together with passages written by John Ponet (a political exile during Queen Mary's reign in England) and King James. By their contrasting viewpoints, these documents further demonstrate some of the competing political ideas current when *Macbeth* was written and first performed. Machiavelli's pragmatic approach to power and Ponet's assertion that subjects can rightfully overrule their king differ sharply from King James's theories of divine right. In most selections, spelling from the original documents has been regularized and modernized for clarity.

BRIEF HISTORICAL CHRONOLOGY

1034–1040	King Duncan rules Scotland.
1040–1057	Macbeth rules Scotland.
1513	Machiavelli's *The Prince* offers a practical guide to Italian state rulers.
1556	John Ponet's *A Short Treatise of Politic Power* advocates the right of rebellion.
1558	Elizabeth I becomes the Tudor Queen of England.
1559	*A Mirror for Magistrates* is published.
1567	James Stuart becomes King James VI of Scotland.
1598	King James writes *The True Law of Free Monarchies*, expressing his views about the rights of kingship.
1599	King James writes *Basilicon Doron*, a pamphlet of political instruction for his son and heir, Henry.
1603	James VI of Scotland becomes James I of England.
1605	Dr. Gwinn's Latin playlet, *Tres Sibyllae*, is performed at Oxford.
1606	Probable date of *Macbeth*'s composition and first performance.
1625	James dies; his son succeeds to the throne as King Charles I.
1649	Charles I is beheaded in the Civil War.

MACHIAVELLI'S POLITICAL VIEWS

Italian political writer Niccolò Machiavelli addresses his ideas to the prince or ruler of the state. In the following three selections from *The Prince*, he offers advice based on his perception of the presence of ambition and corruption in the political sphere. The first quotation argues that a ruler's evil or cruelty may be justified if it is exercised quickly and is used to increase the prince's security, consequently providing subjects with greater peace and stability. Machiavelli's second citation explains that it is better for a ruler to be feared than to be loved because fear of punishment instills greater loyalty and security than admiration. Third, he advocates the necessity of practicing deception, of being as cunning as a fox, because successful governors need only appear to be good rather than actually to be good. Although many in England saw this advice as evil and ungodly, others recognized that government in an imperfect world could not be godly and that a secular, practical approach, therefore, seemed much more appropriate. As you read, consider whether some of these ideas have a place in *Macbeth*, and if so, are they reflected in the behavior of good kings or in Macbeth's tyranny?

NICCOLÒ MACHIAVELLI, *THE PRINCE* (1513), HARVARD
CLASSICS COLLECTION
(New York: Collier, 1910)

[1] It may be asked how Agathocles and some like him, after numberless acts of treachery and cruelty, have been able to live long in their own country in safety, and to defend themselves from foreign enemies, without being plotted against by their fellow-citizens, whereas, many others, by reason of their cruelty, have failed to maintain their position even in peaceful times, not to speak of the perilous times of war. I believe that this results from cruelty being well or ill employed. Those cruelties we may say are well employed, if it be permitted to speak well of things evil, which are done once for all under the necessity of self-preservation, and are not afterwards persisted in, but so far as possible modified to the advantage of the governed. Ill-employed cruelties, on the other hand, are those which from small beginnings increase rather than diminish with

time. They who follow the first of these methods, may, by the grace of God and man, find, as did Agathocles, that their condition is not desperate; but by no possibility can the others maintain themselves.

Hence we may learn the lesson that on seizing a state, the usurper should make haste to inflict what injuries he must, at a stroke, that he may not have to renew them daily, but be enabled by their discontinuance to reassure men's minds, and afterwards win them over by benefits. Whosoever, either through timidity or from following bad counsels, adopts a contrary course, must keep the sword always drawn, and can put no trust in his subjects, who suffering from continued and constantly renewed severities, will never yield him their confidence. Injuries, therefore, should be inflicted all at once, that their ill savour being less lasting may the less offend; whereas, benefits should be conferred little by little, that so they may be more fully relished. (33–34)

[2] And here comes in the question whether it is better to be loved rather than feared, or feared rather than loved. It might perhaps be answered that we should wish to be both; but since love and fear can hardly exist together, if we must choose between them, it is far safer to be feared than loved. For of men it may generally be affirmed that they are thankless, fickle, false, studious to avoid danger, greedy of gain, devoted to you while you are able to confer benefits upon them, and ready, as I said before, while danger is distant, to shed their blood, and sacrifice their property, their lives, and their children for you; but in the hour of need they turn against you. The Prince, therefore, who without otherwise securing himself builds wholly on their professions is undone. For the friendships which we buy with a price, and do not gain by greatness and nobility of character, though they be fairly earned are not made good, but fail us when we have occasion to use them.

Moreover, men are less careful how they offend him who makes himself loved than him who makes himself feared. For love is held by the tie of obligation, which, because men are a sorry breed, is broken on every whisper of private interest; but fear is bound by the apprehension of punishment which never relaxes its grasp.

Nevertheless a Prince should inspire fear in such a fashion that if he do not win love he may escape hate. For a man may very well be feared and yet not hated, and this will be the case so long as he does not meddle with the property or with the women of his citizens and subjects. And if constrained to put any to death, he should do so only when there is manifest cause or reasonable justification. (57–58)

[3] But since a Prince should know how to use the beast's nature wisely, he ought of beasts to choose both the lion and the fox; for the lion cannot

guard himself from the toils, nor the fox from wolves. He must therefore be a fox to discern toils, and a lion to drive off wolves.

To rely wholly on the lion is unwise; and for this reason a prudent Prince neither can nor ought to keep his word when to keep it is hurtful to him and the causes which led him to pledge it are removed. If all men were good, this would not be good advice, but since they are dishonest and do not keep faith with you, you, in return, need not keep faith with them; and no prince was ever at a loss for plausible reasons to cloak a breach of faith. Of this numberless recent instances could be given, and it might be shown how many solemn treaties and engagements have been rendered inoperative and idle through want of faith in Princes, and that he who was best known to play the fox has had the best success.

It is necessary, indeed, to put a good colour on this nature, and to be skilful in simulating and dissembling. But men are so simple, and governed so absolutely by their present needs, that he who wishes to deceive will never fail in finding willing dupes. . . .

It is not essential, then, that a Prince should have all the good qualities which I have enumerated above, but it is most essential that he should seem to have them; I will even venture to affirm that if he has and invariably practises them all, they are hurtful, whereas the appearance of having them is useful. Thus, it is well to seem merciful, faithful, humane, religious, and upright, and also to be so; but the mind should remain so balanced that were it needful not to be so, you should be able and know how to change to the contrary. (60–61)

A DEFENSE OF REBELLION

Unlike Machiavelli, John Ponet, English bishop of Rochester and Winchester (1516?–1556), addresses subjects rather than rulers. Writing in exile during Queen Mary's reign, Ponet strongly advocates the corporate right of subjects to punish and displace a tyrant. His position runs contrary to official monarchical claims for complete supremacy over laws and subjects but gains some support from England's parliamentary system, which gave law-making power to the people. The excerpt below from his *A Short Treatise of Politic Power* (1556) argues that natural law speaks through the conscience of subjects, guiding their decision to overthrow an unjust ruler. According to Ponet, rebellion was sometimes justified and necessary.

JOHN PONET, *A SHORT TREATISE OF POLITIC POWER*
(1556; Yorkshire: A Scholar Press Facsimile, 1970) Sig. Gvi[v];
Gxii[v]–Hi

But now to prove the later part of this question affirmatively, that it is lawful to kill a tyrant. . . .

For it is no private law to a few or certain people, but common to all: not written in books, but grafted in the hearts of men: not made by man, but ordained of God: which we have not learned, received or read, but have taken, sucked, and drawn out of nature: whereunto we are not taught, but made: not instructed, but seasoned: and (as St. Paul saieth) man's conscience bearing witness of it.

This law testifieth to every man's conscience, that it is natural to cut away an incurable member, which (being suffered) would destroy the whole body.

Kings, Princes and other governors, albeit they are the heads of a politic body, yet they are not the whole body. And though they be chief members, yet they are but members: neither are the people ordained for them, but they are ordained for the people. . . .

But I beseech thee, what needeth to make one general law to punish by one name a great many offenses, when the law is already made for the punishment of everyone of them particularly. If a prince rob and spoil his subjects, it is theft, and as theft ought to be punished. If he kill and murder them contrary or without the laws of his country, it is murder, and as a murderer he ought to be punished. . . . If he go about to betray his country, and to bring the people under a foreign power, he is a traitor, and as a traitor he ought to suffer. And those that be judges in commonwealths, ought (upon complaint) to summon and cite them to answer to their crimes, and so to proceed, as they do with others.

KING JAMES'S VIEW OF KINGSHIP

James VI of Scotland (later James I of England) was an intellectual king who had a theoretical as well as a practical interest in issues such as kingship and witchcraft. He wrote extensively to present his views and argue his position. Some have called *Macbeth* King James's play because it dramatizes several of the king's favorite concerns. Two of his most famous works are cited here for their relevance to themes in the play. The first, *The True Law of Free Monarchies* (1598), is a pamphlet that expresses James's ideas about the rights and duties of kings and subjects in a monarchy, which he saw as the form of government nearest to perfection and closest to divinity. Partly because his Scottish perspective on kingcraft lacked England's strong parliamentary tradition and partly because his monarchical position gave him a vested interest in his own power, his ideas contrast significantly with Ponet's earlier views on rebellion. James believed that kings, not subjects or Parliament, made and controlled laws. If for Ponet natural law speaks through the people, for James natural law guarantees the hierarchical supremacy of the monarch. In the passage below notice how he uses the family and the body as analogies to support his extreme position for the royal supremacy and authority of monarchs.

In *Basilicon Doron* (1599), an instructional pamphlet addressed to James's son Henry, who was expected to be heir to the throne until he died at a young age, James theorizes about kingship. The book's title is a Greek phrase translated as "kingly gift." The two sections included here express some of James's views about conscience and tyranny, two central issues in Shakespeare's play. James advises his son to heed conscience as the voice of God and to guard against two forms of a diseased mind, "leaprosy," by which he means blindness to sin, and "superstition," which relies on knowledge or fantasy that is not grounded in God's word. On the topic of just government, James distinguishes clearly between good kings and tyrants, contrasting the two in order to teach his son how to govern well. His ideal view of government offers quite a different interpretation of politics than does Machiavelli, who puts little trust in the godly benevolence of the ruler or in the unquestioning goodness and obedience of the people.

When reading these two documents, refer to the portrait illus-
tration of King James included in this section. Although it pictures
James as an older man near the end of his English reign rather
than at the beginning, it symbolically reinforces the official doctrine of kingship he supported, based on absolute authority and
the divine origin of legitimacy. His crown and the orb (or globe)
and scepter in his hands are the standard symbols of monarchy.
The pendant attached to the front of James's mantle depicts the
patron saint of England, St. George who slew the dragon. St.
George and his horse are encircled by a French inscription,
roughly translated, "Shame to those who think evil." Above
James's head is his personal kingly motto *Beati Pacifici*—"Blessed
are the peacemakers"—a biblical verse from the Beatitudes. On his
left lie the scroll of justice and the Word of God (*Verum Dei*).
Beneath the portrait is a verse that affirms in the last line, "But
knowledge makes the KING most like his maker." This picture of
James I deliberately surrounds him with visual signs of ideal kingship that emphasize his goodness. It indicates how art, as well as
metaphor, helped to shape political perception in the seventeenth
century.

KING JAMES, *THE TRUE LAW OF FREE MONARCHIES* (1598)

Kings are called Gods by the prophetical King *David*, because they sit
upon GOD his Throne in earth, and have the count of their administration to give unto him. . . .

By the Law of Nature the King becomes a natural Father to all his Lieges
at his Coronation: And as the Father of his fatherly duty is bound to care
for the nourishing, education, and virtuous government of his children;
even so is the king bound to care for all his subjects. . . . As the kindly
father ought to foresee all inconveniences and dangers that may arise
toward his children, and though with the hazard of his own person press
to prevent the same; so ought the King toward his people. As the father's
wrath and correction upon any of his children that offendeth, ought to
be by a fatherly chastisement seasoned with pity, as long as there is any
hope of amendment in them; so ought the King toward any of his Lieges
that offend in that measure. And shortly, as the Father's chief joy ought
to be in procuring his children's welfare, rejoicing at their weal, sorrow-
ing and pitying at their evil, to hazard for their safety, travel for their rest,
wake for their sleep; and in a word, to think that his earthly felicity and

Portrait of King James I in his old age from an engraving by Simon Van de Passe. *Courtesy of the British Museum*.

life standeth and liveth more in them, nor in himself; so ought a good Prince think of his people. (54–56)

And the proper office of a King toward his Subjects, agrees very well with the office of the head toward the body, and all members thereof: For from the head, being the seat of Judgment, proceedeth the care and foresight of guiding, and preventing all evil that may come to the body or any part thereof. The head cares for the body, so doth the King for his people. As the discourse and direction flows from the head, and the execution according thereunto belongs to the rest of the members, everyone according to their office: so it is betwixt a wise Prince, and his people. As the judgment coming from the head may not only employ the members, everyone in their own office, as long as they are able for it; but likewise in case any of them be affected with any infirmity must care and provide for their remedy, in case it be curable, and if otherwise, . . . cut them off for fear of infecting of the rest: even so it is betwixt the Prince, and his people. And as there is ever hope of curing any diseased member by the direction of the head, as long as it is whole; but by the contrary, if it be troubled, all the members are partakers of that pain, so it is betwixt the Prince and his people.

And now first for the father's part . . . consider, I pray you what duty his children owe to him, and whether upon any pretext whatsoever, it will not be thought monstrous and unnatural to his sons, to rise up against him, to control him at their appetite, and when they think good to slay him, or to cut him off, and adopt to themselves any other they please in his room: Or can any pretence of wickedness or rigor on his part be a just excuse for his children to put hand into him? And although we see by the course of nature, that love useth to descend more than to ascend, in case it were true, that the father hated and wronged the children never so much, will any man, endued with the least sponk of reason, think it lawful for them to meet him with the line? Yea, suppose the father were furiously following his sons with a drawn sword is it lawful for them to turn and strike again, or make any resistance but by flight? (64–65)

I grant indeed, that a wicked king is sent by God for a curse to his people, and a plague for their sins: but that it is lawful to them to shake off that curse at their own hand, which God hath laid on them, that I deny, and may do so justly. . . .

It is certain then (as I have already by the Law of God sufficiently proved) that patience, earnest prayers to God, and amendment of their lives, are the only lawful means to move God to relieve them of that heavy curse. As for vindicating to themselves their own liberty, what lawful power have they to revoke to themselves again those privileges, which by their own consent before were so fully put out of their hands? (67)

Not that by all this former discourse of mine, and Apology for kings, I mean that whatsoever errors and intolerable abominations a sovereign prince commit, he ought to escape all punishment, as if thereby the world were ordained for kings, & they without controlment to turn it upside down at their pleasure: but by the contrary, by remitting them to God (who is their only ordinary Judge) I remit them to the sorest and sharpest schoolmaster that can be devised for them: for the further a king is preferred by God above all other ranks and degrees of men, and the higher that his seat is above theirs, the greater is his obligation to his maker. (69–70)

From *The Political Works of James I*, ed. Charles Howard McIlwain (Cambridge: Harvard UP, 1918)

KING JAMES, *BASILICON DORON* (1599)

And as for conscience, which I called the conserver of Religion, It is nothing else, but the light of knowledge that God hath planted in man, which ever watching over all his actions, as it beareth him a joyful testimony when he does right, so choppeth it him with a feeling that he hath done wrong, whenever he commiteth any sin. And surely, although this conscience be a great torture to the wicked, yet is it as great a comfort to the godly, if we will consider it rightly. For have we not a great advantage, that have within ourselves while we live here, a Count-book and Inventory of all the crimes that we shall be accused of, either at the hour of death, or at the Great day of Judgment; which when we please (yea though we forget) will chop, and remember us to look upon it. . . . Above all them, my Son, labour to keep sound this conscience, which many prattle of, but over few feel: especially be careful to keep it free from two diseases, wherewith it useth oft to be infected; to wit, Leaprosy, and Superstition; the former is the mother of Atheism, the other of Heresies. By a leaprous conscience, I mean *a cauterized conscience*, . . . being become senseless of sin, through sleeping in a careless security as King *David's* was after his murder and adultery, ever till he was wakened by the Prophet *Nathan's* similitude. And by superstition, I mean, when one restrains himself to any other rule in the service of God, than is warranted by the word, the only true square of God's service?

As for a preservative against Leaprosy, remember ever once in the four and twenty hours, either in the night, or when ye are at greatest quiet, to call yourself to account of all your last day's actions, either wherein ye have committed things ye should not, or omitted the things ye should do, either in your Christian or Kingly calling. . . .

And for keeping your conscience sound from that sickness of superstition, ye must neither lay the safety of your conscience upon the credit of your own conceits, nor yet of other men's humors, how great Doctors that ever they be; but ye must only ground it upon the express Scripture: for conscience not grounded upon sure knowledge, is either an ignorant fantasy, or an arrogant vanity. (16–17)

For the part of making, and executing of Laws, consider first the true difference betwixt a lawful good King, and an usurping Tyrant. . . . The one acknowledgeth himself ordained for his people, having received from God a burden of government, whereof he must be countable: the other thinketh his people ordained for him, a prey to his passions and inordinate appetites, as the fruits of his magnanimity: And therefore, as their ends are directly contrary, so are their whole actions, as means, whereby they press to attain to their ends. A good King, thinking his highest honour to consist in the due discharge of his calling, employeth all his study and pains, to procure and maintain, by the making and execution of good Laws, the welfare and peace of his people; and as their natural father and kindly Master, thinketh his greatest contentment standeth in their prosperity, and his greatest surety in having their hearts, subjecting his own private affections and appetites to the weal [commonwealth] and standing of his Subjects, ever thinking common interest his chiefest particular: whereby the contrary, an usurping Tyrant, thinking his greatest honour and felicity to consist in attaining . . . to his ambitious pretences, thinketh never himself sure, but by the dissension and factions among his people, and counterfeiting the Saint while he once creep in credit, will then (by inverting all good Laws to serve only for his unruly private affections) frame the commonweal ever to advance his particular: building his surety upon his people's misery: and in the end (as a stepfather and an uncouth hireling) make up his own hand upon the ruins of the Republic. And according to their actions, so receive they their reward: For a good King (after a happy and famous reign) dieth in peace, lamented by his subjects, and admired by his neighbours; and leaving a reverent renown behind him in earth, obtaineth the Crown of eternal felicity in heaven. And although some of them (which falleth out very rarely) may be cut off by the treason of some unnatural subjects, yet liveth their fame after them, and some notable plague faileth never to overtake the committers in this life, besides their infamy to all posterities hereafter: Whereby the contrary, a Tyrant's miserable and infamous life, armeth in end his own Subjects to become his burreaux: and although that rebellion be ever unlawful on their part, yet is the world so wearied of him, that his fall is little meaned by the rest of his Subjects, and but smiled at by his neighbours. And besides the infamous memory he leaveth behind him here, and the endless pain he sustaineth hereafter, if oft falleth out, that the committers not only escape unpunished, but farther, the fact will remain as allowed by the Law in diverse ages thereafter. It is easy then for you (my Son) to make a choice of one of these two sorts of rulers, by following the way of virtue to establish your standing; yea, in case ye fell in high way, yet should it be with the honourable report, and just regrate of all honest men. (18–19)

From *The Political Works of James I*, ed. Charles Howard McIlwain (Cambridge: Harvard UP, 1918)

QUESTIONS FOR WRITTEN AND ORAL DISCUSSION

1. Explain succession and its importance in the seventeenth century. How is it addressed by Plowden and by Gwinn's *Tres Sibyllae*?

2. What similarities do you see in the excerpt from *Tres Sibyllae* and the first scene of *Macbeth*? How do you think King James would have reacted to each performance?

3. Study the description of the Chain of Being in Ulysses' speech in *Troilus and Cressida*. What is the foundation of order? How is the hierarchy described? What is the cause of chaos?

4. Discuss how the beliefs of the Elizabethan World Picture are expressed in *Macbeth*. How do the links in the universal Chain of Being affect the movement from order to chaos and back to order? How are natural and political order connected? Refer particularly to Act 2.4 and Macbeth's soliloquy in 2.1.

5. Explain Plowden's use of the body as a political analogy in his *Commentaries*. How does the analogy define the relationship between the king and his subjects? How does it account for the effect of the king's death on the state? What is the difference between the king's two bodies?

6. *A Mirror for Magistrates* relies on examples from history to provide moral and political lessons. Can *Macbeth* be seen as a mirror for magistrates? Does the drama offer lessons, and if so, what are they? How is Scotland's past reflected in Shakespeare's present?

7. In *The True Laws*, how does King James use the analogies of family and body to describe the duties of the king and his subjects? Do his comparisons seem reasonable or not?

8. According to *The True Laws* and *Basilicon Doron*, how should subjects respond to tyranny? How will a tyrant be punished? What are the limitations on a king's actions?

9. Divide a sheet of paper into two columns, one for tyrants and the other for just kings. List the qualities of each according to King James's description in *Basilicon Doron*. Make a similar list for the tyrants and kings in *Macbeth*. How closely do the two resemble each other?

10. In *Basilicon Doron*, James writes about the importance of conscience and the hazards of a diseased mind. How do his observations apply to Macbeth? Does Macbeth suffer from "leaprosy" or "superstition" or both? Give examples.

11. Compare Ponet's attitude toward rebellion with the views of King

James. How do their ideas about the state as body contrast? Suggest reasons for their differences. Which viewpoint seems more acceptable to you and why?

12. If rebellion seems legitimate or justifiable in *Macbeth*, what reasons are provided in the play? When is violence acceptable? When is it not? Is the overthrow of Macbeth consistent with King James's view or Ponet's?

13. Machiavelli was admired and hated in Shakespeare's England. Reading the selections from *The Prince*, can you find reasons for both reactions? Does his advice seem practical and necessary or evil and immoral?

14. Write an essay applying Machiavelli's philosophy to the issue of kingship in *Macbeth*. What parts do cruelty, fear, and deception play in the drama? Is Macbeth a machiavellian?

15. Write an essay on the topic of ideal kingship in *Macbeth*. What qualities seem to characterize an ideal monarch, and do any of the characters meet the standard?

16. Some argue that Shakespeare's Duncan is a good king because he is a moral, generous man. Others suggest that he is a weak king who does not have the political wisdom and insight to be an effective ruler. Is he too trusting? Considering his leadership in Act 1, discuss the merits or failings of his kingship.

17. Read Malcolm and Macduff's discussion of kingship in Act 4.3. Hold a class debate with one side supporting the necessity of Malcolm's deception and the other side arguing against his behavior as unsuitable for a future king.

18. Write an essay about tyranny in *Macbeth*. What makes Macbeth a tyrant, and when does he become one? Does he have any redeeming qualities as a political leader?

19. Imagine you are King James and have just seen *Macbeth* for the first time. Write a diary entry responding to the play's presentation of kingship. Are you flattered or uneasy with the portrayal of tyranny and king killing? Were you entertained or instructed?

20. Power is relative because it can be measured only in comparison with the power that other people have. Make a graph charting Macbeth's power and explain its rise and fall in comparison to the other characters. When is he most powerful? When does he begin to lose control?

21. Legitimacy is as important in *Macbeth* as it is in the political writing of the time. There is a difference between power and legitimacy, be-

tween might and right. In Shakespeare's play, where do rulers find their legitimacy, and if they have no legitimacy, how do they achieve their power?

22. Imagine Macbeth and Machiavelli sitting down to a discussion about kingship. Write a dialogue between them. Would Machiavelli have any advice for Macbeth? Would Macbeth defend his actions using Machiavelli's words?

23. One of the political debates in the seventeenth century centered on the relationship between religion, specifically Christianity, and the state. Divine providence was believed to play an active part in political life. Many saw good kingship as virtuous and godly, and bad kingship as evil and immoral. Earthly actions had heavenly consequences. What role does providence play in *Macbeth*? Who acknowledges its influence? How is Christianity expressed in the political struggle?

SUGGESTED READINGS

Bullough, Geoffrey. *Narrative and Dramatic Sources of Shakespeare*. Vol. 7. London: Routledge, 1973.

Mack, Maynard. *Killing the King: Three Studies in Shakespeare's Tragic Structure*. New York: Yale UP, 1973.

Muir, Kenneth. Critical Introduction. *Macbeth*. London: Routledge, 1984.

Paul, Henry N. *The Royal Play of Macbeth*. New York: Macmillan, 1950.

Raab, Felix. *The English Face of Machiavelli, A Changing Interpretation*. London: Routledge, 1964.

Tillyard, E.M.W. *The Elizabethan World Picture*. New York: Random, 1944.

Wells, Robin Headlam. *Shakespeare, Politics and the State*. London: Macmillan, 1986.

TREASON AND EQUIVOCATION: THE GUNPOWDER PLOT

The Gunpowder Plot was one of the biggest and most controversial events in England when *Macbeth* first appeared on stage in 1606, and exploring the magnitude of this incident will help modern audiences and readers appreciate its influence on the atmosphere and themes in Shakespeare's play. The plot was a treasonous conspiracy initiated by a group of discontented Catholics who planned to blow up Parliament House with a large quantity of gunpowder on the opening day of the legislative session in November 1605.

Had the plot succeeded, it would have been politically cata-
strophic, for the explosion would have killed not only the king but
also his heirs and all the lords attending the session. Government,
as the English knew it, would have been virtually annihilated.
Moreover, the treachery threatened the religious and hereditary
foundations of monarchy itself, based on God's divine appointment of the king and continued political stability through royal
family succession. According to Protestants and loyal monarchists,
this attempt to destroy the whole system was, therefore, not only
an act of anarchy and cruelty but also an evil attack against God
himself.

The conspirators, however, were guided by their own religious
convictions. They intended to rid England of its Protestant king
and sympathizers and to replace him with a Catholic ruler who
would support their faith. Their plan ended with a sensational discovery when Guy Fawkes, the man appointed to ignite the explosives, was caught on the eve of the parliamentary session waiting
beneath the House of Lords with a lantern in his hand and several
slow-burning matches in his pocket. The other conspirators fled
London hoping to stir up a rebellion among Catholic nobles in the
rural areas; but finding virtually no support, they were quickly captured and charged with treason. Within a few months they were
convicted and hanged.

Once the immediate danger was over, the government realized
the magnitude of the disaster that had been prevented and encouraged a widespread public celebration; November 5 became
Guy Fawkes Day, a national event that is still recognized in England
today with bonfires and effigies of Guy Fawkes burned to com-
memorate victory for the law and the Crown. Even in North America colloquial use of the word "guy" derives from the name of the
infamous English conspirator. Although "guy" began as a deroga-
tory term for the effigies used to ridicule the traitor, it has since
then developed less negative connotations.

The bare facts of the Gunpowder story may appear simple now,
but the conspiracy in 1605 marked the culmination of generations
of religious and political tensions in England. Reports favored one
side or the other, and contradictory accounts of the treason leave
questions still unresolved about the guilt of all the conspirators on
trial, the involvement of others who escaped, and the corruption
of government tactics used to expose the treason and promote

peace. Some versions of the event even speculate that the plot was a setup designed by the Protestant government to destroy Catholics. Although this interpretation seems unlikely, the extent of deception in the plot's exposure remains unknown. What we do know is that those in power after the attempted treason had nothing to lose and everything to gain from denouncing the Powder Plot as a horrific and monstrous deed and the traitors as appallingly evil men. Certainly at the time that Shakespeare was likely writing *Macbeth*, during or shortly after the Gunpowder trials, the political climate in England was charged with fear and controversy about threats to public safety and national security.

Dramatic Context

Two central themes in *Macbeth* reflect an urgent political context: treason and equivocation. Treason is the most obvious connection. When all ears in England were tuned to the Gunpowder trials for crimes against England's Scottish-born king, Shakespeare was crafting his own version of Scottish treachery. In the first act of the play, Duncan condemns the Thane of Cawdor to death for conspiring with Norway against Scotland:

> No more that Thane of Cawdor shall deceive
> Our bosom interest.—Go pronounce his present death,
> And with his former title greet Macbeth. (1.2.65–67)

Yet while the traitor is being executed offstage, Macbeth is plotting a treasonous crime of even greater magnitude as he contemplates killing the king and usurping the throne. Duncan's bloody death suggests the horrible end that James I managed to escape. And the demise of both Thanes of Cawdor, Macbeth and his predecessor to the title, was a victory of justice that every loyal English and Scottish subject could applaud.

Equivocation is an equally important theme that links the play and the Powder Plot. To equivocate is to evade the truth not by deliberately lying but by answering ambiguously through hairsplitting logic and mental reservations so that the truth remains unclear. Such deception was associated with the Catholics and particularly with the Jesuits, an offshoot of the Catholic Church in Rome that sent missionaries to England during Elizabeth I's reign.

The Jesuit priests, who were alleged to be involved in the Powder Treason, advocated equivocation as a doctrine to protect themselves and their religious followers against questions, threats, and punishment by the Protestant government.

During the Gunpowder trials, "equivocation" became a central controversy because some Catholic conspirators practiced it in court while others were accused of doing so. A crucial document, an unpublished treatise commonly known as *The Treatise of Equivocation*, surfaced as a piece of evidence implicating Father Henry Garnet, an influential Jesuit priest who had eluded the investigations of Protestant court officals for several decades. Comments in his handwriting covered the margins of the treatise, and the issue of equivocation rose to prominence especially during his prolonged prosecution because he was most notorious for advocating and practicing equivocation both as a missionary before the Powder Plot and as an accused traitor during his trial.

"Equivocation" was therefore a contentious term in 1606, and Shakespeare clearly draws on its popularity in his thematic developments in *Macbeth*. The witches are the chief equivocators who speak in riddles to foretell Macbeth's future and to deceive him with a false sense of security. Their promises are seductive precisely because they sometimes articulate truths that are confirmed by fact, thus making their prophecies all the more believable. When Macbeth does become Thane of Cawdor immediately after the witches foretell it, he consequently feels he has less reason to doubt their claim that he will become "King hereafter." Lines such as "Fair is foul, and foul is fair" (1.1.11) and "nothing is, but what is not" (1.3.142) echo throughout the play, emphasizing how ambiguities and uncertainties about language can foster deception and lead to corrupted values and moral chaos.

The tangled web of treason and equivocation that defines the darkness of Shakespeare's play reflects the currents of fear surrounding the biggest, most ominous political news story of that time.

English Background

The significance of the Gunpowder Plot and reactions to it can be understood better in light of the long history of tension and violence surrounding the relationship of church and state in England. The most immediate problems stemmed from Queen Elizabeth's policies toward the Catholics but originated with the English Reformation and the rule of Henry VIII. King Henry's break from Rome initiated a long battle among Tudor successors over the supremacy of the newly formed Protestant Church of England against the Catholic Church in Rome and the political powers supported by each of them. Edward VI, Henry's child-heir, was a Protestant king. His sister Mary followed as a Catholic queen who gained a reputation as Bloody Mary for violently persecuting Protestant subjects during her monarchy. Then Queen Elizabeth came to the throne, reestablishing the Protestant Church and passing laws against the practice of Catholicism. These laws, known as the Recusancy Laws, included fines for Catholics who failed to attend Protestant services.

Although Elizabeth's unusually long reign marked a time of reasonable political stability, several plots against her life exposed the civil unrest of Catholics hoping to overthrow their ruler and replace her with someone sympathetic to their religion. At times during Elizabeth's reign, especially when attempts against her life revealed the political threat of Catholicism, government attacks against the Catholics or Papists became severe. Some people were imprisoned; others executed. Thus secrecy in defying Protestantism became paramount among those who accepted the pope's authority. Equivocation for them meant self-preservation.

The history of Jesuit priests in England during Elizabeth's reign provides equally important background to the Gunpowder Plot. When Henry Garnet came to England as a Jesuit missionary in 1585, most members of Elizabeth's court simply hoped that the Catholic "problem" would die out. The remaining Catholics were part of an aging population still loyal to Elizabeth's predecessor, Queen Mary, and Garnet was one of only two Jesuit priests. But by Elizabeth's death in 1603, there were countless priests working underground, using assumed names, encouraging oppressed Catholics, and nurturing a growing church dedicated to Rome and loyal to the supremacy of the pope. Because the pope had passed a decree in 1578, known as a papal bull, excommunicating Elizabeth from the Catholic Church, the English government recognized Catholics as traitors who did not acknowledge complete loyalty to their queen. Church and state were inseparable, and divided loyalties were considered dangerous. The Papists in England were therefore seen not simply as heretics of the faith but as a threat to national security.

Most Catholics, in fact, were not a political threat and were willing to wait and hope for a successor who would tolerate their faith. When it became apparent that James VI of Scotland was likely to succeed, Catholics were even more hopeful. They recognized the possibility of his sympathies toward them because although he was a Protestant himself, his mother had been a staunch Catholic. Furthermore, when some English Catholics sent a representative to Scotland prior to 1603 to ask for James's understanding, he indicated his willingness to be open-minded.

A minority of Catholics were not patient enough to wait, and at the end of Elizabeth's reign dissension became more apparent between various factions in the Catholic community. Not only were the Catholics who wanted to wait peacefully for a new monarch at odds with those Catholics who wanted to seek foreign support from Spain but also the Jesuit priests trained on the Continent were at odds with the "natural" or secular priests from England and each distrusted the other. Some were even willing to expose the identities of others to the Protestant authorities. This background of tension within the Catholic community, combined with Protestant persecution of the Catholics, helps to explain not only the deep-seated anger and antagonism that initiated the Gunpowder Plot but also the strong fear and moral victory characterizing the subsequent reactions to its outcome.

Scottish Background

If English subjects knew a history of treasonous plots against their queen, James VI, King of Scotland, was no less familiar with such dangers. His father, Lord Darnley, had been murdererd in a conspiracy that also involved destroying his residence with gunpowder. His mother, Mary Queen of Scots, had been executed by Protestants in England, and James himself faced several threats against his life. The last of these attempts before he became King of England was the Gowrie Conspiracy on April 5, 1600. Like Shakespeare's Duncan, James was visiting a subject, the Earl of Gowrie, a man purported to be an opponent of the king and to whom James supposedly owed money. Someone tried to kidnap the king, but followers discovered him locked in his chambers before he was harmed. The Earl of Gowrie was blamed for the attack and immediately executed. Like Shakespeare's King Duncan, James was betrayed by a man who was both his subject and his host. Macbeth's words suggest the parallels:

> He's here in double trust:
> First, as I am his kinsman and his subject,
> Strong both against the deed; then, as his host,
> Who should against his murtherer shut the door,
> Not bear the knife myself. (1.7.12–16)

The failed Gowrie Conspiracy was widely publicized beyond Scotland's borders and undoubtedly contributed to the political consciousness in 1606 when Shakespeare was reinventing Scottish history. Just two years earlier John Chamberlain, an English noble, commented in a letter about a play performed on the same subject:

> December 18, 1604: The tragedy of Gowrie, with all the Action and Actors hath been twice represented by the King's Players, with exceeding Concourse of all sorts of People. But whether the matter or manner be not well handled, or that it be thought unfit that Princes should be played on the Stage in their Lifetime, I hear that some great Councillors are much displeased with it, and so 'tis thought shall be forbidden.
>
> From *Winwood's Memorials*, vol. 2 (London, 1725) 41

Shakespeare avoided the hazards of dramatizing the reigns of living princes or kings, but the parallels between his play and recent history would not likely have escaped the minds of his audience.

Dissent and Dissatisfaction

It soon became apparent when James came to power as King of England in March 1603 that the union between England and Scotland did not solve the religious tensions and political unrest as the Catholics had hoped. Initially, the king was somewhat lenient. Although he did not rigorously enforce fines against the Catholics, neither did he make the changes that many Catholics anticipated, and he became more cautious about his tolerance when he realized the potential for public unrest if too many Papists openly declared their religion. In a desperate attempt for change, some of the more radical Catholics instigated two more treasonous plots—the Bye Plot and the Main Plot. Neither succeeded but both were important precursors to the more treacherous Gunpowder Plot. In response to these failed attempts, James tightened security measures. On February 22, 1604, all Jesuits and Catholic priests were ordered to leave the country. A new Recusancy Act was passed and fines were increased. Contrary to expectations when James became king, the country seemed to be moving further and further away from a harmonious resolution of long-standing religious strife.

The Conspiracy

The Powder Treason conspiracy began in spring 1604 shortly after official anti-Catholicism grew stronger. Five men joined forces to plot against the king: Robert Catesby, Thomas Winter, John Wright, Guy Fawkes, and Thomas Percy. Catesby was the instigator, and under his leadership these five men met in May to devise a plan, marking the earnestness of their intent by taking an oath of secrecy and sealing it with the sacrament of Holy Communion. On May 24 Thomas Percy rented a house near the Parliament building, and from there the men prepared to dig a tunnel through which they could place gunpowder under the House of Lords in time for the opening of the legislative session in 1605. Digging underground was difficult for five men unaccustomed to manual labor. They began early in December but took a break over Christmas and resumed their digging later in January of the next year. By March, however, they learned that they could rent cellar space under the Parliament building, thus eliminating the need for a tunnel. Without arousing too much suspicion, they were now able to begin hauling gunpowder into the rented space, concealing it under fuel supplies that were legitimately stored in the vault to be used for Lord Percy's house across the street.

The membership of the conspirators grew as the plot developed. First, the five original participants required more laborers simply to dig the tunnel, so they recruited Robert Keyes and Christopher Wright. Even after the tunnel was no longer necessary, however, Catesby and his followers still needed supporters with money to supply troops and weapons for the national uprising planned after the explosion at Parliament. Five wealthy men were added: John

Grant, Robert Winter, Sir Everard Digby, Ambrose Rookwood, and Francis Tresham. This expansion created new difficulties in maintaining secrecy and consensus among the conspirators. Some of them wanted to warn several members of the House of Lords who were either relatives or Catholics or both not to be present at the opening day of the legislature. Robert Catesby remained the chief advocate for complete secrecy, but as the day of disaster drew nearer, he could no longer maintain control over his confederates.

The Failed Plot

Less than a month before the opening day of Parliament, an anonymous bomb threat alerted the government of impending danger. On October 26 Lord Mounteagle, who was a member of the House of Lords, a former Catholic, and the employer of Thomas Percy, received an anonymous letter that marked the beginning of the end for the conspirators. Although no one ever discovered the source of the letter and even the conspirators could not extort a confession from the traitor in their midst, this leaked document sparked a well-planned and effective reaction from the authorities. Mounteagle immediately presented the letter to the Earl of Salisbury, who was secretary of state in charge of national security. Salisbury then reported to the king, and together they agreed that the best way to obstruct the plot and discover the identities of the conspirators was to keep quiet until the day they could catch the men on the verge of accomplishing their murderous deed. Thus on November 4, the day before the legislative session was scheduled to open, several government officials searched the cellar beneath the House of Lords, where they found Guy Fawkes standing guard over a supply of coal and firewood concealing thirty-six barrels of gunpowder.

Fawkes was immediately arrested. When the other conspirators fled London, the center of the action shifted to the government. Fawkes held the key source of information to expose the other traitors, and yet he remained adamantly silent through five days of questioning until, after physical torture, he finally offered a written confession. This confession was the first of several to follow the treasonous attempt, and although Fawkes failed to identify all his accomplices, he did provide the government with some valuable information as they continued their investigation. Prior to acquir-

ing Fawkes's confession, the authorities already managed to uncover the names of many of the conspirators and issue arrest
warrants for them. What remained was to track down the men
before they fled the country.

The conspirators, however, were more anxious to continue their
plans for overthrowing the government than to escape with their
lives. They seemed guided by destiny, not unlike Macbeth, when
he says, "I am in blood / Stepp'd in so far, that, should I wade no
more, / Returning were as tedious as go o'er" (3.4.135–137). Even
when the explosion failed, the plotters continued unsuccessfully
to attempt a full-scale rebellion. Within a few days most of them
were discovered at the home of a Catholic supporter in Stafford-
shire. Robert Catesby and Thomas Percy were killed in the confrontation while the rest were captured and taken to London to
join Guy Fawkes awaiting trial for high treason.

Although by mid-November the government had imprisoned all
the men implicated directly in the plot, another more challenging
search attempted to discover the Jesuit priests whom the authorities believed were also connected in the Catholic conspiracy
against the Crown. Because the Jesuits were well practiced in secrecy through years of evading the government, they were more
difficult to locate than the active plotters. The priests used assumed
names and often sought refuge in hiding places located in the
homes of their supporters. On January 15 the government council
issued a proclamation for the arrest of three priests, John Gerard,
Oswald Tesimond, and Henry Garnet, who had long-standing rep-
utations for their successful work among English Catholics and
who were known to associate directly with many of the conspirators. Gerard and Tesimond managed to escape from England. Garnet, however, was eventually captured after a seven-day search of
the house wherein he was hiding with another priest. Although
the sheriff and his attendants never did find the priests' tiny concealed place, Garnet and his companion opted to surrender rather
than risk starvation. The manhunt ended when they were taken
into custody on January 27.

The Trials

The trials of the conspirators who were already imprisoned began coincidentally the same day Garnet was caught. Their day in

court was swift and simple; they were easily convicted by jury and had little to say for themselves but to plead for mercy. On January 30 and 31 the eight surviving confederates were executed and made a public spectacle for their crime. By the time Garnet reached London in February, all the main plotters were dead. His examination and trial are the most sensational, however, because the question of his guilt was more open ended, because he did not bend easily under the pressure of interrogation, because his fame and success as an undercover missionary for several decades piqued the public interest in his story, and because the Crown was determined not simply to connect him with the Gunpowder Plot but to make him an example of the treasonous behavior of foreign Jesuits in general.

From the time Garnet was captured until his trial on March 28, he was examined over twenty times by members of the king's council. The government wanted and needed proof that Garnet not only was guilty of a capital offense by virtue of being a Jesuit priest but also knew of the Powder Treason and willingly participated in it. However, strong evidence indicated that he used his connections with Rome to discourage English Catholics from using violence against the Crown. The government employed its own corrupt means to extort a confession from Garnet, even setting up a seemingly private link between Garnet's Tower cell and that of a companion priest so that planted eavesdroppers might overhear conversations that would incriminate the two prisoners. Ultimately, government officials resorted to physical torture and thus forced a confession as they had earlier with Guy Fawkes.

Equivocation was the key issue in Garnet's trial. The Jesuit admitted to a vague knowledge of some trouble being planned by a group of Catholics but explained that because his specific knowledge of the plot came to him while he was acting as priestly confessor, he was unable to divulge what he had heard. Garnet dutifully kept his sacred promise to remain silent unless he was threatened with torture, and in doing so he remained true to his religious faith. The Protestant authorities were scandalized that Garnet would risk the safety of his king to maintain his priestly vow. His confession supplied the evidence they needed to charge him as an accessory to the crime. Nevertheless, the council examined him four more times between his confession and his trial, still trying to prove that he had inspired the plot himself.

While equivocation is a pervasive theme throughout *Macbeth*, there are direct allusions to Father Garnet in the Porter scene after Duncan's murder. Pretending to be the gatekeeper of hell, the Porter associates devilry with equivocation at a time when Protestant England considered the Jesuits to be the devil's own agents—not much different than witches—because of their false speaking and their willingness to compromise their loyalty to God's appointed king. Second, and more specifically, the Porter's comment about an imaginary farmer "that hang'd himself on th'expectation of plenty" (2.3.4–5) might have reminded the public that "Farmer" was one of Henry Garnet's aliases used to protect his Jesuit identity.

Third, Shakespeare likely alludes to Garnet's recent trial and execution when the Porter says, "Faith, here's an equivocator, that could swear in both scales against either scale; who committed treason enough for God's sake, yet could not equivocate to heaven" (2.3.8–11). The black humor of the remark depended on a highly charged contemporary context in which laughter would have come at the expense of the Jesuit priest who tried to save his soul by equivocating and whose "holy" deception, according to the Porter and to most loyal English Protestants, landed him in the fiery pit of hell. This allusion is doubly ironic because in another incident, the conspirators who fled London after Fawkes's arrest accidentally ignited some damp gunpowder that was drying near a fireplace. Even some of the traitors saw this unexpected explosion as a sign of God's judgment. As the Porter implies, the plot designed to turn Parliament into an "everlasting bonfire" served the alleged evil instigators with their own punishment. Shakespeare increases the satire in these Gunpowder Plot allusions by allowing an "average-guy" Porter the subtle wit to expose such clever equivocation while at the same time making him completely inept and unaware of the monstrous murder happening during his own watch.

When Father Garnet was finally brought to trial on March 28, it was a brief affair because the evidence of his previous examinations had already convinced the Crown of his guilt. He was not allowed counsel, nor was he able to present his own testimony, and those who could have been witnesses for him had already been executed. On May 3 he too was hanged as the last and, by official accounts, the worst of the Gunpowder traitors.

The Aftermath

The magnitude of the Powder Treason did not allow it to fade easily from public attention. The mood throughout the country continued to be an intense mixture of fear and celebration. Fear arose from the belief that one failed disaster did not prevent the success of another attempt. In spite of his public pleas for calm and reason, King James apparently and perhaps understandably lived the months following the plot in terror and carefully managed the security around him. High anxiety across England cultivated an atmosphere ripe for overreaction, and in March 1606 a rumor of the king's assassination sparked widespread panic until the news proved to be a false alarm. The Catholic community, especially Jesuits, appeared more suspicious than ever, preventing any immediate hope for increased religious toleration.

Given these fragile conditions, an attitude of victory could be sustained most easily by a simplistic interpretation of the plot: Good conquered evil, God and his appointed triumphed over the devil and his servants. The language of official propaganda and of popular literature reflected this attitude. In November 1605 the *King's Book* published the Crown's version of the plot. Another book, titled *The Black Year*, appeared next year recording the current events of the time. On November 5 ministers began preaching annual sermons against the Powder Treason. The title of one ballad, *The Devil in the Vault*, suggested the symbolic darkness that many recognized in the fact that Guy Fawkes was apprehended at the "witching hour" of night.

This contemporary mood illuminates the themes and language in *Macbeth*. Terror, darkness, deception, violence, and an overwhelming sense of evil revolve around the supernatural forces, the treason, and the tyranny that drive the plot of the play. Shakespeare was not writing in a vacuum, and it is unlikely that people who came to the theater to be entertained were ready, willing, or even able to escape the prevailing mood on the streets.

The remainder of this section begins with a brief summary of events surrounding the Gunpowder Plot and includes a variety of documents that chronicle the actions and responses. These excerpts come from personal letters, a parliamentary speech, a court confession, and a record of Garnet's trial and execution. Spelling has been regularized and modernized for clarity.

BRIEF CHRONOLOGY OF THE GUNPOWDER PLOT

1603, Mar. 24	James VI of Scotland becomes James I, King of England.
1603, July 17	James promises to remove fines against the Catholics.
1604, Feb. 22	Priests are ordered to leave England.
1604, Apr.	Conspirators begin to join forces and plot against the king.
1604, May	Five conspirators take an oath to confirm their intent.
1604, Aug.	New Recusancy Act passed, increasing fines.
1604, c. Dec. 11	Five conspirators begin digging the tunnel.
	Break for Christmas.
1605, c. Jan. 18	Work continues.
1605, Mar.	Conspirators rent cellar at Parliament House and give up digging the tunnel.
1605, Oct. 26	Lord Mounteagle receives anonymous letter.
1605, Nov. 4	Guy Fawkes discovered.
1605, Nov. 5	Conspirators flee London.
1605, Nov. 8	Capture of conspirators.
1606, Jan. 27	Trial of conspirators (Father Garnet caught).
1606, Jan. 30	Digby, Winter, Grant, and Bates hanged.
1606, Jan. 31	Winter, Rookwood, Keys, and Fawkes hanged.
1606, Feb. 14	Garnet imprisoned in Tower.
1606, Mar. 28	Trial of Garnet at Guildhall.
1606, May 3	Garnet hanged.

DISCOVERING THE PLOT

The first excerpt is the anonymous letter delivered to Lord Mounteagle, warning him about an impending political conspiracy without divulging the particular details of the plot itself. When reading
it, try to determine how much specific information is actually provided. That letter is followed by Guy Fawkes's confession extracted
from him after several days of imprisonment and torture in the
Tower. In spite of his initial unwillingness to communicate, his
account appears to provide a consistent and believable chronology
of events.

ANONYMOUS LETTER TO LORD MOUNTEAGLE
(OCTOBER 26, 1605)

my lord out of the love i bear to some of your friends i have a care of
your preservation therefore i would advise you as you tender your life to
devise some excuse to shift of your attendance at this parliament for god
and man hath concurred to punish the wickedness of this time and think
not slightly of this advertisement but retire yourself into your country
where you may expect the event in safety for though there be no appearance of any stir yet I say they shall receive a terrible blow this parliament and yet they shall not see who hurts them this counsel is not to
be condemned because it may do you good and can do you no harm for
the danger is passed as soon as you have burnt the letter and i hope god
will give you the grace to make good use of it to whose holy protection
i commend you.

From Philip Sidney, *A History of the Gunpowder Plot* (London: The Religious
Tract Society, 1905) 70–71

GUY FAWKES'S CONFESSION, 1605

I confess that a practice in general was first broken unto me, against his
Majesty, for relief of the Catholic cause, and not invented or propounded
by myself. And this was first propounded unto me by about Easter last
was twelvemonth beyond the seas, in the low-countries, of the archduke's obeisance, by Thomas Winter, who came thereupon with me into
England, and there we imparted our purpose to three other gentlemen

more, namely, Robert Catesby, Thomas Percy, and John Wright, who, all five, consulting together, of the means how to execute the same; and taking a vow, among ourselves, for secrecy, Catesby propounded to have it performed by gunpowder, and by making a mine under the upper house of Parliament; which place we made choice of, the rather, because, religion have been unjustly suppressed there, it was fittest that justice and punishment should be executed there.

This being resolved amongst us, Thomas Percy hired an house at Westminster for that purpose, near adjoining to the Parliament House, and there we began to make our mine about December 11, 1604. The five that first entered into the work were Thomas Percy, Robert Catesby, Thomas Winter, John Wright, and myself, and soon after we took another unto us, Christopher Wright, having sworn him also, and taken the Sacrament for secrecy. When we came to the very foundation of the wall of the house, which was about three yards thick, and found it a matter of great difficulty, we took unto us another gentleman, Robert Winter, in like manner, with the Oath and Sacrament as aforesaid. It was about Christmas, when we brought our mine unto the wall, and about Candlemas, we had wrought the wall half through; and, whilst they were in working I stood as a sentinel, to descry any man that came near, whereof I gave warning, and so they ceased, until I gave notice again to proceed. All we seven lay in the house, and had shot and powder, being resolved to die in that place, before we should yield or be taken. As they were working upon the wall, they heard a rushing in a cellar, of removing of coals; whereupon we feared we had been discovered, and they sent me to go to the cellar, who finding that the coals were a selling, and that the cellar was to let, viewing the commodity thereof for our purpose, Percy went and hired the same for yearly rent. We had before this provided and brought into the house twenty barrels of powder, which we removed into the cellar, and covered the same with billets and faggots, which we provided for that purpose.

About Easter, the Parliament being prorogued till October next, we dispersed ourselves, and I retired into the low-countries, by advice and direction of the rest, as well to acquaint Owen [a Jesuit agent] with the particulars of the plot, as also lest by my longer stay I might have grown suspicious, and so have come in question. In the meantime, Percy, having the key of the cellar, laid in more powder and wood into it. I returned about the beginning of September next, and, then, receiving the key again of Percy, we brought in more powder and billets to cover the same again, and so I went for a time into the country till October 30.

It was further resolved amongst us that the same day that this action should have been performed, some other of our confederates should have surprised the person of Lady Elizabeth, the King's eldest daughter, who was kept in Warwickshire, at the Lord Harrington's house, and presently have proclaimed her for Queen, having a project of a proclamation ready for the purpose; wherein we made no mention of altering of religion, nor would have avowed the deed to be ours until we should have had power enough to make our party good, and then we would have avowed both.

Concerning Duke Charles, the King's second son, we had sundry consultations how to seize on his person, but because we found no means how to compass it, the duke being kept near London, where we had not forces enough, we resolved to serve our turn with the Lady Elizabeth.

The Names of other principal persons that were made privy afterwards to this horrible conspiracy.

–Everard Digby Knight,

–Ambrose Rookewood,

–Francis Tresham,

–John Grant,

–Robert Keyes.

From Philip Sidney, *A History of the Gunpowder Plot* (London: The Religious Tract Society, 1905) 112–114

KING JAMES'S SPEECH FROM THE THRONE

On November 9, four days after the Powder Treason was discovered, King James delivered a speech to Parliament announcing the postponement of the parliamentary session until the panic and danger had subsided and presenting to the public the Crown's official version of the event. His account balances a forceful condemnation of the attempted explosion against a call for a peaceful, measured response. James details the horrific potential consequences of the conspiracy's success, denounces the purpose, and takes credit himself for preventing the plot by interpreting the "dark phrases" in the anonymous letter. At the same time he thanks God for his good fortune and asks the public not to panic but, rather, to carefully distinguish between the traitorous Roman Catholics involved in the plot and the many Catholic subjects who remained loyal to the throne. During the succeeding trials, the Crown encouraged the public to accept that Jesuits were the evil forces behind the plot and that the treason represented an act of universal destruction. Pay attention to the language King James uses to reinforce this official version of the plot as a battle between good and evil by reminding others of the godliness of his own monarchical position. Consider how the personal nature of James's remarks compares with Macbeth's compelling inner struggle.

A SPEECH IN THE PARLIAMENT HOUSE,
AS NEAR THE VERY WORDS AS COULD BE GATHERED AT THE
INSTANT (November 9, 1605)

And now I must crave a little pardon of you, That since Kings are in the word of GOD itself called Gods, as being his Lieutenants and Vice-gerents on earth, and so adorned and furnished with some sparkles of Divinity; to compare some of the works of GOD the great KING, toward the whole and general world, to some of his works toward me, and this little world of my Dominions, compassed and severed by the Sea from the rest of the earth. [Here James provides several examples prior to the Gunpowder Plot of attempts to destroy his life in which God intervened to save him]. . . .

In this great and horrible attempt, whereof the like was never either heard or read, I observe three wonderful, or rather miraculous events.

1

First, in the cruelty of the Plot itself, wherein cannot be enough admired the horrible and fearful cruelty of their device, which was not only for the destruction of my Person, nor of my Wife and posterity only, but of the whole body of the State in general; wherein should neither have been spared, or distinction made of young nor of old, of great nor of small, of man nor of woman: The whole Nobility, the whole reverend Clergy, Bishops, and most part of the good Preachers, the most part of the Knights and Gentry; yea, and if that any in this Society were favourers of their profession, they should all have gone one way: The whole Judges of the land, with the most of the Lawyers, and the whole Clerks: And as the wretch himself which is in the Tower, doth confess, it was purposely devised by them, and concluded to be done in this house; That where the cruel Laws (as they say) were made against their Religion, both place and persons should all be destroyed and blown up at once. . . .

2

Secondly, how wonderful it is when you shall think upon the small, or rather no ground, whereupon the practisers were enticed to invent this Tragedy. For if these Conspirators had only been bankrupt persons, or discontented upon occasion of any disgraces done unto them; this might have seemed to have been a work of revenge. But for my own part, as I scarcely ever knew any of them, so cannot they allege so much as a pretended cause of grief: And the wretch himself in hands doth confess, That there was no cause moving him or them, but merely and only Religion. . . . Wherein their following obstinancy is so joined to their former malice, as the fellow himself that is in hand, cannot be moved to discover any signs or notes of repentance, except only that he doth not yet stand to avow, that he repents for not being able to perform his intent.

3

Thirdly, the discovery hereof is not a little wonderful, which would be thought the more miraculous by you all, if you were as well acquainted with my natural disposition, as those are who be near about me: For as I ever did hold Suspicion to be the sickness of a Tyrant, so was I so far upon the other extremity, as I rather condemned all advertisements, or apprehensions of practises. And yet now at this time was I so far contrary to myself, as when the Letter was showed to me by my Secretary, wherein a general obscure advertisement was given of some dangerous blow at this time, I did upon the instant interpret and apprehend some dark phrases therein, contrary to the ordinary Grammer construction of them, (and in an other sort than I am sure any Divine, or Lawyer in any University would have taken them) to be meant by this horrible form of blowing us up all by Powder; And thereupon ordered that search to be made, whereby the matter was discovered, and the man apprehended: whereas if I had apprehended or interpreted it to any other sort of danger, no worldly provision or prevention could have made us escape our utter destruction.

. . . And the more have We all cause to thank and magnify GOD for this his merciful Delivery; And specially I for my part, that he hath given me yet once leave, whatsoever should come of me hereafter, to assemble you in this Honourable place; And here in this place, where our general destruction should have been, to magnify and praise him for Our general delivery. . . . And therefore may I justly end this purpose, as I did begin it with this Sentence, *The Mercy of God is above all his works.*

It resteth now that I should shortly inform you what is to be done hereafter upon the occasion of this horrible and strange accident. As for your part that are my faithful and loving Subjects of all degrees, I know that your hearts are so burnt up with zeal in this errand, and your tongues so ready to utter your dutiful affections, and your hands and feet so bent to concur in the execution thereof, (for which as I need not to spur you, so can I not but praise you for the same:) As it may very well be possible that the zeal of your hearts shall make some of you in your speeches rashly to blame such as may be innocent of this attempt; But upon the other part I wish you to consider, That I would be sorry that any being innocent of this practice, either domestical or foreign, should receive blame or harm for the same. For although it cannot be denied, That it was the only blind superstition of their errors in Religion, that led them to this desperate device; yet doth it not follow, That all professing that *Romish* religion were guilty of the same. . . . And for my part I would wish with those ancient Philosophers, that there were a Crystal window in my breast, wherein all my people might see the secretest thoughts of my heart, for then might you all see no alteration in my mind for this accident, further then in these two points. The first, Caution and wariness in government, to discover and search out the mysteries of this wickedness as far as may be: The other, after due trial, Severity of punishment upon those that shall be found guilty of so detestable and unheard of villany. And now in this matter if I have troubled your ears with an abrupt speech, undigested in any good method or order; you have to consider that an abrupt, and unadvised speech doth best become in the relation of so abrupt and unorderly an accident.

From *The Political Works of James I*, ed. Charles Howard McIlwain (Cambridge: Harvard UP, 1918) 281–289

FATHER GARNET'S ARRAIGNMENT AND EXECUTION, MARCH 28–MAY 3, 1606

Portrayed unfairly as the evil instigator of the plot, Father Garnet received the most publicity during the trials. Several excerpted passages from an account of his arraignment record the official charges against him on March 28, 1606, and his final response moments before his execution on May 3. Try to determine whether Garnet appears remorseful or deceptive at his end. Following this excerpt, a personal letter from English nobleman John Chamberlain on April 2, 1606, also provides an account of the Crown's case against Garnet. Notice Chamberlain's tone and consider the balance between opinion and fact in his description.

*A TRUE AND PERFECT RELATION OF THE WHOLE PROCEEDING
AGAINST THE LATE MOST BARBAROUS TRAITORS, GARNET A
JESUIT AND HIS CONFEDERATES*
(London: Robert Barker, 1606; STC 11618) Fff2–Fff3

That this *Garnet* . . . together with *Catesby* lately slain in open Rebellion, and with *Oswald Tesmond a Jesuit*, otherwise *Oswald Greenwell*, as a false Traitor against the most mighty, & most renowned King our sovereign Lord King James, the 9 of June last, traitorously did conspire and compass,

To depose the King and to deprive him of his government

To destroy and kill the King, and the noble Prince *Henry*, his eldest Son: such a King and such a Prince, such a Son of such a Father, whose virtues are rather with amazed silence to be wondered at, than able by any speech to be expressed.

To stir sedition and slaughter throughout the kingdom.

To subvert the true Religion of God, and whole government of the kingdom.

To overthrow the whole State of the Commonwealth. . . .

This *Garnet*, together with *Catesby* and *Tesmond*, had speech and conference together of these treasons, and concluded most traitorously, and devilishly. (0–02)

Then *Garnet* said, Good countrymen, I am come hither this blessed day of *The invention of the holy Cross*, to end all my crosses in this life; The cause of my suffering is not unknown to you; I confess I have offended the King, and am sorry for it, so far as I was guilty, which was in concealing it, and for that I ask pardon of his Majesty; The treason intended against the King and State was bloody, myself should have detested it, had it taken effect. And I am heartily sorry, that any Catholics ever had so cruel a design. . . .

Then addressing himself to execution, he kneeled at the Ladder foot, and asked if he might have time to pray, and how long. It was answered, he should limit himself: none should interrupt him. It appeared he could not constantly or devoutly pray; fear of death, or hope of Pardon even then so distracted him: For oft in those prayers he would break off, turn and look about him, and answer to what he overheard, while he seemed to be praying. When he stood up, the Recorder finding his behaviour as it were an expectation of a Pardon, wished him not to deceive himself, nor beguile his own soul, he was come to die, and must die; requiring him not to Equivocate with his last breath, if he knew anything that might be danger to the King and State, he should now utter it. *Garnet* said, It is no time now to Equivocate: how it was lawful, and when, he had showed his mind elsewhere. But saith he, I do not now Equivocate, and more than I have confessed, I do not know. . . . Being upon the Gibbet, he used these words, I commend me to all good Catholics, and I pray God preserve his Majesty, the Queen, and all their posterity, and my Lords of the Privy Counsel, to whom I remember my humble duty, and I am sorry that I did dissemble with them: but I did not think they had had such proof against me, till it was showed me; But when it was proved, I held it more honour at that time to confess, than before, to have accused.

MR. JOHN CHAMBERLAIN'S LETTER TO MR. RALPH WINWOOD ON APRIL 5, 1606

Garnet the Jesuit was arraigned at *Guildhall* the 28th of the last. . . . The King was present but unseen, as likewise diverse Ladies. It lasted long, from eight in the Morning till seven at Night. The Sum of all was, that *Garnet*, coming into *England* in 1586, *hath had his Finger in every Treason since that time*, and not long before the Queen's Death, had *two Breves* sent him by the *Pope*, the one to the Nobility and Gentry, the other to the *Arch-priest* and Clergy of *England*, that . . . they should take Care . . . *to make Choice of such a Prince, as either should be Catholic, or promise and swear not only to tolerate, but to further that Religion to his utmost. . . .* But for the *late hellish Conspiracy* he was proved to be *privy to it*, both from *Catesby*, and *Tesmond* or *Greenway* a *Jesuit*. To which he answered, that from *Catesby* he had it but *in general terms*, and from *Tesmond sub sigillo Confessionis* [under the seal of confession]. To which Answer, tho' it were insufficient, yet it was replied, that *Catesby* having imparted to him the Particulars *of the very same Plot to be performed in the Queen's time, it was not likely he would conceal them from him now*; and the continual Intercourse 'twixt him and the *chief Actors*, with his *Directions* and *Letters* by *Winter* and *Wright* to the King of *Spain*, by *Fawkes* to the *Archduke*, and by Sir *Edward Bainham* (*Captain* of the *damned Crew*) to the *Pope*, show that he could not but be acquainted, and *one* of the *principal Directors* in it; as likewise his coming to the Rendezvous in *Warwickshire, the very next Day after it should have been performed.* To all which he had no other Answer, *but that having it in Confession he was not to reveal it*; but protested that he had *dissuaded it*, and prayed against it, and that he made no question, but God heard his Prayer.

But how far these Men are to be believed in their Protestations and Oaths, my Lord *Salisbury* made known by two notable Instances; having first showed, *that by reason of their impudent Slanders and Reports*, we are driven to take *another Course* than they do in other Countries by way of *Torture*; for if they die in Prison, they give out we have *starved* or *tortured them to Death*; if they kill *themselves, we make them away*; so that we are feign to *flatter* and *pamper them*, and get out matters by fair means as we can: So that by the Cunning of his Keeper, *Garnet* being brought into a *Fool's Paradise*, had diverse Conferences with *Hall, his fellow Priest in the Tower*, which were overheard by *Spials* set on purpose. With which being charged, he stiffly denied it; but being still urged, and some Light given him that they had notice of it, *he persisted still, with Protestation upon his Soul and Salvation, that there had passed no such Interlocution*; till at last being *confronted* with *Hall*, he was driven to *confess*: And being now asked in this Audience, how he could salve this *lewd Perjury*, he answered, *that so long as he thought they had no Proof he was not bound to accuse himself; but when he saw they had Proof, he stood not long in it*. And then fell into a large Discourse defending *Equivocations*, with many weak and frivolous Distinctions. . . .

In Conclusion he was found guilty and in Truth behaved himself very gravely, and temperately, for the manner, as likewise he was used; with good respect and good Words. . . . One thing I must not forget, how my Lord *Admiral* nicked it, in saying to him, *Garnet thou hast done more good in that Pulpit this Day* (for he stood in a Pew by himself,) *than in all the Pulpits that ever thou cam'st in.* . . .

Yours most assuredly,
JOHN CHAMBERLAIN

From *Winwood's Memorials*, vol. 2 (London, 1725) 205–206

KING JAMES'S RUMORED ASSASSINATION ON MARCH 22, 1606

The following is an account of the rumored assassination of King James in 1606. Public attention to trials following the Gunpowder Plot may have inspired the rumor and most certainly added to the panic it caused. Try to determine the balance between fear and reason conveyed in this report.

JOHN NICHOLS, ED., *THE PROGRESSES, PROCESSIONS, AND MAGNIFICENT FESTIVITIES OF KING JAMES THE FIRST, HIS ROYAL COURT, FAMILY AND COURT*, VOL. 2
(New York: Burt Franklin, 1828) 38–41

Saturday, the 22d of March, about half an hour before seven o'clock in the morning, was suddenly spread throughout the Court and the City of London, for certain news that the King was slain at Oking, which is about twenty miles Westward from London, and the same news held firm until past nine o'clock, in which space the Court being sore frighted, as well the great Lords as others, speedily shut the Court-gates with double guard in all places, and thereupon London did the like; the Lord Mayor gave forthwith precepts unto the wards to leave trained soldiers, and they to repair unto their known London Captains. . . . [F]or two hours space and more the news grew more and more, that not only the King was slain, but with him, in his defence, the Earl of Montgomery, Sir John Ramsay, and Sir James Hay, which treason, some said, was performed by English Jesuits, some by Scots in woman's apparel, and others said by Spaniards and Frenchmen. Most reports agreed that the King was stabbed with an envenomed knife, which bitter news was more grievous unto all sorts of people than can well be here expressed, great weeping and lamentation both in old and young, rich and poor, maids and wives. The Counsel, upon extraordinary expedition having true knowledge of his Majesty's safety, to quiet the people's distracted minds, made present Proclamation as followeth:

Where a seditious rumor hath been raised this morning, that some ill accident should be befallen our person, and thereupon the people thereabouts have been raised in arms by direction from Constable to Constable, but with uncertain knowledge from whom the first ground should be raised. . . . We do hereby make it known unto all our loving subjects, that, God be thanked, we remain in good and perfect health. And do require them to contain themselves from assemblies, or gathering together in arms or in conventicles: assuring themselves, that after due examination of this seditious rumor, we will make known to them the authors and intent thereof. And whosoever shall not obey this our commandement, we shall hold them for seditious, and breakers of our peace. And do command all our Lieutenants, Deputy Lieutenants, Justices of Peace, Mayors, Sheriffs, and all other our Officers, Ministers, and loving subjects, to do their duties in containing our people within their due obedience, and to advertise us, or our Privy Counsel, of all disturbers thereof.

Given at our Palace of Westminster, the two and twentieth day of March in 1605, and in the third year of our Reign of Great Britain.

This was proclaimed at the Court-gate a little past nine of the clock, and in Cheapside at eleven of the clock, by which time London's universal fear and grief was half abated.

The aforesaid terrible rumor came to the Commons House of Parliament somewhat before eight of the clock and continued until toward ten, in which space, the whole Assembly being mightily perplexed, sent every half quarter of an hour unto the Earl of Salisbury and others of the Counsel to be truly ascertained, and for almost two hours space they received news that the King was stabbed, smothered in his bed, and shot with a pistol as he was riding.

At the heavy hearing whereof the whole House began seriously to debate what was then best for them to do; some said let us rise and go hence for our better safety, least we be suddenly surprised, &c. Some said one thing and some another, but in brief it was agreed that they should sit still in their accustomed peaceable manner, until the truth were known, lest their sudden rising should add more terror both to Court, City, and Country, continually sending Gentlemen of the House, for almost two hours space, to learn news, by which time a special swift messenger sent by the Lords, brought certain knowledge of the King's perfect health and safety, who until then had not heard of any rumor of treason, and that his Majesty would come to White Hall about two or three o'clock, and that afternoon the Prince, the Counsel, with other Lords and Burgesses, met the King about Knightesbridge, and thousands of people flocking that way, ravished with joy to behold the King.

Also that afternoon, the Lord Mayor and Aldermen went to Court, where the Recorder, in all humble and hearty manner, signified unto his Highness the deep sorrow that his subjects sustained by the late flying news, and the unconceivable joy they now possessed upon the assurance of his Majesty's safety, &c. unto whom the King cheerfully returned all princely thanks and knowledgment of their singular love and loyalty, assuring them his Royal merit should ever equal their zeal and duty.

Conclusion

Language and action unite in the controversy surrrounding the Gunpowder Plot. Equivocation is the language of deception, and treason is the action of political betrayal leading to personal and national chaos. In word and in deed, *Macbeth* brings these concerns to life on stage. But whereas those responding to the contemporary political scene attempted to simplify the experience using propaganda and a well-staged drama of court justice, Shakespeare allows his audience to enter into the mind of the traitor himself, to experience the evil from the perspective of one who is blinded by his own convictions and tempted by seductive prophecies that echo the desires of his own heart. If Shakespeare had chosen to dramatize the Gunpowder Plot rather than a historical narrative with similar themes, perhaps he would not have relied on the *King's Book* or King James's official speech from the throne but would have appealed to his own imagination to shed some light on the ambitions of Robert Catesby or the even more ambiguous role of Henry Garnet.

QUESTIONS FOR WRITTEN AND ORAL DISCUSSION

1. What clues does the letter to Mounteagle present about the nature of the Gunpowder Plot? Do you think that King James was as clever as he claimed to be for having deciphered the "dark phrases" in the message?

2. What are the three miracles or wonders that King James identifies in his speech?

3. Language manipulation is central to *Macbeth* and the Powder Treason. In the Gunpowder Plot language is manipulated not only by the traitors' equivocation but by government propaganda. Discuss what propaganda is. What elements of political propaganda appear in King James's speech to Parliament in 1605? How does he attempt to convince others that his position is the only right one?

4. Do you think there are propagandists in *Macbeth*, as well? If so, who are they? Does the "good" side distort experience to make it appear good?

5. Remorse is a response that is often considered when a criminal is judged or pardoned. What does Duncan say about the remorse of the original Thane of Cawdor at his death? Discuss whether Guy Fawkes and Henry Garnet appear remorseful in their confessions. Does that make them more or less sympathetic? How does Macbeth respond to his fall at the end of the play? How does his response affect our attitudes toward him then?

6. Considering that Garnet's trial and final words are recorded by Chamberlain and others rather than himself, do you think those reports appear biased? In what ways? When Garnet is quoted, does he equivocate as he speaks on his own behalf?

7. The language in *Macbeth* includes many antonyms or pairs of opposites: black and white, dark and light, good and evil, angels and devils. Suggest how these literary patterns reflect attitudes in England toward the Powder Treason.

8. Rumor, like propaganda and equivocation, is another form of false speaking. Read the rumor about King James's assassination in 1606 and then write an imaginary account of what or who might have initiated it. Decide whether you think it was an honest mistake or a purposeful deception and how the Gunpowder Plot and trials may have played a part.

9. Discuss how fear manifests itself in the account of James's assassination. Compare this display of fear with the fear expressed in *Macbeth*, considering both the causes and effects of each.

10. A tragedy about the Gowrie Conspiracy was censored because authorities were suspicious of current events or recent history portrayed on stage. Discuss how Shakespeare adopts a safer approach in *Macbeth* that allowed it to escape censorship. If you were one of the Crown's censors, how would you react to the play? Write a personal letter expressing your concerns and your reasons for not interfering.

11. The Porter scene has sometimes been considered out of place in Shakespeare's tragedy and therefore added later by someone else or included simply for comic relief. Given the political relevance of its allusions to the Gunpowder Plot, do you think the humor is appropriate? Does the scene fit thematically in the play? Can you think of any allusions or references to current events in movies or television shows you have recently seen? Why do you think they were included, and what effect did they have on you?

12. Does the treason committed by Macbeth and Lady Macbeth seem more or less serious and horrible than the plot planned by the Gunpowder conspirators? Why or why not?

13. The witches represent evil in *Macbeth* just as the Jesuits did to Protestant authorities during the Gunpowder Plot. Discuss the differences and similarities between Shakespeare's three women and the Jesuits and other Powder Plot conspirators.

14. Discuss the relationship of church and state in the Gunpowder Plot. Does the "holy" cause or motivation make the treason seem more or less horrific? Why?

15. Pretend you are Robert Catesby, the ringleader, and compose (and optionally perform) a soliloquy about your initial plans for the plot. What are his motivations, and how does he rationalize his purpose? In assuming the character's part, decide how you will portray him. Is he evil, even machiavellian (see "Machiavelli's Political Views" in this chapter), or is he admirable because he willingly dedicates his life to his beliefs?

16. Compose and perform a soliloquy for Henry Garnet after he has found out about the Powder Plot while acting in the confidential role of priestly confessor. What struggle of conscience does he experience, and how does he resolve it? Compare your dramatization of Garnet with Macbeth's soliloquy in Act 1 when he contemplates murdering Duncan.

17. Enact a classroom rendition of the Gunpowder trials, casting characters for the judge, Crown prosecutor, jury, convicted criminal(s), and spectators, including King James, who was present but unseen

during the proceedings. Choose which traitor(s) you will try and decide how to present grounds for a guilty verdict.

18. Imagine you are a foreign ambassador at the court of Scotland during the Macbeth crisis. Write a report on the political climate there and how your government might aid the country.

SUGGESTED READINGS

Caraman, Philip. *Henry Garnet, 1555–1606, and the Gunpowder Plot*. New York: Farrar, Strauss and Co., 1964.

Gardiner, Samuel Rawson. *What the Gunpowder Plot Was* (1897). Rpt. New York: Greenwood Press, 1969.

Hotson, Leslie. *I, William Shakespeare do appoint Thomas Russell, Esquire . . .* Freeport, NY: Books for Libraries Press, 1970.

Parkinson, C. Northcote. *Gunpowder, Treason and Plot*. London: Weidenfeld and Nicholson, 1976.

Sidney, Philip. *A History of the Gunpowder Plot: The Conspiracy and Its Agents*. London: The Religious Tract Society, 1905.

Wills, Garry. *Witches and Jesuits: Shakespeare's Macbeth*. New York: Oxford UP, 1995.

TOIL AND TROUBLE: WITCHCRAFT IN ENGLAND AND SCOTLAND

Perhaps the most difficult characters in *Macbeth* for modern audiences to understand are the witches. Although witchcraft is by no means entirely dead in our own culture, it does not have the prominence and widespread acceptance that it had in the sixteenth and seventeenth centuries in Scotland and England. Ours is a society influenced more by science than superstition. Ever since the eighteenth-century revival of Shakespeare on stage, producers, directors, and actors have been troubled by the role of the witches. Some have been tempted simply to make a mockery of the witchcraft scenes, casting the three "Weird Sisters" as comic, laughable characters.

For Macbeth the witches are by no means harmless old hags intruding on his private thoughts, and for us to appreciate the magical, supernatural influence in the play, we must attempt to understand the attitudes of a Jacobean audience. Although witchcraft was not universally believed in Shakespeare's time, and occasional detractors spoke out against the fears and beliefs held by many, nevertheless the period from 1550 to the end of the seventeenth century was a time of witch hysteria, accompanied by rigorous witch hunts. The most intense trials and persecution of witches occurred in the decade or more before Shakespeare wrote *Macbeth*, and one of the chief supporters of the witch trials was King James himself.

Dramatic Context

Many modern critics have pointed out that Shakespeare's own portrayal of the three witches in *Macbeth* is ambiguous. Part of the confusion and uncertainty arises from the vagueness of Shakespeare's main source, Holinshed's *Chronicles*. In his historical narrative of King Duff's reign in Scotland, Holinshed tells of rebels attempting to overthrow the king by seeking assistance from witches who are discovered one night secretly burning a wax image of the king and chanting incantations to try to destroy him through the power of evil spirits. Holinshed offers two inconsistent descriptions of the witches, calling them "either the weird sisters, that is (as ye would say) the goddesses of destiny, or else some nymphs or fairies, endued with knowledge of prophecy by their necromatical science" (vol. 5, 269). These two alternative descriptions are quite different. "The weird sisters" signify the Fates of Greek or Scandinavian mythology, who are three goddesses with supernatural powers over human beings. The word "weird" derives from Old English "wyrd," which means fate or destiny. "Nymphs or fairies" are also supernatural beings, but in Renaissance England they were more directly related to devils or demons than to either goddesses or our own modern conception of fanciful, harmless, effeminate creatures.

Shakespeare's women are called "the Weird Sisters," not fairies. The original text actually identifies them as "wayward sisters," and although some scholars suggest that that means wandering women rather than mythological goddesses, most believe instead that "wayward" simply approximates the pronunciation of "weird" and that Shakespeare was in fact using Holinshed's expression. The play also refers to the characters by numerous other terms: "the instruments of darkness," "midnight hags," "juggling fiends," and "oracles." Oddly enough, Macbeth and Banquo never use the term "witch" at all, although their references to the bearded women as

The Three Weird Sisters in *Macbeth at the Stratford Festival, Ontario, Canada, 1983*. L-R: Elizabeth Leigh-Milne, Seana McKenna, and Paddy Campanaro. Photo by Robert Ragsdale. *Courtesy of Stratford Festival.*

"hags" is virtually synonymous. Witches or hags, as opposed to Fates, nymphs, or fairies, were human beings who were believed to possess special powers because they had made pacts with the devil.

Shakespeare's presentation of the witches is as confusing as Holinshed's, for *Macbeth* appears to bring together the mythological dimension with contemporary popular witch lore. The ambiguity revolves around the question of how much power the witches actually have. Are they demons in human form or human beings assisted in their incantations by evil spirits? To what extent do their prophecies influence or simply foretell the future? Clearly, the witches do not completely determine Macbeth's actions. If they did, Macbeth would simply be a victim rather than a tragic figure who suffers the consequences of his own choices. As he wades deeper and deeper into his own darkness, pulling the kingdom down with him, the Weird Sisters act less as goddesses than as tempters whose foreknowledge spurs Macbeth to his own corruption. They are not the Greek Fates, but they are not simply nasty, meddling old women either. Their character is confusing and disturbing, but their function as instruments of darkness is undeniable. In the service of evil rather than good, they equivocate in their prophecies, encouraging destructive behavior and contributing to the mystery, eeriness, and fear in the play.

Witchcraft Beliefs

Witchcraft was indeed a subject of great fear in Scotland and England in Shakespeare's time. People were superstitious, believing in the supernatural and in the power of witches to inflict harm and influence events in many different ways. Allegedly, they could cause sickness and death in both humans and animals; they could raise storms and interfere with daily household activities. These malicious acts were known as *maleficium*: injury or damage motivated by spite or revenge and attributed to the witch's affiliation with the devil. Concern arose from anxiety about the harm that witches could cause and also from religious opposition to women who would deny the existence of God in favor of satanic worship. Some saw witches as criminals; others saw them as heretics; many saw them as both.

Witch lore included several other popular beliefs. Witches were thought to bear a physical mark somewhere on their bodies that would identify them as agents of the devil. If the spot were pricked, supposedly it would not hurt or bleed. This belief inspired witch hunters to examine the bodies of those whom they suspected of witchcraft. People also thought that witches possessed familiars or imps, demonic creatures often taking the shape of animals such as cats or toads and acting to assist the witches in their horrible charms. In Act 1.1 of *Macbeth*, the witches address two familiars, saying, "I come, Graymalkin!" and "Paddock calls" (1.1.8–9). The first refers to a grey cat; the second, to a toad. Not everyone shared the same assumptions about witches, but most were superstitious enough to fear the harm or evil that witchcraft could inflict on their lives.

This fear, verging on paranoia, led to witch hunts and trials. Many believed that any ill occurrence without clear natural causes resulted from witchcraft or sorcery. They responded to alleged witches with cruelty, prejudice, and persecution. Countless individuals, mostly women, were accused of practicing witchcraft. They were brought to trial, encouraged or compelled to make confessions, often tortured, and even sentenced to death without concrete evidence or a fair hearing. Sometimes witnesses were small children or the witch's neighbors, whose testimony had questionable credibility. Whereas some people undoubtedly did practice magic, conjuring, and witchcraft and believed they had special supernatural powers, numerous other innocent people suffered because they became targets of widespread hysteria and were not able or allowed to defend themselves. Spurred by panic and malice, rather than reason, the accusers often acted unjustly, and the results were potentially horrific for anyone who fell under suspicion.

Scholars of the witch craze in the Renaissance point out that the movement reflects theological, political, and social attitudes of the time. It is difficult to know exactly why witchcraft and witch beliefs became much more common in the sixteenth century than earlier. People did not simply become more superstitious. Although there are no clear answers, some theories exist. Theologically, the Reformation may have had some effect. By emphasizing the power of the devil and God's just punishment of evil, Protestantism encouraged an aggressive attack against those who were perceived to be in league with Satan. Furthermore, when unexplained tragedies occurred, it was easier to blame witches or outside forces than to assume the alternative—that God was punishing the sufferers for their own sins by sending disaster, disease, and hardship (Larner 200–201).

Politically, when witchcraft became a threat to reigning monarchs, it inspired much more attention and fear because it became associated with treason. In England, during the first few years of Elizabeth's reign, several plots against her life involved conjuring and sorcery. Not long after that, in 1563, the government passed a law against witchcraft, and the queen's men were constantly wary of similar conspiracies against her. In Scotland, after King James's life was threatened by a witchcraft plot in 1590, he became very active in the specific trial of that case, subsequently writing his own treatise on witchcraft. For James especially, the theory of the divine right of kings helped to cultivate his fascination with and terror of witches, for if he saw himself as the servant of God, witches were then servants of the devil, and any confrontation between them became not simply personal or political but cosmic in its implications. Such prominent interest in witchcraft at the state level raised its profile among the public as well.

Finally, socially, the increase in witch hunts and witch trials says something about the contemporary community environment. Most people accused or suspected of being witches were women. Often old, poor, and powerless, they usually subsisted at the bottom of the social system. These facts suggest that when witchcraft became a popular notion and practice, people found it easier to blame those who were defenseless than other more privileged people who had their own sources of power and protection. Also, however, the poor were perhaps more tempted by the allurement of witchraft because they had no other socially acceptable means to assert themselves and provide for their needs (Thomas 520–522). They saw magic as their way out of a bad situation or as a means of retaliation by cursing others who treated them as outcasts. Some of their accusers were motivated by revenge against neighbors with whom they had quarreled. Often, it seems, these accusers may have treated the alleged witch unjustly in the past and thus had reason to fear or suspect retaliation. Any unexplained misfortune simply confirmed their expectations (Thomas 552–553). Thus many witchcraft fears resulted partly from tensions in the community, from unneighborly behavior that led to hostility, suspicion, and concerns about black magic (Thomas 561). In short, witch mania flourished in Shakespeare's time because the theological, political, and social climate allowed it and perhaps encouraged it to do so.

England and St. Osyth

The experiences with witchcraft in Scotland and England were not identical, but both are reflected in *Macbeth*. Witchcraft concerns in England focused primarily on *maleficium* or the personal harm that could come through the curses of old women. Shakespeare's witches engage in such activities themselves, as they indicate in conversation in Act 1.3., where they talk about killing swine and causing storms while sailors are at sea. Historically, fears about this harmful magic in England varied in intensity from one area and period to another.

In the 1580s, witch trials were especially common and hysteria particularly pronounced in the county of Essex. One of the most famous trials took place in 1582 in the Essex village of St. Osyth. Initially, one woman was brought to trial for allegedly bewitching a neighbor's baby, causing it to fall out of its cradle and break its neck. Accusations grew, however, in the climate of hysteria, and before long, thirteen women had been arrested. Hearsay and gossip served as adequate evidence against them as witnesses came forward with stories that twenty-three people had suffered the effects of sorcery in various ways, ranging from harm to their livestock to personal sickness or even death. In the end, the judge condemned to execution only six of the accused, but historical accounts of the trial suggest that much of the evidence was circumstantial and that prejudice prevailed over justice and impartiality. The St. Osyth trial was only one of several very prominent court cases against witchcraft in Essex from the mid-sixteenth century to the end of the seventeenth century, and Essex consequently became known as "the witch county."

The St. Osyth trial is significant partly because it sparked the sceptical response of several men, including Reginald Scot, who wrote a treatise against the irrational paranoia manifest in the court case. Scot was less recognized in his own time than a century later, but his writing indicates that beliefs in witches were not universal, and that at least some people in Elizabethan England were willing to scrutinize the credibility of witch accusations and question the evidence of black magic. His *Discovery of Witchcraft*, published in 1584, two years after the St. Osyth trial, offers the strongest opposition to the widespread attack against witches. Basing his position on the view that only God has power surpassing human capabilities, Scot discounts the existence of the supernatural, rejects the effects of magic, and explains misfortune either as an act of God or as having natural or psychological causes. This argument reflected an extreme position in Renaissance England because it relied so completely on reason and denied any other explanation. Witchcraft, as far as Scot was concerned, simply did not exist.

Scotland and North Berwick

In Scotland the response to witchcraft was more severe than in England partly because Scotland felt a stronger influence from continental Europe, where witch mania was more extreme, but also because King James became directly involved. Like some European nations, the Scots associated witchcraft with devil worship and believed that witches practiced their evil in assemblies or covens where rituals or black sabbaths were performed. The gathering around the caldron in Act 4.1. in *Macbeth* has closer ties to this Scottish belief than to English witch lore. Unlike in England, the Scots' criminal prosecution of witches also allowed more openly for torture as a means of compelling confessions and inflicted harsher penalties on the convicted. The Scottish Witchcraft Act in 1563 declared that not only those who practiced witchcraft but also those who consulted with witches could be punished by death.

The greatest outbreak of witch hunts and criminal trials occurred in the 1590s, and the most famous court case took place in North Berwick in 1591 against a group accused of using witchcraft in a treasonous plot against the king's life. Like the St. Osyth trial in Essex, this court case began with only one individual, a young maidservant, Geilles Duncan, whose reputation for charming the sick and whose nightly excursions away from her master's home aroused his suspicion. After being arrested, questioned, and tortured, she not only confessed to practicing witchcraft herself but also accused a number of others of doing the same. As they too were arrested and made confessions, their activities gradually began to point to treason.

The people who participated directly in this conspiracy included Dr. Fian, a schoolmaster and conjurer, and a group of women, some of whom were peasants and maidservants, several of whom were reputable members of Scotland's noble class. In total thirty-nine people were arrested, and their testimonies unfolded a tale that included, first, using sorcery to raise a storm on the seas in 1590 when King James was bringing home his new bride, Queen Anne, to Scotland from Denmark and, second, trying to kill the king by casting a spell on a wax effigy of him.

Also indirectly incriminated was a nobleman, Francis Stuart, Earl of Bothwell, who, according to the professed witches, initially sought them out to enact these curses against James's life. Bothwell was the king's relative and next in line to the Scottish throne if James had no heirs. Furthermore, because Bothwell's father, James Stuart, had murdered King James's father many years before, Bothwell continued to be considered the king's enemy. He managed to escape the North Berwick trial and flee Scotland to spend the remainder of his life on the Continent. Many of the witches, however, were convicted and executed. This story about a nobleman involved in witchcraft, allegedly attempting to assassinate his own king and usurp the throne, rings familiar in the details of *Macbeth*. Shakespeare was not only borrowing Scotland's ancient history from Holinshed to shape his tragedy but was also drawing on relatively recent political experience.

King James

King James reacted strongly to the North Berwick trial once he realized it involved treason against him. He became particularly incensed when one noblewoman, Barbara Napier, was originally found guilty but later acquitted on charges of treason. Following her acquittal, James chose to oversee the remainder of the court case, hearing some of the confessions himself. He became more strongly convinced than ever that witchcraft placed him in serious personal danger. In the years immediately after the trial, he composed his treatise on demonology in which he theorized about how witches practice their magic, how they ought to be punished, and how people should protect themselves from this particular manifestation of the devil's power. *Demonology* was republished in England early in the seventeenth century, and so English subjects were aware of James's keen interest in witchcraft before he ascended the throne in 1603. Shakespeare may have been directly flattering James's knowledge of the subject by including witches in *Macbeth*. Alternatively, he may simply have been capitalizing on the public interest in demonology, which had grown with the Scottish king's arrival in England.

The tone of fascination and superstition surrounding witchcraft that had been well established in England and in Scotland before the union of the two countries under King James continued and even intensified after 1604. A new statute was passed against witchcraft, imposing the harsh penalties in England that already existed in Scotland and encompassing a broader range of offenses. Severe persecution of witches remained active and popular for many years, and the new statute was not revoked until 1736. Oddly enough, however, James himself gradually became more and more of a sceptic. Even in his early years as England's king, he personally examined many accused witches and exposed a number of them as imposters using fraudulent means to convince others of their power. Through these experiences, James came to realize that imagination or pretense rather than superstition was often involved in many accusations and confessions of witchcraft.

Theatrical Tradition

Although King James grew more sceptical, popular attitudes about witchcraft continued to be expressed not only in pamphlets, treatises, sermons, gossip, and accounts of trials but also in the literature of the time. Shakespeare's *Macbeth* was one of several plays that included witches as minor or major characters. The role of witchcraft varied in the dramas. One play used it as an element of political satire. Several others shaped the main plot around contemporary witch trials, and some simply included traditional and popular witchcraft beliefs, capitalizing on the sensationalism that would have appealed to audiences steeped in the superstitions of their time. Even Christopher Marlowe's earlier well-known play, *Dr. Faustus* (1588), based on the German Faust legend, reflects concerns and fears about the power of sorcery, for although the play does not include witches, it centers on the devastatingly tragic outcome for one man who sells his soul to the devil in the way that contemporary English and Scottish witches were believed to do.

As strange, unfamiliar, and even unbelievable as the witches in *Macbeth* may seem today, examining the political climate, the religious beliefs, and the prevailing popular attitudes of 400 years

ago suggests that Shakespeare was writing within his own tradition, responding to contemporary concerns, and at the same time
leaving some unanswered questions about the power and the presence of the supernatural. What are those three characters who begin his play? Fates? Old hags? Mad people? Evil tempters? Prophets?
Macbeth's personal demons? How much can be determined by
concentrating on the dramatic context? How much is our interpretation necessarily shaped by our own personal and social values
and traditions?

The remainder of this section includes a brief chronology of significant dates and excerpts from some of the history books, tracts,
treatises, pamphlets, and plays that were current in Shakespeare's
time. Each document includes an introduction, clarifying the purpose and historical context. Spelling has been regularized and
modernized throughout.

BRIEF CHRONOLOGY OF WITCHCRAFT IN ENGLAND AND SCOTLAND

1563	Elizabeth I imposes a statute against witchcraft. Scottish Witchcraft Act also passed.
1582	St. Osyth witch trial in England.
1584	Reginald Scot's *The Discovery of Witchcraft* published, arguing that most fears of witchcraft are unfounded.
1591	North Berwick trial in Scotland.
1597	King James VI's *Demonology* published, expressing his belief in witchcraft.
1603	James VI of Scotland becomes James I of England.
1604	James I imposes a new statute against witchcraft.
1606	Probable date of *Macbeth*'s composition.
1613–1616	Period in which Thomas Middleton's *The Witch* was likely composed, including songs of the witches later incorporated into *Macbeth*.
1621	*The Witch of Edmonton* composed, dramatizing the contemporary witch trial of Elizabeth Sawyer.
1736	The statute against witchcraft finally revoked.

THE BEWITCHING OF KING DUFF

Witches appear on several occasions in Holinshed's *Chronicles of England, Scotland and Ireland*, and their presence in this historical source of *Macbeth* likely influenced Shakespeare's decision to give witchcraft a prominent place in his own play. In one incident that parallels *Macbeth*, a witch prophesies to a gentleman that he will murder the king who trusts him as an ally and friend. Although the gentleman is horrified by the witch's prediction, nevertheless, like Macbeth, he does subsequently murder the king in his private chamber. In another section of Holinshed's history, the reign and murder of King Duff are more directly connected to Shakespeare's plot and also include a story of bewitchment. The following excerpt describes how witches from Forres, the same town that is home to *Macbeth*'s witches, cast a spell on King Duff, which leads to a serious illness. Only when soldiers discover the witch meeting and destroy the wax image used to cast the spell does the king recover from his sickness. This story is interesting not only for the treasonous witchcraft it shares with *Macbeth*, along with mention of the proper names Ross and Cathness, but also for its curious resemblance to the well-publicized witch plot against King James's life in 1590.

RAPHAEL HOLINSHED, *CHRONICLES OF ENGLAND, SCOTLAND AND IRELAND* [1587], *VOL. 5*
(London, 1808; New York: AMS Press, 1965) 233–234

But about that present time there was a murmuring amongst the people, how the king was vexed with no natural sickness, but by sorcery and magical art, practiced by a sort of witches dwelling in a town of Murrey land, called Fores.

Whereupon, albeit the author of this secret talk was not known: yet being brought to the king's ear, it caused him to send forthwith certain witty persons thither, to inquire of the truth. They that were thus sent, dissembling the cause of their journey, were received in the dark of the night into the castle of Fores by the lieutenant of the same, called Donwald, who continuing faithful to the king, had kept that castle against the rebels to the king's use. Unto him therefore these messengers declared the cause of their coming, requiring his aid for the accomplishment of the king's pleasure.

The soldiers, which lay there in garrison, had an inkling that there was some such matter in hand as was talked of amongst the people; by reason that one of them kept as concubine a young woman, which was daughter to one of the witches as his paramour, who told him the whole manner used by her mother & other her companions, with their intent also, which was to make away the king. The soldier having learned this of his lemman, told the same to his fellows, who made report to Donwald, and he showed it to the king's messengers, and therewith sent for the young damsel which the soldier kept, as then being within the castle, and caused her upon strict examination to confess the whole matter as she had seen and knew. Whereupon learning by her confession in what house in the town it was where they wrought their mischievous mystery, he sent forth soldiers about the middest of the night, who breaking into the house, found one of the witches roasting upon a wooden broach an image of wax at the fire, resembling in each feature the king's person, made and devised (as is to be thought) by craft and art of the devil: an other of them sat reciting certain words of enchantment, and still basted the image with a certain liquor very busily.

The soldiers finding them occupied in this wise, took them together with the image, and led them into the castle, where being strictly examined for what purpose they went about such manner of enchantment, they answered, to the end to make away the king: for as the image did waste afore the fire, so did the body of the king break forth in sweat. And as for the words of enchantment, they served to keep him still waking from sleep, so that as the wax ever melted, so did the king's flesh: by the which means it should have come to pass, that when the wax was once clean consumed, the death of the king should immediately follow. So were they taught by evil spirits, and hired to work the feat by the nobles of Murrey land. The standers by, that heard such an abominable tale told by these witches, straightwise break the image, and caused the witches (according as they had well deserved) to be burnt to death.

It was said, that the king at the very same time that these things were a doing within the castle of Fores, was delivered of his languor, and slept that night without any sweat breaking forth upon him at all, & the next day being restored to his strength, was able to do any manner of thing that lay in man to do, as though he had not been sick before any thing at all. But howsoever it came to pass, truth it is, that when he was restored to his perfect health, he gathered a power of men, & with the same went into Murrey land against the rebels there, and chasing them from thence, he pursued them into Rosse, and from Rosse into Cathnesse, where apprehending them, he brought them back unto Fores, and there caused them to be hanged up, on gallows and gibbets.

REGINALD SCOT'S SCEPTICAL VIEW OF WITCHCRAFT

Reginald Scot's *The Discovery of Witchcraft* (1584) was the first English study of its kind. In response to the genuine terror surrounding the Essex trials, Scot argues from a rational position that fears about witchcraft are based on unfounded superstition and that people being persecuted as witches were either innocent victims of public paranoia or imposters pretending to possess evil powers. The unpopularity of his position required him to publish his book independently, and when James became England's king in 1603, he ordered all copies of Scot's book to be burned. A few copies survived as a record of his views, and his book was later republished. Of the two excerpts included here, the first is from Scot's introductory chapter, in which he presents his main position that the belief in witches is unfounded because only God has the superhuman power that people so readily attributed to women acting as agents of the devil. The second excerpt offers a description of the people accused of witchcraft and the reasons they aroused suspicion. Scot pictures them as the stereotypical ugly old women that Shakespeare describes in *Macbeth* and explains that their poverty and mistreatment may have made them understandably tempted to curse their wealthier neighbors. If these neighbors then experienced any harm, not only the sufferers but even the cursing old women might believe that their ill-wishes and incantations were the cause of the misfortune. According to Scot, however, witchcraft was nothing more than a system used to support or justify malicious behavior and abuse of the poor.

REGINALD SCOT, *THE DISCOVERY OF WITCHCRAFT* [1584],
INTRO. BY HUGH ROSS WILLIAMSON
(Arundel: Centaur Press, 1964) 25–31

Chapter 1

The fables of Witchcraft have taken so fast hold and deep root in the heart of man, that few or none can (nowadays) with patience endure the hand and correction of God. For if any adversity, grief, sickness, loss of children, corn, cattle, or liberty happen unto them; by & by they exclaim upon witches. As though there were no God in Israel that ordereth all things according to his will; punishing both just and unjust with griefs, plagues, and afflictions in manner and form as he thinketh good: but that certain old women here on earth, called witches, must needs be the contrivers of all men's calamities, and as though they themselves were innocents, and had deserved no such punishments. . . .

Such faithless people (I say) are also persuaded, that neither hail nor snow, thunder nor lightning, rain nor tempestuous winds come from the heavens at the commandment of God: but are raised by the cunning and power of witches and conjurers; insomuch as a clap of thunder, or a gale of wind is no sooner heard, but either they run to ring bells, or cry out to burn witches; or else burn consecrated things, hoping by the smoke thereof, to drive the devil out of the air, as though spirits could be fraied away with such external toys:. . . .

But certainly, it is neither a witch, nor devil, but a glorious God that maketh the thunder. I have read in the scriptures, that God maketh the blustering tempests and whirlwinds: and I find that it is the Lord that altogether dealeth with them, and that they blow according to his will. . . .

But little think our witchmongers, that the Lord commandeth the clouds above, or openeth the doors of heaven, as *David* affirmeth; or that the Lord goeth forth in the tempests and storms, as the Prophet *Nahum* reporteth: but rather that witches and conjurers are then about their business.

. . . But if all the devils in hell were dead, and all the witches in *England* burnt or hanged; I warrant you we should not fail to have rain, hail and tempests, as now we have: according to the appointment and will of God, and according to the constitution of the elements, and the course of the planets, wherein God hath set a perfect and perpetual order.

I am also well assured, that if all the old women in the world were witches; and all the priests, conjurers: we should not have a drop of rain, nor a blast of wind the more or the less for them. For the Lord hath bound the waters in the clouds, and hath set bounds about the waters, until the day and night come to an end: yea it is God that raiseth the winds and stilleth them: and he saith to the rain and snow; Be upon the earth, and it falleth. The wind of the Lord, and not the wind of the witches, shall destroy the treasures of their pleasant vessels, and dry up the fountains; saith [*Hosea*]. Let us also learn and confess with the Prophet *David*, that we our selves are the causes of our afflictions; and not exclaim upon witches, when we should call upon God for mercy. (25–26)

Chapter 3

One sort of such as are said to be witches, are women which be commonly old, lame, bleary-eyed, pale, foul, and full of wrinkles; poor, sullen, superstitious, and papists; or such as know no religion: in whose drowsy minds the devil hath gotten a fine seat; so as, what mischief, mischance, calamity, or slaughter is brought to pass, they are easily persuaded the same is done by themselves; imprinting in their minds an earnest and constant imagination hereof. They are lean and deformed, showing melancholy in their faces, to the horror of all that see them. They are doting, scolds, mad, devilish; and not much differing from them that are thought to be possessed with spirits; so firm and steadfast in their opinions, as whosoever shall only have respect to the constancy of their words uttered, would easily believe they were true indeed.

These miserable wretches are so odious unto all their neighbors, and so feared, as few dare offend them, or deny them anything they ask: whereby they take upon them; yea, and sometimes think, that they can do such things as are beyond the ability of human nature. These go from house to house, and from door to door for a pot full of milk, yeast, drink, pottage, or some such relief; without the which they could hardly live: neither obtaining for their services and pains, nor by their art, nor yet at the devil's hands (with whom they are said to make a perfect and visible bargain) either beauty, money, promotion, wealth, worship, pleasure, honor, knowledge, learning, or any other benefit whatsoever.

It falleth out many times, that neither their necessities, nor their expectation is answered or served, in those places where they beg or borrow; but rather their lewdness is by their neighbors reproved. And further, in tract of time the witch waxeth odious and tedious to her neighbors; and they again are despised and despited of her: so as sometimes she curseth one, and sometimes another; and that from the master of the house, his wife, children, cattle, &c. to the little pig that lieth in the sty. Thus in process of time they have all displeased her, and she hath wished evil luck unto them all; perhaps with curses and imprecations made in form. Doubtless (at length) some of her neighbors die, or fall sick; or some of their children are visited with diseases that vex them strangely: as apoplexies, epilepsies, convulsions, hot fevers, worms, &c. Which by ignorant parents are supposed to be the vengeance of witches. Yea and their opinions and conceits are confirmed and maintained by unskillful physicians: according to the common saying . . . Witchcraft and enchantment is the cloak of ignorance: whereas indeed evil humors, & not strange words, witches, or spirits are the causes of such diseases. Also some of their cattle perish, either by disease or mischance. Then they, upon whom such adversities fall, weighing the fame that goeth upon this woman (her words, displeasure, and curses meeting so justly with their misfortune) do not only conceive, but also are resolved, that all their mishaps are brought to pass by her only means.

The witch on the other side expecting her neighbours' mischances, and seeing things sometimes come to pass according to her wishes, curses, and incantations . . . being called before a Justice, by due examination of the circumstances is driven to see her imprecations and desires, and her neighbors harms and losses to concur, and as it were to take effect: and so confesseth that she (as a goddess) hath brought such things to pass. Wherein, not only she, but the accuser, and also the Justice are foully deceived and abused; as being through her confession and other circumstances persuaded (to the injury of God's glory) that she hath done, or can do that which is proper only to God himself.

Another sort of witches there are, which be absolutely coseners. These take upon them, either for glory, fame, or gain, to do any thing, which God or the devil can do: either for foretelling of things to come, betraying of secrets, curing of maladies, or working of miracles. But of these I will talk more at large hereafter. (29–31)

TREASONOUS WITCHCRAFT IN SCOTLAND
IN 1591

News From Scotland is an anonymous pamphlet published in 1591 that describes the events in the North Berwick trials of the witches charged in the treasonous plot against King James. The first section below reports the confessions of two of the primary women charged in the trial, Agnis Tompson and Agnis Sampson. Tompson tells of a black sabbath where several hundred witches gathered to dance and make music with the devil. She also confesses by what means she tried to bewitch the king to death, applying the charm of a poisonous toad to a piece of his clothing and conjuring up a storm on the sea to destroy his ship traveling home from Denmark. Sampson, too, testifies before the king, frightening him with accounts of her supernatural power by relating private words he spoke to his queen when no one else was present. The second excerpt focuses on the trial of the conjurer, Dr. Fian. After being tortured, he confessed his practice of witchcraft and sorcery, but later he was allegedly visited by the devil and escaped prison. When recaptured, he denied his confession, and even further torture could not compel him to reinstate his earlier testimony. Finally, the king and his counsel condemned him to be burned to death.

NEWS FROM SCOTLAND [1591], ED. G. B. HARRISON,
ELIZABETHAN AND JACOBEAN QUARTOS
(New York: Barnes and Noble, 1966)

Item, the said *Agnis Tompson* was after brought again before the King's Majesty and his Counsel, and being examined of the meetings and detestable dealings of those witches, she confessed that upon the night of All Hallow's Eve last, she was accompanied as well with the persons aforesaid, and also with a great many other witches, to the number of two hundred: and that all they together went by Sea each one in a Riddle or Cive, and went in the same very substantially with Flagons of wine making merry and drinking by the way in the same Riddles or Cives, the Kerke [Church] of North Barrick [Berwick] in Lowthian, and that after they had landed, took hands on the land and danced this reel or short dance, singing all with one voice.

> Commer go ye before, commer go ye,
> Gif ye will not go before, commer let me.

At which time she confessed, that this *Geilles Duncan* did go before them playing this reel or dance upon a small Trump, called Jew's Trump, until they entered into the Kerk of North Barrick.

These confessions made the King in a wonderful admiration, and sent for the said *Geilles Duncan*, who upon the like Trump did play the said dance before the King's Majesty, who in respect of the strangeness of these matters, took great delight to be present at their examinations.

Item, the said *Agnis Tompson* confessed that the Devil being then at North Barrick Kerk attending their coming in the habit or likeness of a man, . . . and having made his ungodly exhortations, wherein he did greatly inveigh against the King of Scotland, he received their oaths for their good and true service toward him, and departed: which done, they returned to Sea, and so home again.

At which time the witches demanded of the Devil why he did bear such hatred to the King, who answered, by reason the King is the greatest enemy he hath in the world: all which their confessions and depositions are still extant upon record.

Item, the said *Agnis Sampson* confessed before the King's Majesty sundry things which were so miraculous and strange, as that his Majesty said they were all extreme liars, whereat she answered, she would not wish his Majesty to suppose her words to be false, but rather to believe them, in that she would discover such matter unto him as his majesty should not any way doubt of.

And thereupon taking his Majesty a little aside, she declared unto him the very words which passed between the King's Majesty and his Queen at Upslo in Norway the first night of their marriage, with their answer each to other: whereat the King's Majesty wondered greatly, and swore by the living God, that he believed that all the Devils in hell could not have discovered the same: acknowledging her words to be most true, and therefore gave the more credit to the rest which is before declared.

Touching this *Agnis Tompson*, she is the only woman, who by the Devil's persuasion should have intended and put in execution the King's Majesty's death in this manner.

She confessed that she took a black Toad, and did hang the same up by the heels, three days, and collected and gathered the venom as it dropped and fell from it in an Oyster shell, and kept the same venom close covered, until she should obtain any part or piece of foul linen cloth, that had appertained to the King's Majesty, as shirt, handkerchief, napkin or any other thing which she practiced to obtain by means of one *John Kers*, who being attendant in his Majesty's Chamber, desired him for old acquaintance between them, to help her to one or a piece of such a cloth as is aforesaid, which thing the said *John Kers* denied to help her to, saying he could not help her to it.

And the said *Agnis Tompson* by her depositions since her apprehension saith, that if she had obtained any one piece of linen cloth which the King had worn and fouled, she had bewitched him to death, and put him to such extraordinary pains, as if he had been lying upon sharp thorns and ends of Needles.

Moreover she confessed that at the time when his Majesty was in Denmark, she being accompanied with the parties before specially named, took a Cat and christened it, and afterward bound to each part of that Cat, the chiefest parts of a dead man, and several joints of his body, and that in the night following the said Cat was conveyed into the midst of the sea by all these witches sailing in their [R]iddles or Cives as is aforesaid, and so left the said Cat right before the Town of Lieth in Scotland: this done, there did arise such a tempest in the Sea, as a greater hath not been seen: which tempest was the cause of the perishing of a boat or vessel coming over from the town of Brunt Island to the town of Lieth, wherein was sundry Jewels and rich gifts, which should have been presented to the now Queen of Scotland, at her Majesty's coming to Lieth.

Again it is confessed, that the said christened Cat was the cause that the King's Majesty's ship at his coming forth of Denmark, had a contrary wind to the rest of his Ships, then being in his company, which thing was most strange and true, as the King's Majesty acknowledgeth, for when the rest of the Ships had a fair and good wind, then was the wind contrary and altogether against his Majesty: and further the said witch declared, that his Majesty had never come safely from the Sea, if his faith had not prevailed above their intentions. (13–17)

As touching the aforesaid Doctor *Fian, alias John Cunningham*, the examination of his acts since his apprehension, declareth the great subtlety of the devil, and therefore maketh things to appear the more miraculous: for being apprehended by the accusation of the said *Geilles Duncan* aforesaid, who confessed he was their Register, and that there was not one man suffered to come to the Devil's readings but only he: the said Doctor was taken and imprisoned, and used with the accustomed pain, provided for those offenses, inflicted upon the rest as is aforesaid. (18)

After that the depositions and examinations of the said doctor *Fian alias Cunningham* was taken, as already is declared, with his own hand willingly set thereunto, he was by the master of the prison committed to ward, and appointed to a chamber by himself, where forsaking his wicked ways, acknowledging his most ungodly life, showing that he had too much followed the allurements and enticements of satan, and fondly practiced his conclusions by conjuring, witchcraft, enchantment, sorcery, and such like, he renounced the devil and all his wicked works, vowed to lead the life of a Christian, and seemed newly connected toward God.

The morrow after upon conference had with him, he granted that the devil had appeared unto him in the night before, appareled all in black, with a white wand in his hand, and that the devil demanded of him if he would continue his faithful service, according to his first oath and promise made to that effect. Whom (as he then said) he utterly renounced to his face, and said unto him in this manner, *Avoid Satan, avoid,* for I have listened too much unto thee, and by the same thou hast undone me, in respect whereof I utterly forsake thee. To whom the devil answered, *That once ere thou die thou shalt be mine.* And with that (as he said) the devil break the white wand, and immediately vanished forth of his sight.

Thus all the day this Doctor *Fian* continued very solitary, and seemed to have care of his own soul, and would call upon God, showing himself penitent for his wicked life, nevertheless the same night he found such means, that he stole the key of the prison door and chamber in the which he was, which in the night he opened and fled away to the Salt pans, where he was always resident, and first apprehended. Of whose sudden departure when the King's Majesty had intelligence, he presently commanded diligent inquiry to be made for his apprehension, and for the better effecting thereof, he sent public proclamations into all parts of his land to the same effect. By means of whose hot and hard pursuit, he was again taken and brought to prison, and then being called before the king's highness, he was reexamined as well touching his departure, as also touching all that had before happened.

But this Doctor, notwithstanding that his own confession appeareth remaining in record under his own hand writing, and the same thereunto fixed in the presence of the King's Majesty and sundry of his Counsel, yet did he utterly deny the same.

Whereupon the [K]ing's [M]ajesty perceiving his stubborn willfulness, conceived and imagined that in the time of his absence he had entered into new conference and league with the devil his master, and that he had been again newly marked, for the which he was narrowly searched, but it could not in any wise be found, yet for more trial of him to make him confess, he was commanded to have most strange torment. . . .

And notwithstanding all these grievous pains and cruel torments he would not confess any thing, so deeply had the devil entered into his heart, that he utterly denied all that which he had before avouched, and would say nothing thereunto but this, that what he had done and said before, was only done and said for fear of pains which he had endured.

Upon great consideration therefore taken by the King's [M]ajesty and his Counsel, as well for the due execution of justice upon such detestable malefactors, as also for example sake, to remain a terror to all others hereafter, that shall attempt to deal in the like wicked and ungodly actions, as witchcraft, sorcery, conjuration, & such like, the said Doctor *Fian* was soon after arraigned, condemned, and adjudged by the law to die, and then to be burned according to the law of that land, provided in that behalf. (25–29)

KING JAMES'S VIEWS ON DEMONOLOGY

King James composed his *Demonology* after the North Berwick trial. The first section included here, from his preface to the reader, explains as his purpose for writing the book the need to recognize the seriousness of witchcraft and to discount sceptical views of men such as Reginald Scot. The study itself is organized as a dialogue between two characters, Philomathes and Epistemon. In the following excerpts, [1] they address the question of why more women than men practice witchcraft, [2] they discuss the many ways that witches can inflict harm on others, [3] they speculate about the three kinds of people who are likely to suffer bewitchment, and [4] they explain the king's responsibility as God's representative to participate in the judgment and punishment of witches.

KING JAMES THE FIRST, DEMONOLOGY [1597], ED. G. B. HARRISON, ELIZABETHAN AND JACOBEAN QUARTOS *(New York: Barnes & Noble, 1966)*

The Preface to the Reader

The fearful abounding at this time in this country, of these detestable slaves of the Devil, the Witches or enchanters, hath moved me (beloved reader) to dispatch in post, this following treatise of mine, not in any wise (as I protest) to serve for a show of my learning & engine, but only (moved of conscience) to press / thereby, so far as I can, to resolve the doubting hearts of many; both that such assaults of Satan are most certainly practiced, & that the instruments thereof, merits most severely to be punished: against the damnable opinions of two principally in our age, whereof the one called SCOT an Englishman, is not ashamed in public print to deny, that there can be such a thing as Witch-craft.

[1] PHILO[MATHES]. What can be the cause that there are twenty women given to that craft, where there is one man?
EPI[STEMON]. The reason is easy, for as that sex is frailer than man is, so is it easier to be entrapped in these gross snares of the Devil, as was over well proved to be true, by the Serpent's deceiving of *Eve* at the beginning, which makes him the homelier with that sex sensine.

[2] EPI[STEMON]. To some others at these times he [the Devil] teacheth, how to make pictures of wax or clay: That by the roasting thereof, the persons that they bear the name of, may be continually melted or dried away by continual sickness. To some he gives such stones or boulders, as will help to cure or cast on diseases: And to some he teacheth kinds of uncouth poisons, which Mediciners understands not (for he is far cunninger than man in the knowledge of all the occult proprieties of nature). . . .

They can make men or women to love or hate other, which may be very possible to the Devil to effectuate, seeing he being a subtle spirit, knows well enough how to persuade the corrupted affection of them whom God will permit him so to deal with: They can lay the sickness of one upon another, which likewise is very possible unto him: . . .

They can raise storms and tempests in the air, either upon Sea or land, though not universally, but in such a particular place and prescribed bounds, as God will permit them so to trouble: Which likewise is very easy to be discerned from any other natural tempests that are meteors, in respect of the sudden and violent raising thereof, together with the short enduring of the same. . . .

They can make folks to become frenetic or Maniac, which likewise is very possible to their master to do, since they are but natural sicknesses: and so he may lay on these kinds, as well as any others. They can make spirits either to follow and trouble persons, or haunt certain houses, and affray oftentimes the inhabitants: as hath been known to be done by our Witches at this time. And likewise they can make some to be possessed with spirits, & so to become very Demoniacs: and this last sort is very possible likewise to the Devil their Master to do, since he may easily send his own angels to trouble in what form he pleases, any whom God will permit him so to use.

PHILO[MATHES]. But will God permit these wicked instruments by the power of the Devil their master, to trouble by any of these means, any that believes in him?

[3] EPI[STEMON]. No doubt, for there are three kind of folks whom God will permit so to be tempted or troubled; the wicked for their horrible sins, to punish them in the like measure; The godly that are sleeping in any great sins or infirmities and weakness in faith, to waken them up the faster by such an uncouth form: and even some of the best, that their patience may be tried before the world, as JOB'S was. For why may not God use any kind of extraordinary punishment, when

it pleases him; as well as the ordinary rods of sickness or other adversities. (43–47)

[4] PHILO[MATHES]. But what is their power against the Magistrate?
EPI[STEMON]. Less or greater, according as he deals with them. For if he be slothful toward them, God is very able to make them instruments to waken & punish his sloth. But if he be the contrary, he according to the just law of God, and allowable law of all Nations, will be diligent in examining and punishing of them: GOD will not permit their master to trouble or hinder so good a work. (50)

WITCHCRAFT ON THE JACOBEAN STAGE

Two witch plays written a number of years after *Macbeth* reflect the diverse views toward sorcery that continued in Jacobean society and on stage. Thomas Middleton's *The Witch* (c. 1613–1616) is a satire or a dark comedy, rather than a tragedy. Middleton clearly uses witchcraft material from Reginald Scot's writing to present his witches as almost wickedly humorous rather than frightening and evil, although they do have real power over the other characters. Several songs from Middleton's play were later incorporated into the published version of *Macbeth*, and a portion of one of the scenes is included here (see Chapter 1). Hecate and her companion witches dance and chant a song to cast a spell on Almachildes, a man from court society whom the Duchess wants bewitched. This one scene clearly influenced the addition of Hecate in the black sabbath or gathering of witches interpolated in *Macbeth*'s Act 3.5.

THOMAS MIDDLETON, *THE WITCH* [c. 1613–1616], ED.
ELIZABETH SCHAFER, NEW MERMAIDS
(London: A & C Black, 1994) 5.2.59–85

HECATE:	Stir, stir about, whilst I begin the charm.
	A charm song about a vessel
	Black spirits and white, red spirits and grey,
	Mingle, mingle, mingle, you that mingle may.
	Titty, Tiffin, keep it stiff in.
	Fire-drake, Puckey, make it lucky.
	Liard, Robin, you must bob in.
	Round, around, around, about, about—
	All ill come running in, all good keep out!
[STADLIN]:	Here's the blood of a bat.
HECATE:	Put in that, oh put in that.
[HOPPO]:	Here's libbard's bane.
HECATE:	Put in a grain.
[STADLIN]:	The juice of toad, the oil of adder.
[HOPPO]:	Those will make the younker madder.
HECATE:	Put in—there's all—and rid the stench.

FIRESTONE: Nay, here's three ounces of the red-haired wench.
ALL [THE WITCHES]: Round, around, around, about, about—
                    All ill come running in, all good keep out!
HECATE: So, so, enough. Into the vessel with it.
                    There 't hath the true perfection. I am so light
                    At any mischief—there's no villainy
                    But is a tune methinks.
FIRESTONE: [*Aside*] A tune! 'Tis to the tune of damnation then, I
                    warrant you, and that song hath a villainous burden.
IIECATE: Come, my sweet sisters, let the air strike our tune,
                    Whilst we show reverence to yond peeping moon.

                    Here they dance the witches' dance and exeunt.

   The Witch of Edmonton, a collaborative play written by several
playwrights in approximately 1621, dramatizes the contemporary
story of Elizabeth Sawyer, a woman executed as a witch that year.
This is a much later play than *Macbeth*, but it reflects attitudes that
existed as early as Reginald Scot's writing in the 1580s. Although
this stage tragedy affirms the current fears about witchcraft, it portrays Sawyer as a tormented victim rather than as a true witch, as
a woman driven to attempt sorcery by a cruel, vindictive society
that persecutes her for being poor. Her speech at the beginning
of Act 2 establishes sympathy with the audience, reflecting a current view that witchcraft partly resulted from social injustice.

       THE WITCH OF EDMONTON [1621], ED. SOIREF ONAT
              (New York: Garland, 1980) 2.1.1–15

   Sawy. And why on me? why should the envious world
   Throw all their scandalous malice upon me?
   'Cause I am poor, deform'd and ignorant?
   And like a Bow buckl'd and bent together,
   By some more strong in mischiefs [than] my self?
   Must I for that be made a common sink,
   For all the filth and rubbbish of Men's tongues
   To fall and run into? Some call me Witch;
   And being ignorant of my self, they go
   About to teach me how to be one: urging,
   That my bad tongue (by their bad usage made so)
   Forespeaks their Cattle, doth bewitch their Corn,
   Themselves, their Servants, and their Babes at nurse.

This they enforce upon me: and in part
Make me credit to it.

Conclusion

The documents in this chapter attempt to inform modern readers and audiences about the widespread acceptance of witchcraft
in Shakespeare's time. Interest in and concern about the supernatural found a variety of expressions, from facts recorded in history books to theories expounded in treatises, from current events
reported in pamphlets to popular beliefs reflected on stage. Yet
although witchcraft was a common subject and superstition a part
of culture, views about the power and presence of witches were
not wholly uniform and consistent. Many people unconditionally
feared and believed in witchcraft, others were strong sceptics, and
still others believed in the existence of witchcraft but were aware
that fraud was practiced and that much of the persecution against
alleged witches was unjust. Conflicting theories evolved to explain
apparent manifestations of witchcraft either as the result of spiritual evil, as the equivalent of modern psychological illness, or as a
sign of political tensions and social unrest. Given the diversity of
attitudes, it would be impossible to say that Shakespeare's portrayal of witches simply represents the view of his time. It is much
more interesting to try to understand how his presentation of the
supernatural fits into the spectrum of beliefs in his day, to consider
why his witches have such a compelling presence in *Macbeth* although they appear in only four scenes, and to ask what continues
to give this magical world of witches such a curious appeal for us
today.

QUESTIONS FOR WRITTEN AND ORAL DISCUSSION

1. Compare Holinshed's account of King Duff's bewitchment with Agnis Tompson's confession in *News from Scotland* about her effort to bewitch King James. What similarities do you notice? How are witchcraft and treason connected in both narratives, and how might you explain the parallels?

2. Compare the witches in Holinshed's *Chronicles* and *News from Scotland* with Shakespeare's Weird Sisters, particularly in Act 1.3. How are their practices similar, especially with regard to storms and treason?

3. Compare Holinshed's King Duff and Shakespeare's King Duncan. How are their experiences with sorcery similar? How do they differ?

4. Both Scot and King James appeal to God, but each makes quite different arguments about witchcraft. How does Scot use his faith in God to dismiss the power of witches? Conversely, how does James use theology to confirm the presence of witchcraft?

5. In Chapter 3 of *Discovery of Witchcraft*, how does Scot explain witchcraft beliefs? For what different reasons did the alleged witches and others fear and accept the power of the supernatural?

6. Make a list of witchcraft practices confessed in *News from Scotland* and a parallel list summarizing James's account of witchcraft acts in *Demonology*. How do they compare, and how might you explain the similarities?

7. In *Demonology*, Epistemon identifies "three kinds of folks" who might be tempted by witchcraft. Who are they? Does Macbeth resemble any of them?

8. How does King James describe the influence of witchcraft on monarchs and their response? How does that explanation justify or reflect his active role in witchcraft trials?

9. Imagine you are King James hearing the confessions of Agnis Tompson and Agnis Sampson. Write a diary entry that reflects your concern about their attacks against your life. Are they credible? Are you frightened or relieved by the results of the trial?

10. Summarize the crimes of Dr. Fian, his contradictory testimonies, and his punishment. Consider how his experience compares with Macbeth's. How does their contact with the supernatural differ? Do you think Fian is a fraud or a confused, bewitched man? Is Macbeth motivated more by private ambitions or by the Weird Sisters' prophecies?

11. Compare 4.1 in *Macbeth* with 5.2 in Middleton's *The Witch*. Consider

how their language, characters, setting, and action are similar. Do you think the inclusion of excerpts from Middleton adds to *Macbeth*?

12. Elizabeth Sawyer's speech in *The Witch of Edmonton* portrays witches quite differently than does *Macbeth* or Middleton's *The Witch*. Describe the differences. What do these contemporary characters on stage indicate about seventeenth-century attitudes toward witchcraft and sorcery?

13. Compare Macbeth's and Banquo's responses to the witches and consider how their shared experience affects their friendship and their goals. Refer especially to Acts 1.3, 2.1, and 3.1, as well as to Macbeth's soliloquy in Act 1.7. How ambitious is Banquo? Which man exhibits more courage? Do both suffer the torments of conscience?

14. Consider Lady Macbeth's character in relationship to the witches. What does she have in common with them? How does her effect on Macbeth compare? Refer especially to Acts 1.5 and 1.7.

15. Discuss the political element of witchcraft in *Macbeth*, *Demonology*, and Holinshed's *Chronicles*. To what extent do the witches influence political events? To what extent do the power and beliefs of political figures increase the power of witchcraft practices and superstitions?

16. Discuss the religious foundation of witchcraft beliefs in the Elizabethan and Jacobean periods. How does the widespread acceptance of Christianity influence popular superstitions? What kind of God and devil did the people believe in?

17. Discuss the social aspect of witch hysteria in the period. How does prejudice conflict with reason? How do fears and superstition reflect tensions between the strong and the weak? What is gained and lost socially by accepting the existence of witchcraft?

18. Discuss the role of gender in witchcraft practices. What do superstitions suggest about sixteenth- and seventeenth-century views of women? Is there more than one view presented in the documents in this chapter?

19. Write an essay summarizing the range of beliefs in witchcraft during Shakespeare's time and indicating how his portrayal of witches fits into the spectrum of viewpoints.

20. Research one of the prominent trials in England or Scotland in the 1500s and 1600s. Write and act out a dramatic scene with judge, jury, witnesses, and the accused. If the witch was convicted or released, what were the reasons? Will you choose to present witchcraft as a real or imagined problem and why?

21. Discuss modern stereotypes of witches in relationship to historical

attitudes in the Renaissance. How do they compare? What are the dangers or limitations of relying on stereotypes?

22. Write your own dialogue, using King James's treatise as a guideline, to debate or discuss the influence of the witches in *Macbeth*. How much power do they have? How evil or harmful are they?

23. Imagine yourself as a spectator at the North Berwick trial and write a response to it. Are the testimonies convincing? Do you believe the witnesses or question their credibility?

24. Newspapers and magazines are today's equivalent of pamphlets like *News from Scotland*. Provide your own newspaper coverage of the North Berwick trial, including several of the following: a report of the events, an editorial providing a commentary, a letter to the editor expressing public opinion (or two letters offering opposing opinions), a press release from the king, and an editorial cartoon depicting some aspect of the case.

SUGGESTED READINGS

Haining, Peter, ed. *The Witchcraft Papers: Contemporary Records of the Witchcraft Hysteria in Essex, 1560–1700*. London: Robert Hale and Co., 1974. Excerpted historical documents and edited summaries describing the experiences of "the witch county."

Hart, Roger. *Witchcraft*. East Sussex: Wayland, 1971. A short study of the history of witchcraft, including illustrations and excerpted documents.

Larner, Christina. *Enemies of God: The Witch-Hunt in Scotland*. London: Chatto and Windus, 1981.

Miller, Arthur. *The Crucible*. 1954. A modern play dramatizing the Salem witch hunts of 1692 and suggesting their relationship to political hysteria in the United States in the 1950s.

Thomas, Keith. *Religion and the Decline of Magic*. New York: Charles Scribner's Sons, 1971. A comprehensive study of magic and witchcraft up to the end of the seventeenth century.

Wills, Garry. *Witches and Jesuits: Shakespeare's Macbeth*. New York: Oxford UP, 1995.

3

Performance and Interpretation

Chapter 3 traces *Macbeth*'s journey through history, exploring its stage life and examining the play as script and text through the eyes of different actors, spectators, scholars, and critics over the ages. Although the discussion progresses chronologically, each section also addresses issues whose relevance is not bound by a particular time or place.

The first segment, "The Jacobean Stage," places *Macbeth* in the context of England's theatrical activity at the turn of the seventeenth century, using documentary evidence and educated assumptions about acting companies, playhouses, and the diverse membership of audiences to provide insight into the play's early performances. The study questions also consider general interest in staging, in how to create an acting space where the script is transformed into drama.

"From the Restoration to the Nineteenth Century" studies how political and cultural changes influenced the staging of *Macbeth* after the theatrical revival following the English revolution. Beyond such specific historical interest, this section considers more broadly ways in which Shakespeare's text is open to different interpretations and how those possibilities translate into producers' choices about ghosts and witches, and actors' decisions about the qualities of guilt and nobility that Macbeth and Lady Macbeth share.

"The Twentieth Century" surveys some of the main perform-ances of *Macbeth* over the last 100 years, addressing the impact of a rising film industry and exploring ways in which dramatic rep-resentations are subject to experiments, adaptations, and innova-tions. This exchange opens up questions about competing visions of the play, inviting students to weigh the issue of "relevance" and to see how new settings can reveal *Macbeth* as both a timeless and a time-bound story, a story that is continually refashioned out of and into different cultures.

"Currents of Criticism" examines some of these concerns from a literary perspective, surveying a variety of approaches to *Mac-beth*. Although it is difficult to enter into this discussion without appearing unduly theoretical, topical categories and selective doc-umentary excerpts are designed to make the overview as simple as possible while still demonstrating that there is no one way to read or watch *Macbeth* and that even contradictory viewpoints find sup-port in the play itself. In light of dissenting and evolving ideas about what *Macbeth* "means," students should be encouraged to realize that consensus is rarely as valuable as a willingness to en-gage in ongoing debate.

THE JACOBEAN STAGE

Shakespeare is both an Elizabethan and a Jacobean playwright because his dramatic career from 1590 to 1613 spanned the En-glish reigns of Queen Elizabeth (1558–1603) and King James (1603–1625). Although *Macbeth* is an early Jacobean play, it nevertheless exists within the theatrical tradition that became enor-mously popular during the last half of Elizabeth's reign. Today, with very little documentary evidence about *Macbeth*'s early stage history, we can attempt to understand or recreate the atmosphere, style, and reception of the first performances primarily by piecing together an array of theatrical records, public accounts, and dra-matic references from the period. Into that picture, we can also add one specific reference to a performance of *Macbeth* and some strong suggestions about another likely appearance.

Actors

Actors in Shakespeare's time belonged to acting companies whose right to perform publicly depended on the patronage or support of English aristocrats. During Elizabeth's reign, several such companies evolved gradually out of a long tradition of traveling players and wandering minstrels. The development of these companies and the construction of theater buildings helped to legitimize drama as a form of entertainment and increase its popularity. Initially Shakespeare wrote for a troupe supported by the Lord Chamberlain and known as the Chamberlain's Men. The company played in London and also traveled to the countryside, particularly when the plague threatened the city, inciting a ban on public performances to prevent the spread of disease. When James became England's king, he gave actors preferential status by assuming the patronage of the Chamberlain's Men, which, then renamed the King's Men, became the leading company in London. As members of the royal household, the King's Men not only continued to perform regularly in public theaters but also were commissioned to entertain at court numerous times throughout the year. *Macbeth*, like Shakespeare's other Jacobean plays, would have been performed by this company.

Playhouses

Publicly, the King's Men performed at a playhouse called the Globe, located on the south side of the Thames River in a theater district of London known as Bankside. The Globe was built in 1599 by two brothers, Richard and Cuthbert Burbage, and also involved the participation of five other actors as shareholders, one of whom was Shakespeare. His position is unique among the theatrical men of his time because he was not only a playwright but also an actor and a businessman. As the Globe became the main venue for his plays, he became a reasonably wealthy man. After 1609 Shakespeare expanded his financial interests to the Blackfriar's Theater, another playhouse where the King's Men also began performing.

The Globe was a large, three-story, polygonal building with an unroofed center or yard that was open to the air and provided standing room for spectators to crowd around the stage. This yard was surrounded by three levels of roofed galleries with benches for wealthier spectators, who paid a higher price to sit and watch the performance. Some gallants even sat on the stage itself or in balcony seats above it, where they could be seen as well as see. The yard, galleries, and stage provided room for between 2,000 and 3,000 people, but with much more cramped seating and standing arrangements than exist at theaters and concert halls today.

The stage platform in the Globe was a thrust or apron stage, extending out into the yard and providing relatively intimate interaction with the audience surrounding three sides. Two doorways at each side of the back wall allowed for entrances and exits while a third larger curtained opening between them could also be used as an entrance or a discovery space for secret or interior action. A trap door in the stage floor supplied another opportunity for unexpected appearances or disappearances. A canopy extended over the stage, and behind the back wall was a tiring room or dressing room, roofed as the galleries were and including a second story that could be used not only for spectators but also for performers in two-tiered action such as the balcony scene in *Romeo and Juliet*.

Staging

Several other details about Elizabethan and Jacobean theaters can help us understand early performances of *Macbeth*. The stage was relatively bare, with the exception of simple props, such as a king's throne, a table, a few chairs, and a bed that could be rolled out when needed. Without elaborate sets or curtains to draw, setting and scene changes were marked simply by actors' entrances, exits, and dialogue. Words were therefore more important for the audience than the physical stage design. In *Macbeth*, for example, when Duncan and Banquo describe Macbeth's castle, they allow viewers to imagine what cannot be seen:

DUNCAN: This castle hath a pleasant seat; the air
                      Nimbly and sweetly recommends itself
                      Unto our gentle senses.
BANQUO: This guest of summer
                      The temple-haunting martlet, does approve,
                      By his loved mansionry, that the heaven's breath
                      Smells wooingly here. (1.6.1–6)

The irony of this pleasant scene soon becomes apparent as the audience listens to the murderous plot devised by the king's host and hostess.

Costuming and lighting also affected the visual experience of the play. Although sets were simple, costumes were probably elaborate, particularly for the royal characters. Sometimes servants of English aristocrats received items of clothing in estate settlements, and because the garments were too fancy for their station, they sold these items to theater companies for costumes. With royal characters attired in rich robes, ceremonial scenes such as coronations might have appeared quite spectacular.

Lighting, however, relied again on the audience's imagination. Plays at the Globe were necessarily performed during daylight hours, and as a result viewers could see each other as clearly as they could see the stage. Activity in the yard and galleries could and apparently did occasionally distract from the action of the play. Moreover, darkness such as that which pervades the atmosphere of *Macbeth* would have been created primarily by the language itself and possibly by a few torches to indicate night. The candle Lady Macbeth carries in her sleepwalking scene would have been an important indication of the setting, particularly if the midafternoon sun happened to be beaming down on the stage. After 1609, when the King's Men also began performing at the Blackfriar's, which was a smaller, indoor playhouse, the audience's experience would have been quite different: darkness would have been real and candles and torches would have had a much more obvious effect.

More similar to productions at the Blackfriar's than the Globe, court performances before the king took place indoors at one of the great halls of a royal residence before a much smaller audience. A raised platform at one end of the hall might have served as a temporary stage, or actors may have cleared a space in the center of the room with the audience surrounding all sides. The king had the best seat in the house, and actors typically performed directly to him. The play script would likely not have changed much from the public theater except for simple adaptations to accommodate the smaller acting space and the absence of a convenient tiring house or dressing room.

Finally, casting in sixteenth- and seventeenth-century plays is worth mentioning. Women did not perform; acting companies were comprised of male actors only. Consequently, roles such as Lady Macbeth and Lady Macduff were played by young men or boy actors whose voices had not yet changed. Furthermore, because the companies were small, comprised of about nine to twelve men with extras occasionally hired, a large cast of characters meant that actors frequently doubled parts. For example, after Duncan's murder, the actor who played Duncan's part likely assumed another role that never shared the stage with the king—perhaps the Doctor or one of Banquo's murderers.

Audience

Because Shakespeare's company performed in public as well as at Court, its audiences included a broad spectrum of society from royalty to laborers, servants, and apprentices. Evidence suggests that even a public playhouse such as the Globe attracted its audience from all social classes. Because the price of admission ranged from one penny for standing room in the yard to sixpence (six pennies) for one of the balcony rooms over the stage (Gurr & Orrell 54–55), many people with different incomes could attend the same play. Scholars today still debate about whether England's public playhouses could attract citizens from the lower classes not only because afternoon performances conflicted with working hours for servants and apprentices but also because even the cheapest admission represented a huge sacrifice for London's poorest workers. Nevertheless, records and reports indicate that many people from all classes did attend theaters in spite of the costs. As a popular playwright Shakespeare therefore had to consider a variety of tastes and interests. *Macbeth*, like many of his plays, reflects a potentially eclectic appeal, ranging from the coarse humor of the Porter's scene to Malcolm's philosophizing about the virtues of kingship, from the supernatural eeriness of witchcraft to the final bloody confrontation between Macbeth and Macduff.

Performances of *Macbeth*

Although we know little about *Macbeth*'s early history, we do know that it was played publicly at the Globe on April 20, 1611, because an English astrologer, Simon Forman, describes that performance. Unfortunately, his account is primarily a plot summary and consequently adds little to our understanding of how the play was staged. However, his manuscript helps to confirm what seems most probable anyway, that the play did appear in the popular playhouse where Shakespeare had economic ties.

Circumstantial evidence also suggests that *Macbeth* was performed at the king's court. No concrete proof can confirm this theory, but the royal theme of the play is enough to provoke speculation. The Scottish historical setting, the Banquo legend, the inclusion of witches, and the debate about kingship all reflect personal interests of King James, indicating that Shakespeare may have had a court performance in mind. Furthermore, in 1606, the likely date of *Macbeth*'s composition, King Christian of Denmark, James's brother-in-law, visited England between July 18 and August 10, during which time many festivities took place. The King's Men performed three plays, and scholars believe that *Macbeth* was one of them, possibly performed on August 7, 1606, at Hampton Court.

SIMON FORMAN'S ACCOUNT OF *MACBETH*,
1611

Forman's unpublished manuscript is characterized by erratic punctuation and irregular spelling, with names such as "Mack dove" (Macduff) and "dunston Anyse" (Dunsinane) suggesting inaccuracies that might result from watching and hearing the story rather than reading it. The reference to Duncan making Macbeth Prince of Northumberland is also inaccurate, as is Forman's date, April 20, 1610, since April 20 fell on a Saturday in 1611 rather than 1610. In the following account punctuation has been added and spelling changed for clarity and consistency.

SIMON FORMAN, *THE BOOK OF PLAYS AND NOTES THEREOF*
PER FORMAN'S FOR COMMON POLICY
Ashmolean ms. 208, Bodleian Library, Oxford, 207r–207v

In Macbeth at the Globe, 1610, the 20th of April [Sat.], there was to be observed first how Macbeth and Banquo, 2 noble men of Scotland, riding through a wood, there stood before them 3 women fairies or nymphs and saluted Macbeth, saying 3 times to him: "Hail Macbeth, King of Cawdor, for thou shalt be a king, but shall beget no kings, &c." Then said Banquo, "What, all to Macbeth and nothing to me?" "Yes," said the nymphs. "Hail to the Banquo; thou shalt beget kings, yet be no king." And so they departed & came to the Court of Scotland to Duncan King of Scots and it was in the days of Edward the Confessor. And Duncan bade them both kindly welcome, and made Macbeth forthwith Prince of Northumberland and sent him home to his own castle and appointed Macbeth to provide for him, for he would sup with him the next day at night, and did so. And Macbeth contrived to kill Duncan & through the persuasion of his wife did that night murder the king in his own castle, being his guest. And there were many prodigies seen that night & the day before. And when Macbeth had murdered the king, the blood on his hands could not be washed off by any means, nor from his wife's hands which handled the bloody daggers in hiding them. By which means they became both much amazed and affronted. The murder being known, Duncan's 2 sons fled, the one to England, the other to Wales, to save themselves. They being fled, they were supposed guilty of the murder of their father, which was nothing so. Then Macbeth was crowned king, and then he for fear of Banquo, his old companion, that he should beget kings but be no king himself, he contrived the death of Banquo and caused him to be murdered on the way as he rode. The next night being at supper with his noble men whom he had bid to a feast to the which Banquo should have come, he began to speak of noble Banquo and to wish that he were there. And as he thus did, standing up to drink a carouse to him, the ghost of Banquo came and sat down in his chair behind him. And turning about to sit down again saw the ghost of Banquo, which fronted him so that he fell into a great passion of fear and fury, uttering many words about his murder, by which when they heard that Banquo was murdered, they suspected Macbeth.

Then Macduff fled to England to the king's son, and so they raised an army and came to Scotland and at Dunsinane overthrew Macbeth. In the meantime, while Macduff was in England, Macbeth slew Macduff's wife and children and, after in the battle, Macduff slew Macbeth.

Observe also how Macbeth's queen did rise in the night in her sleep & walk and talked and confessed all & the doctor noted her words.

Conclusion

With few written records about Jacobean stage history or specific details about the appearance of Shakespeare's plays, reconstructing early productions of *Macbeth* requires creative detective work and a vivid imagination. What most researchers have discovered is the importance of the plays themselves as a record of performance. Carefully rereading the lines of *Macbeth* can be the best way to determine how actors may have presented it almost 400 years ago.

QUESTIONS FOR WRITTEN AND ORAL DISCUSSION

1. Study diagrams and written descriptions of the Globe Theater and then construct a model, choosing cardboard, wood, or whatever materials you feel would work well.

2. Act out a scene from *Macbeth* for your classmates, using only simple props and creating a temporary performance space that, like the Globe's thrust stage or the makeshift platforms in Shakespeare's time, allows for intimacy with your audience.

3. Although Forman's review primarily retells the plot, does he use any words that also capture some of the play's emotion? Write a parallel review that emphasizes the psychological experience of *Macbeth* rather than simply the plot details.

4. Consulting Forman's summary, illustrate a "comic book" version of *Macbeth*, deciding how many frames to use and what captions to include in order to present the story.

5. Imagine that Shakespeare's contemporaries had access to radio and telecommunications. As a group project, prepare and act out a preview of *Macbeth* for the daily news, possibly including an interview with an actor or two, a few scenes from the play, and a rating (five stars or two thumbs up?).

6. Design a poster to appear outside the Globe Theater announcing the premiere performance of *Macbeth*.

7. Attending plays was a social event in Shakespeare's time. Consider the effect of watching *Macbeth* in broad daylight where several thousand fellow spectators are as visible as the actors. Write two reports of the event, one from the one-penny position in the yard where you jostle elbows with others crowded around the stage, and one from the balcony seats above the stage where you paid a hefty price not only to see the play but also to be seen by all the spectators below. Try to capture the viewers' personalities. How will your impressions of the play be influenced by your position (both socially and physically) and by the activity around you?

8. Imagine you are directing *Macbeth* at the Globe in 1606. Supply director's notes and diagrams for the staging of one act. Computer graphics may be effective. Where will the actors deliver their lines? How will they use the stage space and to what effect? Where will they enter and exit? If some characters speak lines that others obviously do not hear, how will you position them to make the illusion of separation convincing?

9. Given the absence of many stage directions in *Macbeth*, consider how

much information about staging appears in the lines of the play itself. On a working copy of a scene, circle words and phrases that provide clues about the setting and action. Which words offer clear guidance for the audience to imagine what it cannot see? Which sections might supply helpful hints for actors about specific movements and gestures or the possible use of simple props?

10. If you have a mind for details and like solving puzzles, assume the role of a financial consultant for the King's Men and try to determine how many actors will be needed to play all the minor characters in *Macbeth*. Remember that if Ross and Lennox appear in the same scene, they cannot be played by the same actor. Can you discover opportunities to double roles and save the acting company money for hiring extra performers? Write a report summarizing your findings.

SUGGESTED READINGS

Cook, Ann Jennalie. *The Privileged Playgoers of Shakespeare's England: 1576–1642*. Princeton, NJ: Princeton UP, 1981. Argues from records that only wealthy or privileged citizens attended theaters.

Gurr, Andrew, and John Orrell. *Rebuilding Shakespeare's Globe*. New York: Routledge, 1989. An account of the research involved in a project to reconstruct a new Globe Theater in London modeled after the original.

Hattaway, Michael. *Elizabethan Popular Theatre: Plays in Performance*. London: Routledge, 1982. Argues for the broad appeal of theater entertainment across the spectrum of society in Shakespeare's time.

Harbage, Alfred. *Shakespeare's Audience*. New York: Columbia UP, 1941.

Hodges, C. Walter. *Shakespeare's Theatre*. London: Oxford UP, 1964. An illustrated history of the Globe Theater and dramatic performance in Shakespeare's time.

Paul, Henry N. *The Royal Play of Macbeth*. New York: Macmillan, 1950. The strongest argument for the belief that *Macbeth* was performed before the king at court.

FROM THE RESTORATION TO THE NINETEENTH CENTURY

When the English monarchy was overthrown in 1642, the new Puritan government of Oliver Cromwell closed and eventually destroyed all the playhouses in London, outlawing acting as an idle,

frivolous, even subversive activity. Public play going was not revived again until the Restoration of the monarchy with the coronation of Charles II in 1660. But when drama once again became
a form of public entertainment, it emerged in an entirely different
form than Shakespeare's contemporaries had known it. Radical
changes motivated by the revolution and the regicide of Charles I
led to new political attitudes, social expectations, and cultural
tastes. Play-going became a much more elite activity for considerably smaller audiences numbering in the hundreds rather than the
thousands. The architecture of new indoor playhouses more
closely resembled modern theaters than the open-air thrust stage
of the Globe. Stages were framed by a curtained proscenium
arch—the invisible fourth wall—and sets and props became more
elaborate. In this new cultural and political environment, many
Shakespearean plays were revived. *Macbeth* became particularly
popular, although like the theaters themselves, it changed so dramatically that it could hardly be recognized as the same play that
appeared at the Globe over fifty years earlier.

Davenant's Adaptation

The first revival of *Macbeth* was Sir William Davenant's 1674
adaptation, which significantly altered the text and influenced both
the staging and the interpretation of the play well into the eighteenth century. With many additions, omissions, and revisions to
the text, Davenant's version became known as the "operatic" *Macbeth*, although it was not true opera to the extent that all parts
were sung rather than spoken. Two centuries later Guiseppe Verdi
composed just such a rendition of *Macbeth*, but Davenant's version
did include considerably more music, song, and dance than appeared in the original script. Chiefly, these additions revolved
around the witches, who were transformed from the mysterious
supernatural influences of the Jacobean age to almost comic characters who literally flew onto the stage with broomsticks and
whose expanded role in the play provided opportunity for much
spectacle.

Other additions reflected new theatrical and political developments. Acting companies now included women, so several new
scenes were written to give the female actors larger parts as Lady
Macbeth and Lady Macduff. Political motivation inspired some re-

visions, too, such as a new scene in which Lady Macduff articulates the dangers of regicide, warning against rebellion and celebrating kingship. Her speech clearly addresses a topic of deep concern and immediate relevance for England's newly restored monarchy. Other changes reflect the more puritanical sensibilities and tastes of the time. Lady Macduff's murder scene is reported rather than enacted because "refined" audiences had less tolerance for violence on stage. Also, most directors and producers omitted the Porter scene because they felt that such coarse comedy interfered with the play's dignified, tragic tone. Finally, Davenant radically altered the text itself, rarely leaving more than two or three words untouched, instead revising Shakespeare's poetry allegedly to improve the language and decrease the violence of the imagery.

This new version of *Macbeth* proved immensely popular. One prominent gentleman, Samuel Pepys, records seeing the play twenty-two times over a period of years and particularly expresses his pleasure in the added musical entertainment. On April 19, 1667, he writes in his diary, "To the playhouse, where we saw 'Macbeth', which, though I have seen it often, yet it is one of the best plays for a stage, and variety of dancing and musique, that I ever saw" (3/6/93 in *Shakespere Allusion Book*, vol. 2, 1932). The Restoration adaptation clearly suited and reflected the cultural tastes and political ideas of a new era in theater. Acting styles and dramatic criticism that grew out of these innovations contribute to the long tradition of Shakespearean performance and interpretation that continues today as *Macbeth* and other plays are revised and re-created again and again for new audiences.

The Supernatural

Throughout the eighteenth century the seriousness of the supernatural element in *Macbeth* continued to be downplayed and its dramatic effect sensationalized. The witches remained a comic chorus, numbering sometimes up to fifty characters who danced and sang on stage. They provided spectacle for the audience but no longer played a significant role in the plot because, robbed of their mystery and evil, they had virtually no power over Macbeth. Not everyone agreed with this interpretation. One nineteenth-century actress, Fanny Kemble, complained,

It has always been customary,—heaven only knows why,—to make low comedians act like witches, and to dress them like old fish-women . . . with as due a proportion of petticoats as any women, letting alone witch, might desire, jocose red faces, peaked hats, and broomsticks.

From *Journals* 2: 115, 116 (February 18, 1833, in Sprague 224)

By the late eighteenth century and into the nineteenth century, some productions did attempt to portray the witches more seriously, but by then the change seemed so radical and unusual in the context of Davenant's popular adaptation that most viewers and performers saw it as an innovation rather than a return to Shakespeare's original text. Overall, audiences appeared to prefer a caricatured rendition of evil rather than an ambiguous, ominous, withering presence whose "supernatural soliciting," as Macbeth says, "Cannot be ill; cannot be good" (1.3.130–131).

Banquo's ghost is the second supernatural element in the play that became the subject of controversy and reinterpretation in a more sceptical age than Shakespeare's. One of the few stage directions in the earliest Folio text of the play indicates the appearance of a real actor playing the ghost: "The Ghost of BANQUO enters and sits in MACBETH's place." Many productions of *Macbeth* from Davenant's time onward followed this direction, sometimes adapting it by having the ghost rise eerily from a trap door in the floor rather than walk on and off stage.

Other producers, actors, and spectators found the ghost's presence intrusive. One critic, mistakenly referring to the ghost as Macduff rather than Banquo, says:

I would willingly confine all dumb ghosts beneath the trap-doors . . . otherwise, their mealy faces, white shirts, and red rags stuck on in imitation of blood are rather the objects of ridicule than terror. I cannot help imagining that if the audience were not coldly let into the cause by the rising of the mangled MACDUFF [*sic*], our surprise would be much greater, and our terror more alarming, while the imagination of MACBETH conjur'd up an airy form before him, though he were really looking only on a chair.

From Bonnell Thornton, *The Drury Lane Journal* (March 19, 1752, in Sprague 255)

Apparently many agreed with these objections, for during the nineteenth century Banquo's ghost became more frequently an invisible figure, relegated to Macbeth's imagination or represented
simply by a ghostly light on stage. Perhaps not surprisingly, if a
post-Restoration audience preferred comical witches, they also had
difficulty considering Banquo's ghost seriously.

Whether or not to give the ghost a bodily presence remains an
unresolved question even today. On the one hand, the scepticism
of modern audiences might undermine the effect of a walking
ghost; furthermore, the text clearly indicates that Macbeth is the
only character who sees it. Thus, an imaginary ghost might emphasize Macbeth's guilty conscience. On the other hand, once the
ghost becomes invisible, the audience begins to experience the
scene from the perspective of the Scottish nobles rather than
through the eyes of Macbeth. This shift in point of view potentially
threatens identification with Macbeth, which is so necessary to
maintain interest in and attachment to him as he spirals out of
control, moving further away from the ties of humanity that more
easily invite understanding.

Setting and Costumes

Unlike the bare Jacobean stage, new theaters in the post-
Restoration period were more elaborate and sets consequently
more detailed. A cave became a traditional construct for the witch
scenes, and bushes appeared on stage to represent the outdoors.
Lighting became relatively sophisticated, as did mechanical devices
allowing for the exit of flying witches. Many productions relied on
"modern dress" costumes that typically included an aristocratic
wig and buckled shoes for Macbeth and fashionable gowns for
Lady Macbeth. In general, historical accuracy provoked little interest or concern, although several productions attempted to acknowledge history by introducing costumes that included the
Scots' highland tartan and chain mail armor for Macbeth. Although
these innovations gave a national flavor to the performance, they
represented period dress from several centuries after Macbeth's
era. Furthermore, few producers seemed interested in making
Lady Macbeth's costume either historical or consistent with Macbeth's. In some respects, the approach to costuming in the eighteenth and nineteenth centuries was similar to the practice in the

Jacobean period—often lavish, mostly modern, with little attempt to reflect historical accuracy or cultural realism.

Macbeth and Lady Macbeth

Macbeth and Lady Macbeth present great challenges for actors and demand production choices that reflect not only the complexity of the characters but also a wide range of interpretations and dramatic preferences. Because the two central characters act in partnership, one measure of a successful production is the balance achieved between them. Beyond that, both characters are enigmatic, driven by ambition, complicit in evil, yet somehow fully human in their doubts and fears, their guilt and affections. Embodying the dimensions of their humanity and its depravity defines the play's dramatic center. Since the post-Restoration revival of *Macbeth*, many men and women have played these roles, some achieving an effective balance and compelling characterization, others being less successful. The differences reflect dramatic skills, as well as acting styles and theatrical expectations.

David Garrick began playing Macbeth's role in the 1740s and attempted to return to Shakespeare's original text after Davenant's adaptation had been the acceptable version for seventy years. Although opposition to change ultimately resulted in a compromise between Davenant and Shakespeare, Garrick did offer a strong interpretation of Macbeth's character by portraying him as a sensitive, honorable man—a reluctant murderer who suffered severe psychological consequences for his guilt. One of Garrick's strengths is that he challenged the acting tradition of his time, which favored declamation or recitation in a formal, exaggerated manner. He adopted a natural style instead, using gesture and expression that made the character lifelike and convincing.

Interpretations varied among many of the early actors who played Macbeth's part. Some were formal and dignified; others were more natural. The trend, however, gradually moved from an emphasis on nobility and sensibility to ambition, cowardice, and villainy. Simultaneously, the witches became a more powerful evil presence in the play. Romantic tastes for heroism, along with Victorian sensibilities and propriety, steadily gave way to twentieth-century tolerance for and expectation of experimentation combined with gritty realism.

The evolution of Lady Macbeth's role coincided with these changing representations of Macbeth. Early post-Restoration versions of her part emphasized her power and ambition. When Macbeth was played as a noble, reluctant murderer and the witches as comic diversions, she acted as the criminal impetus, a cold, heartless woman who lured her husband to his evil plot. But as actors began to develop Macbeth's darker side, some actresses portrayed Lady Macbeth with more sensitivity, demonstrating her femininity, her love for her husband, and sometimes even a highly charged sexual energy. By far the most memorable Lady Macbeth was Sarah Siddons, who played the part numerous times between 1785 and 1816. Stressing ambition more than femininity, she presented the part with such conviction and energy that she set the standard for many years to follow.

The Staging of *Macbeth*

Three excerpts below address some of the issues and concerns surrounding the staging of *Macbeth* after its revival in 1674. The first gives an actor's perspective on Lady Macbeth's part, and the other two offer critics' impressions of Macbeth's role. Each not only reflects the artistic judgments and critical impressions of a particular age but also draws attention to some enduring questions about the measure of good acting and the ability to bring Shakespeare's characters to life on stage.

SARAH SIDDONS REHEARSES LADY MACBETH

Sarah Siddons played Lady Macbeth's part for over thirty years, beginning in 1785 when she was only twenty years old. She describes the task of learning the part, admitting her initial naiveté about the difference between memorizing lines and becoming a character. She also provides a vivid account of the horrors bred by her imagination once she began to enter into Lady Macbeth's world. A subsequent incident captures the intensity Siddons brought to her role by describing a disagreement with the producer behind the scenes just before a performance. An audience member once said of Siddons's performance, "I smelt blood! I swear I smelt blood!" Her own reflections here help to suggest why she commanded such a powerful response.

THOMAS CAMPBELL, *LIFE OF MRS. SIDDONS*
(London: Edward Moxton, 1839) 184–187

Mrs. Siddons had played *Lady Macbeth* in the provincial theatres many years before she attempted the character in London. Adverting to the first time this part was allotted to her, she says, "It was my custom to study my characters at night, when all the domestic cares and business of the day were over. On the night preceding that in which I was to appear in this part for the first time, I shut myself up, as usual, when all the family were retired, and commenced my study of *Lady Macbeth*. As the character is very short, I thought I should soon accomplish it. Being then only twenty years of age, I believed, as many others do believe, that little more was necessary than to get the words into my head; for the necessity of discrimination, and development of character, at that time of my life, had scarcely entered into my imagination. But, to proceed, I went on with tolerable composure, in the silence of the night, (a night I never can forget,) till I came to the assassination scene, when the horrors of the scene rose to a degree that made it impossible for me to get further. I snatched up my candle, and hurried out of the room, in a paroxysm of terror. My dress was of silk, and the rustling of it, as I ascended the stairs to go to bed, seemed to my panic-struck fancy like the movement of a spectre pursuing me. At last I reached my chamber, where I found my husband fast asleep. I clapt my candlestick down upon the table, without the power of putting the candle out; and I threw myself on my bed, without daring to stay even to take off my clothes. At the peep of day I rose to resume my task; but so little did I know of my part when I appeared in it, at night, that my shame and confusion cured me of procrastinating my business for the remainder of my life.

About six years afterwards I was called upon to act the same character in London. By this time I had perceived the difficulty of assuming a personage with whom no one feeling of common general nature was congenial or assistant. One's own heart could prompt one to express, with some degree of truth, the sentiments of a mother, a daughter, a wife, a lover, a sister, &c., but, to adopt this character, must be an effort of the judgment alone.

Therefore it was with the utmost diffidence, nay terror, that I undertook it, and with the additional fear of Mrs. Pritchard's reputation in it before my eyes. The dreaded first night at length arrived, when, just as I finished my toilette, and was pondering with fearfulness my first appearance in the grand fiendish part, comes Mr. Sheridan, knocking at my door, and insisting, in spite of all my entreaties not to be interrupted at this to me tremendous moment, to be admitted. He would not be denied admittance; for he protested he must speak to me on a circumstance which so deeply concerned my own interest, that it was of the most serious nature. Well, after much squabbling, I was compelled to admit him, that I might dismiss him the sooner, and compose myself before the play began. But, what was my distress and astonishment, when I found that he wanted me, even at this moment of anxiety and terror, to adopt another mode of acting the sleeping scene! He told me he had heard with the greatest surprise and concern that I meant to act it without holding the candle in my hand; and, when I urged the impracticability of washing out that '*damned spot,*' with the vehemence that was certainly implied by both her own words, and by those of her gentlewoman, he insisted, that if I did put the candle out of my hand, it would be thought a presumptuous innovation, as Mrs. Pritchard had always retained it in hers. My mind, however, was made up, and it was then too late to make me alter it; for I was too agitated to adopt another method. My deference for Mr. Sheridan's taste and judgment was, however, so great, that, had he proposed the alteration whilst it was possible for me to change my own plan, I should have yielded to his suggestion; though, even then, it would have been against my own opinion, and my observation of the accuracy with which somnambulists perform all the acts of waking persons. The scene, of course, was acted as I had myself conceived it; and the innovation, as Mr. Sheridan called it, was received with approbation. Mr. Sheridan himself came to me, after the play, and most ingenuously congratulated me on my obstinacy. When he was gone out of the room I began to undress; and, while standing up before my glass, and taking

off my mantle, a diverting circumstance occurred, to chase away the feelings of this anxious night; for, while I was repeating, and endeavouring
to call to mind the appropriate tone and action to the following words,
'Here's the smell of blood still!' my dresser innocently exclaimed, 'Dear
me, ma'am, how very hysterical you are to-night; I protest and vow,
ma'am, it was not blood, but rose-pink and water; for I saw the property-
man mix it up with my own eyes.' "

DAVID GARRICK'S MACBETH

In a collection of dramatic criticism, Francis Gentleman records his high praise of David Garrick's Macbeth in the eighteenth century, comparing Garrick's achievements to less successful portrayals of other contemporary actors. In the following excerpt, notice the emotions Gentleman identifies in Garrick's interpretation of Macbeth and the relative weaknesses described in Quin's execution of the same role.

FRANCIS GENTLEMAN, *THE DRAMATIC CENSOR*, VOL. 1
(London: J. Bell, 1770) 107–109

Through all the soliloquies of anxious reflections in the first act; amidst the pangs of guilty apprehensions and pungent remorse in the second; through all the distracted terror of the third; all the impetuous curiosity of the fourth, all the desparation [*sic*] of the fifth, Mr. GARRICK shows uniform, unabating excellence; scarce a look, motion, or tone, but takes possession of our faculties: and leads them to just sensibility.

. . . [W]hoever saw the *immortal actor* start at, and trace the imaginary dagger previous to Duncan's murder, without embodying by sympathy, unsubstantial air into the alarming shape of such a weapon? Whoever heard the low, but piercing notes of his voice when the *deed is done*, repeating those inimitable passages which mention the sleeping grooms and murder of sleep, without feeling a vibration of the nerves? Whoever saw the guilty distraction of features he assumes on Banquo's appearance at the feast, without sacrificing reason to real apprehension from a mimic ghost; who has heard his speech, after receiving his death wound, uttered with the utmost agony of body and mind, but trembles at the idea of future punishment, and almost pities the expiring wretch, though stained with crimes of the deepest dye? . . .

Mr. QUIN, whose sole merit in tragedy was declamation or brutal pride, was undescribably cumbersome in Macbeth; his face, which had no possible variation from its natural grace, except sternness and festivity, could not be expected to exhibit the acute sensations of his character; his figure was void of the essential spirit, and his voice far too monotonous for the transitions which so frequently occur; yet, wonderful to be told, he played it several years with considerable applause.

MACREADY AS MACBETH

A century after Francis Gentleman's theatrical reviews, dramatic critic Leigh Hunt similarly examines several actors' presentations of Macbeth, attempting to define what works well and what does not. The following excerpt offers his assessment of William Charles Macready. Recognizing how the complexity of Macbeth's character challenges a player's skill and versatility, Hunt acknowledges that Macready excels in some scenes and fails in others. Notice in the discussion of Macready's weaknesses the distinctions Hunt observes between a dramatic character and a real person and how he feels those differences should affect an actor's part. Also pay attention to his emphasis on the delivery of words as an important aspect of a good performance.

LEIGH HUNT, "TO 'THE TATLER': MONDAY, NOVEMBER 7," IN
DRAMATIC ESSAYS, ED. WILLIAM ARCHER AND ROBERT W. LOWE
(London: Walter Scot, 1894) 233–234

Mr. Macready is admirable in the scenes just before and after the murder, in the banquet scene, and in the death—but these are not the scenes which distinguish the character from all others—and the great difficulty is in the characteristic marking, in which he succeeds to a degree that provokes instead of satisfying us. We see that he has studied the part deeply, we feel assured that he understands it thoroughly, yet he often fails to hit on the right tone to communicate the feeling—and we fancy we can see how. He pitches his design too high, o'erleaps the sense, and "falls on the other." In trying to show an entire absorption in the spirit of the scene, he becomes careless of the expression of particular words, and in such a part as Macbeth, where a life of thought and action is curdled into hours, "words are things," and the lightest of grave import. In such a play, above all others, it is necessary for an artist to remember that he is not acting a long history of the hero's life and death, but a work of art, in which every line should contribute as far as possible to the general effect, and in which he must often endeavour to substitute appropriate symbols of passion for its exact representation. Thus Mr. Macready speaks the first line after he has reached the blasted heath, "So fair and foul a day I have not seen," as a mere casual remark on the weather; so probably Macbeth himself would have uttered it; but the purpose and the space of the poet require that, in these words, the audience should feel a strange contention of the elements, fit for the supernatural appearances which are at hand, and a mood in the mind of the speaker which makes him fit subject for their "supernatural soliciting." Thus he lets the words, "If chance will have me King, why chance may crown me Without my stir," slide from his lips without emphasis, as if he were dismissing the thought from his mind; whereas he is yet busy with the dream of ambition; and that "Chance" to which he inclines to leave his elevation, is only the mightest power in his mind, because it seems to supersede the necessity for criminal action. The hurried and unemphatic tone adopted in these and other passages in the early part of the play, gives great dissatisfaction to old play-goers, which we cannot help partaking, although convinced that these are the results, not, as they suppose, of carelessness or affectation, but of an over-anxiety to avoid bombast and mouthing. In the murder scene, Mr. Macready, at least, equals any one we have ever seen—his whispered intimation that he has done the deed is fearful—in the banquet scene, he far excels Kemble and every one else, and his last scene is a succession of terrible pictures.

QUESTIONS FOR WRITTEN AND ORAL DISCUSSION

1. Sarah Siddons's account of her experience as Lady Macbeth reveals much about the skill and thought required in behind-the-scenes preparation. Discuss what her narrative says about transforming a role into a character. What makes imagination both a necessary and a critical part of the process? What difficulties does Siddons identify in assuming Lady Macbeth's role? Consider whether and how Macbeth's part shares some of the same challenges.

2. What does the dispute between Siddons and Mr. Sheridan reveal about the interpretive balance between actor and producer? Who makes the decisions? Find a partner in class, choose one of Macbeth's or Lady Macbeth's scenes, and work together as actor and producer, deciding on appropriate gestures, expressions, and props. Give a class presentation that may include explanations of your choices, the effect you hope to achieve, and short recitations of selected parts.

3. Francis Gentleman divides his analysis of Garrick's Macbeth into several parts. In the first paragraph, what different qualities does he feel Garrick captures successfully in his portrayal of Macbeth? In the second paragraph, what emotional reactions does Garrick inspire in the audience? Considering these complementary aspects of performance in light of the play's plot, make an act-by-act list with three columns. In the first column, summarize the main events for Macbeth in each act; in the second, enter his responses, as identified by Gentleman; in the third, include the audience's emotional reactions to significant events. Discuss how this exercise increases your awareness or understanding of Macbeth's character and of an actor's challenge in portraying him.

4. According to Gentleman, why does Mr. Quin's portrayal of Macbeth fail?

5. What weaknesses does Hunt identify in Macready's performance of Macbeth, and why does he suggest they occur?

6. According to Hunt, what distinguishes "a long history" from a "work of art"? How does this difference become important in *Macbeth*, and how might it affect an actor's delivery of the part? Consider how Hunt's analysis of Macready's Macbeth and Gentleman's discussion of Quin's unsuccessful performances demonstrate that completely different approaches can result in poor acting.

7. Using Gentleman's and Hunt's accounts of various dramatic interpretations, how would you distinguish between a formal style of acting and a natural style of acting? Choose one of Macbeth's speeches

and have one or two students recite it in several different styles. Ask classmates to vote on the most effective interpretation and explain their preference.

8. How do Siddons, Gentleman, and Hunt reveal the importance of gesture and speech in an effective performance? To appreciate the contribution of each skill, form two small groups to act a scene or portion of one scene in two ways: One group will mime the scene without words, and the other will record the scene on tape as a radio play without actions but including necessary sound effects. Follow the two presentations with a discussion between performers and the remaining audience of classmates about the challenges and results of both approaches.

9. Discuss the staging of the supernatural elements in *Macbeth*. In what different ways might the witches be cast? Discuss whether the illustration of the witches in this book (See Chapter 2) satisfies your perception of Shakespeare's characters. How else might you portray them? Consider also the possibilities for staging Banquo's ghost. How would your choice for the witches affect your decision about the ghost? What would you do with Macbeth's dagger scene? Discuss whether or not decisions about the staging of these scenes need to be made in conjunction with one another. What total impression do you intend to achieve?

10. Comic witches dominated the eighteenth-century stage. How do you think a deliberately comic portrayal would affect your reaction to the play and to Macbeth's rise and fall? Can you imagine *Macbeth* without witches? Discuss what effect the general lack of superstition in modern society might have on a live performance? Do you think that Shakespeare's use of the supernatural detracts from our twentieth-century appreciation of the play? Why or why not? Perhaps compare the possibilities with science fiction movies or plays you may have seen. Does the performance have to be "realistic" to be convincing?

11. Shakespeare's original audiences would likely have enjoyed live instrumental music at a performance of *Macbeth* as well as the witches' songs. Davenant's audiences later responded enthusiastically to additional music and dance, and in modern drama and film, music is often used to create mood. Pretend you are a music producer for *Macbeth* and select music you feel would enhance the play. Record the selections and attach a written report explaining where you would include each piece and what effect you intend to achieve. You may limit the exercise to one act or choose selective scenes throughout the play that spark your musical imagination.

12. Select music from Verdi's opera *Macbeth* (1847) or Sir William Wal-

ton's *Macbeth* Theater Music (1941) and write a response suggesting how the music reflects the action and captures the atmosphere of the play.

13. Decide how you would produce a "modern dress" version of *Macbeth*. Illustrate costumes you would use for the main characters and briefly explain your choices. Alternatively, research the history of eleventh-century Scotland or seventeenth-century England and draw costumes that reflect either period, again briefly explaining your choices.

NOTE

Suggested Readings for this section appear at the end of the next section, "The Twentieth Century."

THE TWENTIETH CENTURY

The twentieth century has seen a wide range of innovations in performances of *Macbeth*, some following a natural development from earlier productions, others reacting against previous styles and interpretations, and all responding in different ways to vast technological, political, and cultural changes over the decades. Technologically, the rise of film and television represents the greatest influence, with movie cameras adding a whole new dimension to the stage and presenting new creative opportunities and challenges for actors and directors. Politically and culturally, improved global communications and growing interest in Shakespeare's drama throughout the world have allowed international perspectives to shape our modern understanding of his plays. *Macbeth*'s Scottish plot has consequently been relocated to a variety of settings, from the downtown streets of urban North America to the tribal villages of Africa, as each new producer attempts to bring freshness and relevance to a centuries-old story.

Any temptation to find such adaptations a perversion of Shakespeare's text should be balanced against an awareness that drama, as a living art form, cannot merely be "reproduced" but is necessarily reinterpreted and re-created with each performance. Being true to Shakespeare's original intent is not simply a transparent and straightforward task because his plays include few stage directions and are filled with ambiguities and multiple possibilities. Furthermore, even Shakespeare himself typically borrowed and reshaped old plot lines into new stories, turning Holinshed's text-book history into Macbeth's compelling personal tragedy. Evalu-ating each dramatization of the play should not, therefore, be limited to superficial judgments about the details of place and time but, rather, ought to consider broader questions about what makes the play current or valid in each new age. The challenge of dra-matic critics is to consider whether each performance interprets and realizes the play's central human truths, whether it presents a coherent and consistent vision, and whether it allows Shake-speare's poetry to exercise its imaginative power. Some produc-tions clearly stretch the limits of re-creation, becoming instead "loosely based" revisions of *Macbeth*. Yet even these deserve to be evaluated according to the performance's goals and the success with which they have been realized.

Interpretive decisions that have influenced twentieth-century productions of *Macbeth* relate not only to setting but also to style and theme. Production styles range from elaborate realism—rely-ing on vivid, detailed scenery and even the special effects of the movie screen—to stark symbolism that simply trusts the power of a dark, almost empty stage. The central thematic question about the source and motivation of Macbeth's crimes continues to inspire new ideas about the play's focus on character, society, and the supernatural. Are there heroes, villains, and victims? How do inner and outer conflicts balance? Should the emphasis be spiritual or psychological? Christian, pre-Christian, or non-Christian? Should the production offer hope or accentuate darkness? And given the typical need to abbreviate the text into a comfortable performance time, even for a play as short as *Macbeth*, what parts should be cut? These are some of the questions directors face. The following brief survey of several modern stage and film productions exposes a variety of answers.

Orson Welles, Harlem (1936)

Macbeth had been performed traditionally as a Scottish play or a virtually "timeless" play in modern dress; Orson Welles's pro-duction at the Lafayette Theater in Harlem in 1936 represented a radical departure. Using an all-black cast, he adopted the jungle of nineteenth-century Haiti as his setting and replaced Shakespeare's three witches with forty-three characters practicing the black magic of voodooism. The supernatural dominated this interpretation of the play as the main source of power and evil. Witches appeared in almost every scene, led by an authentic African witch doctor and accompanied by drums and chanting. The source of corruption became not Macbeth but malevolent spirituality, represented by these voodoo followers. Macbeth appeared as little more than a victim of malignant forces beyond his control rather than a flawed individual suffering a personal conflict within. In order to sustain this consistent theme, Welles made significant changes to the text, eliminating some minor characters, omitting specific references to Scotland, and scattering the Hecate scenes throughout the play. Ultimately, his drama concluded with a dark vision that emphasized the unending control of supernatural powers.

Thematically, the Harlem *Macbeth* focused solidly on evil, perhaps at the expense of tragedy. Stylistically, it was a lavish production with a huge cast and elaborate sets. Politically, it made a bold racial statement by employing only black actors at a time in U.S. history when few blacks had professional status or recognition in the theater business. Although Welles returned to a Scottish setting in his movie version of *Macbeth* in the 1940s, his Haitian stage rendition remains noteworthy for the attention it attracted with its artistic innovations and social intentions.

The following *New York Times* article offers a contemporary preview of the production just prior to its opening night. The Haitian setting and the black cast inspired this writer's greatest curiosity and interest. Notice particularly how Welles defends the "geographically irreverent" location and what conclusions the "scout" or reporter reaches about the innovation.

"MACBETH" THE MOOR
By Bosley Crowther

The bloody business of Shakespeare's "Macbeth" has found itself re-enacted upon a great many stages and under a variety of peculiar circumstances since that monstrous tragedy first fell into the public domain some three hundred years ago. Beardless boys have portrayed the sanguineous queen, school girls have challenged Macduff, Chinamen have played it in Chinese and the corner of some tropical sward has probably served at one time or another for a blasted Scottish heath. But generally—

with possible exceptions—the scene of the action has been, as Shakespeare instructed—Scotland.

Broadway might, therefore, be excused for tilting a quizzical eyebrow—
yes, even looking around—at the recent reports drifting south from Harlem that the Negro Theatre unit of the Federal Theatre Project was whip-
ping into shape a production of the Bard's most slaughterous drama
which was not to have its setting in Scotland at all, but in a West Indian
island—namely Haiti. Old fustians who have torn their share of passions
to tatters and wall-eyed pedants may have blown through their whiskers
at the news, but less devout worshipers at the shrine of Stratford's fore-
most son were heartily stirred by it. And the odds are at even money that
a sizable representation will be present on Thursday night for the first
performance of this geographically irreverent "Macbeth" at Harlem's Lafayette Theatre. . . .

The scout, upon arrival, discovered a good-sized crowd of Negroes
milling around at the back of the theatre, talking, laughing and betraying
themselves as wholly impervious to time. More than 100 persons are in
the company of "Macbeth" and that's about how many were in the
crowd—for these were the Shakespearean thespians themselves waiting
to begin rehearsal.

Not to them, however, but to John Houseman and Orson Welles, su-
pervisor and director, respectively, of the Negro Theatre troupe, it was
that the scout went for information. Why, he wanted to know, had they
mustered the audacity to take "Macbeth" for a ride? What sort of thane
of Cawdor would find himself in Haiti? Whither would Malcolm and Donalbain flee—to Jamaica or possibly Nassau? There were lots of questions
to ask.

Both Mr. Houseman and Mr. Welles, the scout soon found, were
pleased to talk brightly and intelligently, about their unusual creation.
But they were also quite serious about it. This was no deliberate stunt
on their part, no striving to accomplish a freak production just for the
sake of sensation. They had good, sound reasons for it. . . .

"We were very anxious to do one of Shakespeare's dramas in the Negro
Theatre," said he, "and 'Macbeth' seemed, in all respects, the most adaptable—so that's the one we're doing.

"You've heard that the locale we've chosen is Haiti? Well, it isn't Haiti
at all. It's like the island that 'The Tempest' was put on—just a mythical
place which, because our company is composed of Negroes, may be anywhere in the West Indies. As a matter of fact," he added, with a smile,
"the only point in shifting the scene from Scotland was because the kilt
is naturally not a particularly adaptable costume for Negro actors."

"However," he continued, "the witch element in the play falls beau-
tifully into the supernatural atmosphere of Haitian voodooism. We've

taken full advantage of that. Instead of using just three witches, as most productions of 'Macbeth' conventionally do, we have an entire chorus of singers and dancers. And Hecate, who is seldom presented, is the leading spirit in their midst—a sort of sinister Father Divine—a man witch who leads the others."

A man witch? Do you remember Banquo's observation:

". . . you should be women

"And yet your beards forbid me to interpret

"That you are so."

Further, the stormy history of Haiti during and subsequent to the French colonization in Napoleon's day—and the career of Henri Christophe, who became "the Negro King of Haiti" as the result of civil war, and ended by killing himself when his cruelty led to a revolt—form a striking parallel to the bloody story of "Macbeth." The costumes and settings of the production are therefore broadly in this period of Haiti's grimmest turbulence. Place names have been altered without any regard for geographical accuracy, but with particular care to retain the rhythm of Shakespeare's lines. And Malcolm and Donalbain don't flee to "England' but to "the coast."

So far as the acting company is concerned, Mr. Welles said that he finds the present one a whole lot more natural and comprehending than any troupe of professional whites that he has ever seen.

"You see," he said, "these Negroes have never had the misfortune of hearing Elizabethan verse spouted by actors strongly flavoring a well-cured Smithfield. They read their lines just as they would any others. On the whole, they're no better and no worse than the average white actor before he discovered the 'red plush curtain' style."

New York Times, Sunday, April 5, 1936

Laurence Olivier, Stratford-upon-Avon (1955)

One of the most renowned twentieth-century productions of *Macbeth* appeared in Stratford, England, in 1955 with Glen Byam Shaw as director and Laurence Olivier as Macbeth. Unlike Welles, Shaw chose simple sets to represent traditional Scottish scenes. The production concentrated on character rather than location or social corruption, and Olivier's ability to capture the complexity of Macbeth's personality and motivation provided the strength of the performance. His Macbeth was an evil man who had obviously contemplated usurping Duncan's throne long before the witches approached him with the idea in the first act. He was also a sen-

Macbeth and Lady Macbeth played by Laurence Olivier and Vivian Leigh at Strat-ford-upon-Avon, 1955. Angus McBean photograph. *Harvard Theatre Collection, The Houghton Library*.

sitive man, plagued by the voice of his own conscience. The illus-tration in this book reveals a dark, brooding character pondering Duncan's murder while under the attentive eye of his wife, played by Vivian Leigh. As Lady Macbeth, Leigh also rendered an accept-able performance, although she was overshadowed by the power and energy of Olivier. This Stratford *Macbeth* is still widely consid-ered one of the most successful stage productions of the century.

Roman Polanski Film (1971)

Although there have been several film versions of the play, the 1971 production directed by Roman Polanski continues to be the most popular and well known. Polanski strives for naturalism and realism, using the versatility of the camera lens to survey the panoramic vastness of the landscape, to explore the vacuous interior of medieval castles, and to probe the facial expressions of his troubled characters. The setting is primitive Scotland, a savage, brutal place.

Polanski focuses the tragedy not on character or the supernatural but on society itself. He creates this perspective by diminishing Macbeth and Lady Macbeth's prominence and power, projecting sinister motives on several other characters, and including scenes of graphic violence throughout. Ross becomes a self-interested, unscrupulous character who appears willing to claim allegiance to any leader as long as it serves his advantage. The witches, ugly, unkempt women who are more human than supernatural, set an ominous tone at the outset of the play by symbolically burying a severed arm and a dagger on a barren beach. When Macbeth later revisits them in Act 3 to hear more of their prophecies, ironically he rides a white horse, a sign of goodness, but then drinks their brew, a gesture of his complicity in their evil. The play concludes with Donalbain, Duncan's uncrowned son, limping to the witches' cave presumably to hear his own fortunes from the evil forecasters of political unrest. The scene suggests that violence will continue, that society is unredeemable and its corruption irreversible. The power of Polanski's movie resides in its dark, haunting vision generated by the effective blend of symbolism and naturalism.

A *New York Times* review of Polanski's production included here evaluates its representation of Shakespeare's play, considering characterization, lighting, and theme. Notice what liberties the journalist feels Polanski has taken with the text and whether the critic finds this interpretation effective.

FILM: POLANSKI'S AND TYNAN'S "MACBETH"
By Roger Greenspun

So much has been written and rumored about the nudity and violence of Roman Polanski's "Macbeth" that it seems worth insisting that the film is neither especially nude nor unnecessarily violent. There is some nudity—the sleepwalkers scene; a steaming coven of perhaps three dozen weird sisters; more importantly, the naked chest of Duncan before it receives the dagger. And there is much quite energetic violence. But the nakedness seems natural to Polanski's construction of "the single state of man." And the violence, together with the blood it makes flow, is surely part of what "Macbeth" is all about.

*

Shakespeare's play is, of course, about a good deal more, not all of which gets into the movie. "Macbeth" is a drama of unusual dark disruption, and in Polanski's version the countervailing sense of order is either ironically undercut (as in the speeches of a smugly callous Duncan) or cut out entirely. I can imagine a much better "Macbeth," but in point of fact all the other productions I've seen have been much worse.

Polanski has cast a young Macbeth (Jon Finch) and Lady Macbeth (Francesca Annis), who play more for a kind of efficient determination than for terrible grandeur. Both Mr. Finch and Miss Annis are very fine (a quality they share with the entire cast, which has been meticulously prepared down to the smallest role). But what by their youth they gain in accessibility and believable intimacy, they lose in breadth and ultimately in strength of character. Their most striking characteristics, like their most famous speeches, are underplayed even beneath the requirement of ordinary cinematic modesty.

I think that there is a principle of subordination at work here, and that Polanski means to develop a world in which no individual matters too much or, indeed, differs too greatly from his fellows. He has created the most unsettling environment for his drama, not so much by sleight-of-camera tricks (which "Macbeth" freely invites) as by a continual dislocation of time so that, for example, dark night is always seen to descend or leaden morning to rise too quickly to permit the restorative rhythms of the natural day.

*

All this may seem to have little to do with "Macbeth" as written, but I think it represents excellent Shakespearean moviemaking, a real interpretation of the text on the part of Polanski and his co-scenarist Kenneth Tynan. Of their other choices I am less sure, and these would include the creation of an all-purpose villain in Ross (wonderfully frank and open-faced John Stride), whom they make into Banquo's third murderer and who betrays everyone and gladly passes the crown from each dead king to his successor.

Passing the crown (finally, a crown that takes Macbeth's severed head along with it) becomes the theme of the movie, and for Shakespeare's study of kingship, Polanski substitutes a study of succession—even to adding a silent epilogue in which Donalbain seeks prophecies against Malcolm. There is thus no good power, only a transferal of power. And to such a view, everything, even the tragedy of Macbeth, grows less re-markable.

New York Times, Tuesday, December 21, 1971

Trevor Nunn, Stratford-upon-Avon (1976)

Like Orson Welles, Trevor Nunn produced *Macbeth* on both stage and film. Similarly, he incorporated aspects of voodooism into his stage version. Unlike Welles, however, he adopted an artistically stark and simple approach. In a small theater with a thrust stage surrounded by a few hundred spectators, the ritualistic performance relied on minimal sets and props. A chalk circle created the performance space, and actors sat on stools around the circle when they were not playing a part. The interpretation centered on character interaction, visually emphasizing darkness and fostering a surrealistic rather than a realistic atmosphere. Audiences found the performance compelling, and the success of Nunn's theater production credits the power of the imagination that was such an integral part of Shakespeare's own experience with the stage over three hundred years earlier.

Adaptations

Some modern re-creations of *Macbeth* have altered the original text so radically through various cultural settings or specific political situations that these productions often no longer even share *Macbeth*'s title. For their debt to Shakespeare's plot, however, and as a testament to its adaptability, they deserve acknowledgment here. A Japanese movie translated as *Throne of Blood* (1957) set the Scottish tragedy in Japan's feudal Samurai society. Using the artistic techniques of Noh theater, a stylized, ritualistic Japanese drama, director Akira Kurosawa invited comparisons of the violence shared by European and Oriental history.

Umabatha encouraged similar connections between Shakespeare's medieval Scotland and primitive African tribal villages. A Zulu drama with an African writer and cast, *Umabatha* received attention and acclaim at the World Theater Season in London in 1972. Centering on the tribe rather than a Macbeth character, it based its dramatic effect on traditional African music, dance, and costume. With Shakespeare's play, it shared an interest in the social dynamics of power.

A movie titled *Joe Macbeth* (1956) transported Shakespeare's plot to North American urban culture, casting the main character as a Chicago gangster. Another popular approach, attempted more than once and generated by the profound effect of two world wars, has been to replace swords with machine guns, castles with trenches, and to portray Macbeth as a modern soldier, a Nazi, even Hitler himself. All these varied adaptations suggest the endless interpretive possibilities inspired by *Macbeth*'s themes, which continue to defy boundaries of time and place in their ability to haunt the human imagination.

The Curse

Macbeth possesses one of the most colorful performance histories of any English play. From its earliest productions, many people began to believe that *Macbeth* was cursed because shows seemed plagued by inexplicable accidents and misfortunes. Accounts of bad luck—"The Curse"—are especially abundant in the twentieth century because better records exist and because the sensationalism of The Curse not only inspired some actors to become remarkably superstitious but also captured media attention and the public imagination. Doubtless other plays have suffered their misfortunes, but when *Macbeth* provides the scene for yet another unexpected calamity, everyone notices. Typically, even today, many people refuse to name the play when they are in a theater, referring to it instead by code words such as "that play" or "the Scottish play."

Countless stories record disasters occurring at various rehearsals and performances of *Macbeth*. One of the most famous accounts involves Olivier's first appearance as Macbeth in London in 1937, years before his renowned 1955 role at Stratford. Bad luck haunted the production from the start. The director and "Lady Macbeth" were injured in a car accident one night during rehearsal, elaborate stage sets turned out to be the wrong size, Olivier lost his voice and then barely survived when a stage weight crashed onto his seat seconds after he left it, and finally, the theater's elderly patron suffered a fatal heart attack the night of the dress rehearsal (Huggett 150–154). Such unprecedented misfortune converted sceptics of The Curse into believers, and whereas many now find the wealth of anecdotes simply good story material, others accept the superstition with uneasy amusement. They laugh but take it just seriously enough to speak of "the Scottish play" to ward off any unlikely coincidences. Ngaio Marsh's mystery novel *Light Thickens* offers an engaging fictional account of a cast's unhappy encounter with *Macbeth*'s dark reputation.

Conclusion

Dramatic performances always exist within a context. They are influenced by political movements, cultural tastes, social values, technology, tradition, history, and often a bold desire to challenge any or all of these in imaginative new ways. Playhouses and movie theaters are therefore venues for entertainment, but they are also places that express the ebb and flow of ideas through dialogue and debate. Tracing *Macbeth*'s performance history over four centuries illuminates just how alive a play script can be as generations of artists leave their fingerprints on its pages. *Macbeth* has many creators, and together they continue to remind us of the kernel of truth in Ben Jonson's remark about Shakespeare: "He was not of an age, but for all time!"

QUESTIONS FOR WRITTEN AND ORAL DISCUSSION

1. In the newspaper article about the Harlem "voodoo *Macbeth*," what reasons does Welles provide for adopting a Haitian or Caribbean setting? Does the critic find the innovations justifiable? Do you? Can you detect any elements of social commentary in the article, any signs that the review knowingly or unknowingly reflects attitudes about the racial significance of the production as well as its artistic innovations?

2. What strengths and weaknesses does the reviewer note in Polanski's *Macbeth*? What does the article have to say specifically about character, setting, and theme?

3. Watch Polanski's *Macbeth* and write your own review of it or hold a class debate that addresses the effectiveness of the production, considering specific interpretive choices such as the violence, the witches, Ross's duplicitous role, the youthfulness of Macbeth and Lady Macbeth, and the ending when Donalbain visits the witches' cave.

4. Write a response to Polanski's reinterpretation of *Macbeth*'s ending. How does his rendition alter the theme in Shakespeare's *Macbeth*?

5. A popular opinion maintains that the twentieth century cannot effectively portray tragedy because our modern age lacks heroes and because contemporary literature focuses not on kings but on common people such as Willy Loman in Arthur Miller's *Death of a Salesman*. Some modern productions of *Macbeth* similarly downplay its tragic elements by emphasizing social domination or pervasive corruption, and by encouraging a notion of victimhood or communal rather than individual guilt.

  Review the summaries of productions discussed in this chapter and consider how tragedy is reflected in each. Then write an essay about how tragedy has been interpreted and understood in modern times, using *Macbeth* as your central example. Can tragedy exist without heroes? Must Shakespeare's story be adapted to maintain contemporary relevance? Is tragedy compromised if kingly characters are reduced to common soldiers? Arthur Miller's essay "Tragedy and the Common Man" might help you develop your ideas.

6. Look up definitions of "realism," "naturalism," "symbolism," and "ritual." Guided by the production summaries in this chapter, discuss some of the artistic choices available in producing and directing *Macbeth*. What might be the advantages and disadvantages of each approach? Alternatively, choose one approach and provide an analysis of its dramatic potential.

7. Consider Trevor Nunn's ritualistic techniques and try to develop your own version of *Macbeth* that uses simple sets and symbolism.

8. Create a collage of *Macbeth*, using materials and images that capture the play's themes visually and perhaps symbolically.

9. Many modern experiments with *Macbeth* relocate the story to suggest relationships between it and other factual events or specific people. Discuss whether you think these revisions enhance the play by making it more engaging and relevant. What does "relevance" really mean? Does it depend on setting? Can it be achieved in other less obvious ways?

10. If you were to direct *Macbeth*, can you imagine a specific setting that would shed new light on the play? For suggestions, consider some of the contemporary themes examined in Chapter 4 of this book.

11. Using a video camera, film a scene of *Macbeth* as a group assignment. Include production notes indicating choices such as camera angles, lighting, and props.

12. Discuss the effect of parody and enact a satiric version of one scene. How would you play *Macbeth* for laughs? The witches, as the most difficult characters to play seriously, present an obvious choice. As another option, write a humorous song or poem about *Macbeth* and present it to the class.

13. Discuss the history of The Curse in relation to *Macbeth*'s plot. Why do you suppose superstitions surround this play? How do they respond to the belief that twentieth-century scepticism undermines the supernatural element of *Macbeth*?

14. Try to uncover some stories about *Macbeth*'s curse and give a written or oral report of your findings. What strange rituals do actors use to ward off consequences of The Curse?

15. Read Ngaio Marsh's mystery novel *Light Thickens* and write a book review or an essay that describes how the story has increased your understanding of *Macbeth* or taught you a different way to see the play.

SUGGESTED READINGS

Bartholomeusz, Dennis. *Macbeth and the Players*. Cambridge: Cambridge UP, 1969.

Huggett, Richard. *The Curse of Macbeth and Other Theatrical Superstitions*. New York: Picton Books, 1981.

Jorgens, Jack. *Shakespeare on Film*. Bloomington: Indiana UP, 1977.

Kliman, Bernice. *Shakespeare and Performance: Macbeth*. Manchester: Manchester UP, 1993.

Marsh, Ngaio. *Light Thickens*. Boston: Little, Brown, 1982.

Paul, Henry N. *The Royal Play of Macbeth*. New York: Macmillan, 1950.

Rosenberg, Marvin. *The Masks of Macbeth*. Berkeley: University of California Press, 1978.

Sprague, Arthur C. *Shakespeare and the Actors: The Stage Business in His Plays (1660–1905)*. Cambridge: Harvard UP, 1944.

Updike, John. "Tomorrow and Tomorrow and So Forth." In *The Same Door*. New York: Knopf, 1959. 27–40. A short story about a class studying *Macbeth*.

Williams, Gordon. *Macbeth: Text and Performance*. London: Macmillan, 1985.

CURRENTS OF CRITICISM

Macbeth is not only a dramatic script but also a written text, a literary work of art with poetry and themes that challenge and reward critical evaluation. Although ignoring the essential aspect of performance necessarily limits a full appreciation of Shakespeare's play, his drama also invites literary analysis. Even during his lifetime Shakespeare's plays were published to be read as well as seen. Moreover, theatrical, literary, and historical interests need not be mutually exclusive; they can often complement one another.

Critical approaches to *Macbeth* continue to be vast and varied, and one way to put this diversity into perspective is to consider how two seemingly contradictory meanings of the word "contemporary" apply to Shakespearean scholarship. "Historical Context," Chapter 2 of this book, reinforces the fact that Shakespeare's drama can be better understood in light of "contemporary" values and ideas—that is, those present in Shakespeare's time and place. From an entirely opposite perspective, however, Jan Kott's study *Shakespeare Our Contemporary* (1964) argues that Shakespeare is a modern writer to the extent that his works reflect concerns relevant to recent or "contemporary" society. Many stage productions adopt a similar approach, as does Chapter 4 of this book, "Contemporary Applications." The word "contemporary" can mean "then" *or* "now," often, in fact, "then" *and* "now," for even historical studies bear the influences of modern values and culture, which shape interests and interpretations. Partly for that reason, opposing views about the "contemporary" value of *Macbeth* have always existed in creative tension with one another. The focus of Shakespearean criticism has also shifted over the years according to intellectual trends and the advent of new scholarship.

Although attempting to categorize approaches invariably over-simplifies them because good interpretations defy boundaries, classifying nevertheless does help to create some order out of great critical diversity. The following brief summary of major currents in literary analysis endeavors not only to point out the vast range of interpretations that *Macbeth* has stimulated but also to reveal the ways in which these perspectives illuminate the complexity and richness of the play itself.

Dramatic and Structural Approaches

Dramatic and structural approaches primarily address the nature of tragedy, exploring *Macbeth* within its dramatic tradition. Shakespeare's heritage of Aristotle, Seneca, and the morality plays (see Chapter 1) guide this critical discussion as scholars ask, for example, to what extent *Macbeth* conforms to Aristotelian conventions requiring "imitation of action" and eliciting "fear and pity." Other critics emphasize the moral element of tragedy by comparing *Macbeth*'s structure to the morality play's allegorical representation of good and evil. Opponents to this position argue, however, that such moral conclusions can simplify and reduce Macbeth's plight, diminishing tragedy to melodrama rather than recognizing the play's moral ambiguity.

Writing early in the twentieth century, A. C. Bradley maintains that the center of tragedy is not so much plot or morality but character. Exploring Macbeth's and Lady Macbeth's depth and vitality, he argues that Macbeth's main flaw is his poetic imagination and that Lady Macbeth's character development contrasts her husband's.

A. C. BRADLEY, *SHAKESPEAREAN TRAGEDY*
(London: Macmillan, 1904)

This bold ambitious man of action has, within certain limits, the imagination of a poet,—an imagination on the one hand extremely sensitive to impressions of a certain kind, and, on the other, productive of violent disturbance both of mind and body. Through it he is kept in contact with supernatural impressions and is liable to supernatural fears. And through it, especially, come to him the better intimations of conscience and honour. Macbeth's better nature—to put the matter for clearness' sake too broadly—instead of speaking to him in the overt language of moral ideas, commands, and prohibitions, incorporates itself in images which alarm and horrify. His imagination is thus the best of him, something usually deeper and higher than his conscious thoughts; and if he had obeyed it he would have been safe. But his wife quite misunderstands it, and he himself understands it only in part (352). . . .

The greatness of Lady Macbeth lies almost wholly in courage and force of will. It is an error to regard her as remarkable on the intellectual side. In acting a part she shows immense self-control, but not much skill. . . . But the limitations of her mind appear most in the point where she is most strongly contrasted with Macbeth,—in her comparative dullness of imagination. . . . It is not *simply* that she suppresses what she has. To her, things remain at the most terrible moment precisely what they were at the calmest, plain facts which stand in a given relation to a certain deed, not visions which tremble and flicker in the light of other worlds (371). . . .

This want of imagination, though it helps to make Lady Macbeth strong for immediate action, is fatal to her. If she does not feel beforehand the cruelty of Duncan's murder, this is mainly because she hardly imagines the act, or at most imagines its outward show. . . . Nor does she in the least foresee those inward consequences which reveal themselves immediately in her husband, and less quickly in herself (373). . . . [H]er part in the crime was so much less open-eyed than his, that, if the impossible and undramatic task of estimating degrees of culpability were forced on us, we should surely have to assign the larger share to Macbeth. (377)

Bradley remains one of the most influential critics of Shakespearean tragedy, inspiring reaction and counterreaction over the decades. His critics contend that he treats drama too much like prose fiction, a genre that depends heavily on character development. Overall, interest in the meaning of tragedy in *Macbeth* has directed attention to the literary aspect of drama by focusing on character and action as well as on patterns that shape the play's structure and development.

Thematic and Poetic Analysis

Partly in reaction to the powerful influence of Bradley's character analysis and in keeping with literary trends in the mid-twentieth century, many critics turned their attention to language studies, to images, symbols, and themes not easily identified in performance but realized in a close reading of the text. Adopting an approach known as New Criticism, some scholars began to describe the play as a dramatic poem, seeing in it poetic unity sustained by clusters of metaphors and common themes reflected in different scenes and characters.

An early scholar to trace extensive image patterns in Shakespeare's drama, Caroline Spurgeon, contends that the clothing imagery emphasizes Macbeth's diminished moral stature.

CAROLINE SPURGEON, *SHAKESPEARE'S IMAGERY AND WHAT IT TELLS US*
(Cambridge, Cambridge University Press, 1935)

Few simple things—harmless in themselves—have such a curiously humiliating and degrading effect as the spectacle of a notably small man enveloped in a coat far too big for him. Comic actors know this well—Charlie Chaplin, for instance—and it is by means of this homely picture that Shakespeare shows us his imaginative view of the hero, and expresses the fact that the honours for which the murders were committed are, after all, of very little worth to him (324–325). . . .

Undoubtedly Macbeth is built on great lines and in heroic proportions, with great possibilities—there could be no tragedy else. He is great, magnificently great, in courage, in passionate, indomitable ambition, in imagination and capacity to feel. But he could never be put beside, say, Hamlet or Othello, in nobility of nature; and there *is* an aspect in which he is but a poor, vain, cruel, treacherous creature, snatching ruthlessly over the dead bodies of kinsman and friend at place and power he is utterly unfitted to possess. It is worth remembering that it is thus that Shakespeare, with his unshrinking clarity of vision, repeatedly *sees* him. (327)

Other image patterns, such as babies, blood, disease, light, and dark, have also attracted interest, and this close scrutiny of language expands naturally into discussions about larger thematic issues. Critics approach *Macbeth* as a study of various themes: fear, ambition, manliness, power, guilt, evil. G. Wilson Knight, for example, addresses Macbeth's speech, "Why do I yield to that suggestion" (1.3.135–142), calling it "a microcosm of the *Macbeth* vision":

G. WILSON KNIGHT, *THE WHEEL OF FIRE*
(London: Methuen, 1930)

This is the moment of the birth of evil in *Macbeth*—he may have
had ambitious thoughts before, may even have intended the murder, but now for the first time he feels its oncoming reality. This is
the mental experience which he projects into action, thereby plung-
ing his land, too, in fear, horror, darkness, and disorder. In this
speech we have a swift interpenetration of idea with idea, from fear
and disorder, through sickly imaginings, to abysmal darkness, noth-
ingness. "Nothing is but what is not": that is the text of the play.
Reality and unreality change places. We must see that Macbeth, like
the whole universe of this play, is paralysed, mesmerized, as though
in a dream. This is not merely "ambition"—it is fear, a nameless
fear which yet fixes itself to a horrid image. (153)

Language studies have continued to be a part of *Macbeth* criticism, although in recent years a theory known as Deconstruction
has led to conclusions vastly different from those of New Criticism.
Deconstruction contends that language patterns reflect not poetic
unity but instability. The deception Malcolm employs to test Macduff in Act 4, as well as the many contradictory expressions
throughout the play—"Nothing is, but what is not" and "Fair is
foul, and foul is fair"—suggest to some critics that language cannot
be trusted, not by the characters, nor even by Shakespeare's readers. The pervasive theme of equivocation supports this viewpoint.
Meaning becomes very slippery rather than fixed and unified. Thus
although language issues remain an important part of *Macbeth*
studies, they continue to provoke more debate than consensus.

Spiritual and Psychological Interpretation

Because conscience plays such a central role in *Macbeth*'s tragic
struggle, many critics have used spiritual and psychological theories—both historical and modern—to illuminate the drama's character development and world view. For those approaching
Macbeth's evil from a biblical, Christian perspective, "sin" is the
foundation of the tragedy. Interestingly, however, different theological positions yield contradictory conclusions. Some emphasize
the biblical imperative that "the wages of sin is death"; others

point to signs of charity and grace in the play's resolution when once again, "the time is free" (5.9.21) and Malcolm acknowledges "the grace of Grace" (5.9.38). Some say that Macbeth and Lady Macbeth act according to free will as Adam and Eve did when they first sinned in the Garden of Eden; others suggest that given the witches' demonic power, Macbeth has no ability to resist his destiny. Whereas one critic applies the modern philosophy of Søren Kierkegaard, others look to John Calvin or the medieval theology of St. Augustine. Those who believe that the function of evil in *Macbeth* demonstrates Shakespeare's medieval theological heritage see the witches as representatives of the demonic.

For other scholars the presence of evil is a psychological rather than theological phenomenon. Here, again, the approaches vary, with some interpreters relying on early psychological theories appearing in the Renaissance period and others observing how the modern views of Sigmund Freud and Carl Jung can illuminate the main characters' inner conflicts and final self-destruction. One critic traces the descent of the Macbeths into mental illness that robs them of their ability to act rationally. Another describes the husband and wife in Jungian terms as introvert and extravert who act unwisely because they do not understand themselves or the activities of their unconscious minds.

Guilt is such a pervasive element in *Macbeth* that the interior world of the characters necessarily invites analysis and interpretation from a whole variety of perspectives.

Historical, Political, and Cultural Perspectives

Historical and social approaches focus more on the external world of action than the internal world of conscience. Some of these interpretations have received greater attention in Chapter 2 of this text, but a summary here helps to put that discussion into context. Like the other categories of analysis, this one encompasses a broad range of perspectives, based on old and new assumptions, adopting conservative or liberal beliefs, and playing with the two contradictory meanings of the word "contemporary."

Methods are topical and theoretical. Henry Paul, for example, explores *Macbeth*'s topical allusions to specific people and public events at the time of *Macbeth*'s early performances, concluding that *Macbeth* is a royal play with many direct references clearly designed to flatter and please King James. Garry Wills addresses topical interest, too, but not so much in the play's royal themes as in the way its language draws connections between witches and Jesuits, thereby echoing attitudes and concerns about the Gunpowder Plot in 1605.

Relying on past political theories, some scholars advocate a conservative interpretation, suggesting that *Macbeth* reflects dominant, orthodox views about divine right, the fall of tyrants, and the resolution of order through good kingship. These ideas were popular in the mid-twentieth century as part of an approach later labeled Old Historicism. Since then perspectives have become more liberal, arguing for *Macbeth*'s political ambiguity, for its illumination of England's conflicting attitudes toward tyranny, civil disobedience, and succession.

In recent decades cultural studies and the rise of a New Historicism have shifted discussion to modern rather than historical social and political theories as a new way of understanding the play. Where traditionalists saw orthodoxy and moderates suggested ambiguity, new political critics see potential subversion in *Macbeth*'s social and psychological conflicts. Some suggest, for example, that the witches represent a breed of social outcasts whom political authorities and dominant classes depend on as scapegoats in order to maintain their power.

Feminism has bred similar discussions about social inequalities perpetuated between the sexes in the Renaissance period. For some critics, Shakespeare's portrayal of Lady Macbeth as the weaker sex reflects the misogyny of his time. For others, his dramatization of manly and womanly expectations subversively hints at the need for greater gender equality by enacting the devastating consequences when characters like the Macbeths cannot assume the full scope of their humanity, including both masculine and feminine attributes. These contrasting conclusions indicate that even when approached from the same political perspective, Shakespeare provokes debate and disagreement. Is his "contemporary" status a reflection of life then or now? Can it be both and if so, how?

Conclusion

Ultimately, such diverse critical discourse must be measured by its effect on the text as well as the reader. There are many ways to understand *Macbeth*, and new theories have their merit when they expand our vision of the play and its characters. But when theories and ideas threaten to take precedence over the text, making the application seem forced and somehow false, then more is lost than gained in the interpretation. Good readers and hearers of *Macbeth* learn from the critical insights and views of others. Such learning requires a willingness to ask questions, to trust one's own judgment, and to evaluate the analysis as well as using it to evaluate the play. Thus informed, readers can engage with the play's language, actions, and meanings more effectively.

QUESTIONS FOR WRITTEN AND ORAL DISCUSSION

1. According to A. C. Bradley, what is Macbeth's imagination and how is it potentially good and harmful? Does it become Macbeth's redeeming quality?

2. How does Bradley describe Lady Macbeth? What differences does he see between her and Macbeth? Discuss whether you agree that Lady Macbeth is less guilty of Duncan's murder than her husband and why. Could you argue instead that she bears more blame than Macbeth? If so, how?

3. Referring to Caroline Spurgeon's discussion of imagery and character, consider the importance of clothing imagery in *Macbeth*. Find examples in the play and discuss how they contribute to characterization and theme.

4. Suggest how the clothing references would help you make production decisions if you were involved in a performance of the play.

5. Spurgeon suggests that Macbeth is both heroic and unheroic. Do you agree? Find examples in the play to support both observations. Does one seem more true than the other, and how does your conclusion about the balance affect your understanding of *Macbeth*'s tragedy?

6. Write an essay that discusses one of the following image patterns in relation to *Macbeth*'s themes, characterization, and action: disease, babies, blood, sleep, night, nature.

7. Write an essay discussing how Shakespeare develops one of the play's themes in dialogue, soliloquy, and action. Potentially, you could begin by saying, *"Macbeth* is a play about _____," and fill in the blank with one of the following: fear, ambition, manliness, power, guilt, or evil. Then explain why.

8. G. Wilson Knight says, "Reality and unreality change places" in the play. Discuss how this shift occurs in Macbeth. What is "real" in his world? What is "unreal" or imaginary? Which aspect influences him the most, and how does the confusion affect the outcome of the play?

9. *Macbeth*'s language reflects confusion about appearance and reality. Macbeth says, "So foul and fair a day I have not seen" (1.3.38). Lady Macbeth says, "False face must hide what the false heart doth know" (1.7.83). Use these examples and find several others to discuss the sources of ambiguity in the characters' words. When are characters admitting confusion and when deliberately promoting deception? Do their contradictory statements simply describe their world or do they "create" appearances? Discuss how your observations contribute to

an understanding of the main characters and to an interpretation of the evil in *Macbeth*.

10. Debate whether you think evil in *Macbeth* is a spiritual or psychological sickness. Does guilt seem to be related to sin in a God-centered world or solely to conscience in a world where morality is guided by an individual's sense of right and wrong? What, for example, does Macbeth say about the eternal consequences of his crime? Do other characters echo his views or consider them through alternative perspectives? How do your conclusions affect your understanding of the witches and your view of the play's final "justice"?

11. Assume the role of a psychiatrist, a priest, or a marriage counselor who is about to hear a confession from either Macbeth or Lady Macbeth. Compose a dialogue or monologue that records your observations and recommendations.

12. Discuss how Shakespeare portrays women in *Macbeth*—negatively, positively, or with a sense of balance? How does his depiction of women compare to his characterization of men? Does gender play any part in the vision of right and wrong, strength and weakness? Once you have reached a conclusion, consider whether and how your views reflect modern and/or historical ideas about gender roles and expectations.

13. Act out a dialogue between Lady Macbeth and a modern activist in the feminist movement. Or compose a similar dialogue beween Macbeth and an advocate for the men's movement. What will they say to each other about gender roles and expectations? Would Macbeth's or Lady Macbeth's attitudes contradict or support modern views about the rights and roles of men and women?

SUGGESTED READINGS

Bradley, A. C. *Shakespearean Tragedy*. London: Macmillan, 1904.

Brown, John Russell, ed. *Focus on Macbeth*. London: Routledge, 1982.

Halio, Jay L., ed. *Approaches to Macbeth*. Belmont, CA: Wadsworth, 1966.

Hawkes, Terence, ed. *Twentieth Century Interpretations of Macbeth*. Englewood Cliffs: Prentice-Hall, 1977.

Knight, G. Wilson. *The Wheel of Fire*. London: Methuen, 1930.

Muir, Kenneth, ed. *Shakespeare Survey*. Vol. 16 (1966). A journal issue dedicated to *Macbeth* criticism.

Paul, Henry N. *The Royal Play of Macbeth*. New York: Macmillan, 1950.

Schoenbaum, S., ed. *Macbeth: Critical Essays*. New York: Garland, 1991.

Shakespere Allusion-Book, The: A Collection of Allusions to Shakespere From 1591 to 1700. Originally compiled by C. M. Ingleby, L. Toulmin Smith, and F. J. Furnivall, re-ed. and rev. by John Munro, 1909. Vol. 2. Rpt. London: Humphrey Milford, 1932.

Spurgeon, Caroline. *Shakespeare's Imagery and What It Tells Us*. Cambridge: Cambridge UP, 1935.

Wain, John, ed. *Shakespeare's Macbeth*. London: Macmillan, 1968.

Wills, Garry. *Witches and Jesuits: Shakespeare's Macbeth*. New York: Oxford UP, 1995.

NOTE

Entries by Brown, Halio, Hawkes, Schoenbaum, and Wain are all collections of essays or book excerpts representing significant voices in *Macbeth* criticism over the decades and centuries. They provide a good beginning for further study of the play.

4

Contemporary Applications

Because *Macbeth* is an intense drama realized within a living art form, it is open to continual reinterpretation. Like all drama, it exists in the eternal present tense of each performance. Many modern productions of Shakespeare's play demonstrate this capacity for freshness and immediacy by using settings other than medieval Scotland. Producers and directors adapt costumes and scenery to illustrate the connections they see between *Macbeth* and other tragic and political experiences in other times and places.

Beyond the stage, however, the play also shares themes and conflicts with other stories, with historic and current events, and with individual, personal experiences with which some of us can identify. We can hope to direct the discussion from the issue of relevance—why study Shakespeare?—to an appreciation of the poetic language, the dramatic craft, and the representation of values and beliefs in another age and culture. We can also point to the thematic, political, and moral connections that contribute to the appeal of Shakespeare's drama century after century. What, we might ask, makes *Macbeth* seem like such a modern play?

This last chapter of the book selectively traces several of *Macbeth*'s themes as they appear in other examples, both in fact and in fiction. The first part, "Crime and Punishment," looks at the issue of corruption in national politics, in sports, and in a terrorist regime. The three examples, Watergate, the 1988 and 1994 Olympic Games, and Haiti's historic civil unrest are studies of abused power, scandal, and violence in which the players are motivated by ambition, insecurity, or greed and are ultimately exposed. They share with *Macbeth* the pattern of crime and punishment, expose the blindness of desire, and raise similar questions about the dimensions of tragedy, the nature of evil, and the social quest for justice and order.

The second part, "Beyond the Courtroom," examines these questions from another angle, exploring the psychological and social impact of actions and choices that may variously be defined as evil, immoral, criminal, or unjust. Fear and guilt are two responses in Shakespeare's play that receive attention here. They are the side effects or sometimes the ultimate consequences of actions driven by extreme, single-minded visions of success and inspired by the false idols of power and glory. Both the perpetrators of such actions and those around them can face confusing, if not devastating, mental and emotional responses. In one example in 1995, the Oklahoma City bombing triggered a national reaction of fear and insecurity not unlike the reaction to the Gunpowder Plot in 1606 when *Macbeth* was first performed, appealing to the currency of heightened public emotion surrounding that potential political disaster. In another series of examples, the torments of guilt shared by Macbeth and Lady Macbeth are traced through several stories that similarly probe the power of conscience and self-accusation. Guilt as an inner struggle can initiate surprising, unwanted, and unanticipated responses: moral confusion, a sense of self-loathing and discontent, a newfound introspection, a greater awareness of the tragic, causal inevitability of acting out secret desires. The selected stories reflect the psychological complexity of *Macbeth* and suggest that fiction and myth can help to unify human experience and teach us how to understand and define personal and social identity.

As a whole this section on contemporary applications encourages an interdisciplinary approach by studying the boundaries of time and place, questioning the cultural or essential qualities of human experience, and exploring the connections between fact and fiction, story and history. This exercise of looking both outward and inward is designed to expand the meaning of the play itself and invite a fuller appreciation of its "relevance."

CRIME AND PUNISHMENT: A QUEST FOR POWER

Watergate: A Political Scandal

> I have no spur
> To prick the sides of my intent, but only
> Vaulting ambition, which o'erleaps itself,
> And falls on th'other—.
>
> *Macbeth* 1.7.25–28

Watergate is one of the greatest scandals in recent U.S. history. Like *Macbeth*, it is a story about ambition and paranoia that resulted in broad, sweeping political corruption. It began with the arrests of five men attempting to break into the Democratic headquarters in the Watergate office complex in Washington on June 17, 1972. In the months that followed, however, investigations uncovered evidence to link the burglary to a vast Republican scheme of sabotage and espionage against their Democratic opponents. The illegal activities extended back several years in the Nixon administration, were centered at the White House, and ultimately implicated the president himself. His impeachment and resignation in August 1974 marked the culmination of the scandal and greatly challenged the faith of the American people in their political leaders and the democratic system.

The title of one Watergate study, *They Could Not Trust the King*, draws connections between this American crisis and the constitutional crisis that ended with the beheading of James I's son, King Charles I, in England in the seventeenth century. As the title suggests, kings and presidents share similar powers and temptations. Nixon, like Macbeth and Charles I, was driven to extreme measures in his quest for power. Political history is thus played out like a theme with variations from a Scottish medieval castle to the English stage and courts to the American White House. Each time and place is a setting for the corruption of power, the question of moral responsibility and authority, and the betrayal of public trust by leaders who become obsessed with control at the expense of civil or royal obligation.

There are essentially two parts to the Watergate scandal. The first involves all the crimes leading up to the burglary on June 17. The

Republicans engaged in a campaign of "dirty tricks" to undermine the Democrats during the primaries before the 1972 election. Their illegal activities included breaking and entering, phone tapping, undercover investigations of civilians, canceling Democratic campaign rallies, forging letters, and planting spies. Furthermore, the whole operation was financed by illegal campaign money hidden in a secret "security fund" controlled by members of the Committee to Re-elect the President (CREEP).

The second part of the scandal, and perhaps the most shocking violation of public trust, followed the burglary on June 17 with efforts to cover up all the activities and protect those who had committed the crimes. Like Macbeth, those involved in the conspiracy—most significantly the president himself—were anxious to hide their guilt at all costs so they could maintain their power. For Macbeth murder prompted more murder in order to prevent witnesses from exposing him and to consolidate his power. Corruption, he found, led him down a lonely path of fear and distrust. For the Watergate conspirators the cover-up crimes committed to protect themselves included perjury in court, bribery with hush money for the original Watergate defendants, and obstructing justice with the help from the CIA, the FBI, and the privilege of the president's executive power.

As the trail of evidence led closer and closer to President Nixon himself, one of the final outrages of the scandal centered on the discovery of tapes in his possession recording conversations from a secret taping system in his office. Nixon refused to hand the tapes over to the courts, and when he finally agreed to do so, one tape had an eighteen-and-a-half minute gap in the conversation, a strong indication that someone had tampered with the evidence. Early in the investigations Nixon declared in a press conference statement, "What really hurts is if you try to cover up." By the end, it was all too apparent that that was what he and others had been doing. In spite of his bold denial during the Watergate investigations, "I am not a crook," eventually public pressure and evidence against him left him little choice but to resign in the middle of his term in office, a step that had not been taken by any previous president in U.S. history.

The media played an important role in exposing Watergate. The investigative journalism of two *Washington Post* reporters, Carl Bernstein and Bob Woodward, revealed the number of people potentially involved in the scandal and the wide-reaching implications of the initial burglary. The following abbreviated chronology demonstrates the inevitability of the scandal's conclusion by summarizing key events and thus revealing the clear interlocking connections between each decision and action. The remainder of this chapter includes a series of excerpts and editorials from *The Washington Post* exposing the facts and providing a commentary about the motivation and intrigue surrounding this modern tale of ambition and political corruption.

BRIEF CHRONOLOGY OF WATERGATE

1972, June 17	Five men arrested for breaking into the Democratic headquarters at the Watergate building.
1972, Sept. 15	The five burglars and two White House advisors indicted.
1972, Nov. 7	President Nixon and Vice-President Agnew reelected.
1973, Jan.	Trial of the seven indicted men. All but two plead guilty. Jury convicts all.
1973, Apr. 30	Nixon denies involvement in Watergate. Four of his advisors resign. One is dismissed.
1973, July 23	Prosecutor in Watergate trials subpoenas tape recordings of Nixon's White House conversations.
1973, July 25	Nixon refuses subpoena, claiming "executive privilege."
1973, Oct.	House of Representatives begins steps to impeach Nixon.
1973, Nov.	Nixon releases first set of tapes to court.
1973, Nov. 21	18½–minute gap in tape revealed.
1974, Mar. 1	Key players in Nixon's reelection campaign indicted on conspiracy charges.
1974, July	House Judiciary Committee recommends Nixon be impeached.
1974, Aug. 8	Nixon announces resignation.

UNCOVERING THE SCANDAL

Most of the media attention for the first few months after the Watergate break-in focused on the burglary itself and the role of the seven men charged in the crime. By October, however, the persistent investigations of reporters Bernstein and Woodward uncovered enough evidence to suggest a link between the burglary and other illegal activities in Nixon's reelection campaign and at the White House. With front-page headlines on October 10, 1972, Woodward and Bernstein broke that story, alerting the public to the possible scope of the Watergate break-in and its connections to a much broader Republican conspiracy. The following excerpt from that article summarizes their findings. Appearing less than a month before the presidential election, this story could have seriously harmed Nixon's chance of reelection, but the coverup at the White House had already begun, and insufficient evidence to support media suspicions diminished the impact of *The Washington Post* allegations. Nixon was reelected to his second term in office with a resounding majority on November 7, 1972.

FBI FINDS NIXON AIDES SABOTAGED DEMOCRATS
By Carl Bernstein and Bob Woodward

FBI agents have established that the Watergate bugging incident stemmed from a massive campaign of political spying and sabotage conducted on behalf of President Nixon's re-election and directed by officials of the White House and the Committee for the Re-election of the President.

The activities, according to information in FBI and Department of Justice files, were aimed at all the major Democratic presidential contenders and—since 1971—represented a basic strategy of the Nixon re-election effort.

During their Watergate investigation, federal agents established that hundreds of thousands of dollars in Nixon campaign contributions had been set aside to pay for an extensive undercover campaign aimed at discrediting individual Democratic presidential candidates and disrupting their campaigns.

"Intelligence work" is normal during a campaign and is said to be carried out by both political parties. But federal investigators said what they uncovered being done by the Nixon forces is unprecedented in scope and intensity.

They said it included:

Following members of Democratic candidates' families and assembling dossiers on their personal lives; forging letters and distributing them under the candidates' letterheads; leaking false and manufactured items to the press; throwing campaign schedules into disarray; seizing confidential campaign files, and investigating the lives of dozens of Democratic campaign workers.

In addition, investigators said the activities included planting provocateurs in the ranks of organizations expected to demonstrate at the Republican and Democratic conventions; and investigating potential donors to the Nixon campaign before their contributions were solicited.

Informed of the general contents of this article, the White House referred all comment to the Committee for the Re-election of the President. A spokesman there said, "The Post story is not only fiction but a collection of absurdities." Asked to discuss the specific points raised in the story, the spokesman, DeVan L. Shumway, refused on grounds that "the entire matter is in the hands of the authorities." . . .

Both at the White House and within the President's re-election committee, the intelligence-sabotage operation was commonly called the "offensive security" program of the Nixon forces, according to investigators.

Perhaps the most significant finding of the whole Watergate investigation, the investigators say, was that numerous specific acts of political sabotage and spying were all traced to this "offensive security," which was conceived and directed in the White House and by President Nixon's re-election committee.

The investigators said that a major purpose of the sub rosa activities was to create so much confusion, suspicion and dissension that the Democrats would be incapable of uniting after choosing a presidential nominee.

The FBI's investigation of the Watergate established that virtually all the acts against the Democrats were financed by a secret, fluctuating $350,000–$700,000 campaign fund that was controlled by former Attorney General John N. [M]itchell while he headed the Justice Department. Later, when he served as President Nixon's campaign manager, Mitchell shared control of the fund with others. The money was kept in a safe in the office of the President's chief fund-raiser, former Secretary of Commerce Maurice Stans.

According to sources close to the Watergate investigation, much of the FBI's information is expected to be revealed at the trial of the seven men indicted on charges of conspiring to eavesdrop on Democratic headquarters at the Watergate.

"There is some very powerful information," said one federal official, "especially if it becomes known before Nov. 7."

The Washington Post, Tuesday, October 10, 1972

NIXON'S RESIGNATION

Watergate continued to make headlines regularly after Nixon's re-election as Senate hearings and criminal investigations proceeded. By October 1973 the House of Representatives began introducing bills in support of Nixon's impeachment. On August 8, 1974, more than two years after the Watergate burglary, Nixon announced his resignation as President of the United States. For over a year he had been battling the courts over his unwillingness to release the tapes in his possession to the prosecution or the judge. Investigations of the White House remained incomplete. In July the House Judiciary Committee had taken final steps to impeach the president, yet even as he spoke his last words in office, Nixon refused to confess the extent of his involvement in the Watergate scandal. An excerpt from Nixon's resignation speech captures the main details and the tone of his departure from office. Given the inevitability of his resignation, consider whether his concluding address attempts to register any sincerity and nobility or whether it simply acknowledges the necessity of his action. Does he say what he intends to say? Is his speech convincing?

NIXON'S FINALE: AMERICA NEEDS A FULL-TIME PRESIDENT

Good evening.

This is the 37th time I have spoken to you from this office where so many decisions have been made that shaped the history of this nation. Each time I have done so to discuss with you some matter that I believe affected the national interest.

In all the decisions I have made in my public life, I have always tried to do what was best for the nation. Throughout the long and difficult period of Watergate, I have felt it was my duty to preserve, to make every possible effort to complete the term of office to which you elected me.

In the past few days, however, it has become evident to me that I no longer have a strong enough political base in the Congress [t]o justify continuing that effort. As long as there was a base, I felt strongly that it was necessary to see the constitutional process through to its conclusion, that to do otherwise would be unfaithful to the spirit of that deliberately difficult process, and a dangerously destabilizing precedent for the future.

But with the disappearance of that base, I now believe that the constitutional purpose has been served, and there is no longer a need for the process to be prolonged.

I would have preferred to carry through to the finish whatever the personal agony it would have involved, and my family unanimously urged me to do so. But the interest of the nation must always come before any personal considerations.

From the discussions I have had with Congressional and other leaders, I have concluded that because of the Watergate matter I might not have the support of the Congress that I would consider necessary to back the very difficult decisions and carry out the duties of this office in the way the interests of the nation would require.

I have never been a quitter. To leave office before my term is completed is abhorrent to every instinct in my body. But as President, I must put the interest of America first. America needs a full-time President and a full-time Congress particularly at this time with the problems we face at home and abroad.

To continue to fight through the months ahead for my personal vindication would almost totally absorb the time and attention of both the President and the Congress in a period when our entire focus should be on the great issues of peace abroad and prosperity without inflation at home.

Therefore, I shall resign the Presidency effective at noon tomorrow. Vice President Ford will be sworn in as President in that hour in this office. . . .

By taking this action: I hope that I will have hastened the start of that process of healing which is so desperately needed in America.

I regret deeply any injuries that may have been done in the course of the events that led to this decision. I would say only that if some of my judgments were wrong, and some were wrong, they were made in what I believed at the time to be the best interest of the nation.

To those who have stood with me during these past difficult months, to my family, my friends, to many others who joined in supporting my cause because they believed it was right, I will be eternally grateful for your support.

And to those who have not felt able to give me your support, let me say I leave with no bitterness toward those who have opposed me, because al[l] of us, in the final analysis, have been concerned with the good of the country however our judgments might differ.

So, let us all now join together in affirming that common commitment and in helping our new President succeed for the benefit of all Americans.

The Washington Post, Friday, August 9, 1974

THE NATION'S RESPONSE TO WATERGATE

Whereas newspaper articles strive to report the bare facts of daily events, editorials offer opinion or interpretation. Many of the editorials that appeared in *The Washington Post* on August 9 addressed Nixon's resignation and attempted to put his fall from office into perspective. Two of those editorials are included here. Both talk about tragedy. George Will's editorial seeks to guide the response of the American people toward the president's resignation. When he speaks about tragedy, he focuses on themes that also appear in *Macbeth*: ambition, guilt, blame, and healing. William Greider's editorial tries to make sense of the Watergate scandal as a tragedy by comparing it directly to *Macbeth*, drawing connections between Shakespeare's stage and American public office, and thus suggesting both the validity of art and the timelessness of political corruption. Reading these two articles together, try to assess the writers' attitudes toward Nixon and Watergate and consider how the immediacy of the event might influence their perspectives.

A CONSUMING PASSION FOR POWER
By George F. Will

As in all true tragedy, we see in Mr. Nixon's ruination the ravages of a failing to which all men are prey. Mr. Nixon's sin, like all sin, was a failure of restraint. It was the immoderate craving for that which, desired moderately, is a noble goal.

It is a terrible curse to want anything as much as Mr. Nixon wanted power. He wanted it more than he wanted friends. Indeed, he wanted it with a consuming passion that left no room for friendship.

And when, in his final extremity, he looked around for friends to grabble to his soul with hoops of steel, there were no friends there.

But, then, friends could not have helped, once Mr. Nixon was weighed down with scandal. Once the deeds were done, he was done, because the American system works.

A heart weighed down with the weight of woe to the weakest hope will cling, and for two years Mr. Nixon clung to the wicked hope that the rule of law could not reach up to him. His final hope was that the task of breaking a President to the saddle of law would tax the American people's composure to the breaking point.

The dashing of all such hopes is the happy issue of our Watergate affliction.

Mr. Nixon is not as bad as—caught in the tangled web he could not stop weaving—he came to appear. And no one else is as good as they may now be tempted to feel.

It would be wrong for people—journalists, politicians, judges—to preen themselves on their performances during this protracted sorrow. No one did more than his duty, as a professional and a citizen, and many people did less.

In the end Congress was driven to the brink of doing its duty to protect the Constitution. Many journalists did what they are paid to do, reporting things that had been improperly concealed. And the judiciary construed and administered the law.

But no one deserves a garland for doing his duty.

Although the Nixon White House ran amuck as no other has done, and its abuses were uniquely lurid and sinister, there is a sense in which the kind of work we have been doing is work without end.

As our megagovernment grows, its potential for evil grows. Keeping the government reasonably tame and free from active venom is a task comparable to painting the Golden Gate Bridge. It is endless: You just get to one end and then you have to go back and start again from the beginning.

But surely, now, we can and must relax a little.

Oscar Wilde's aphoristic criticism of socialism—"It would take too many evenings"—meant that it is uncivilized to allow politics to become a dominating preoccupation. Watergate has taken too many evenings.

Now there are books to be read, children to be played with, and other humane and civilizing pursuits that have been neglected because the task of getting the government back on the leash demanded a hideously large slice of the republic's energies.

Life under these conditions has not encouraged the softer emotions, but one would have to be dead to all human feelings not to feel deep regret for the suffering endured by Mr. Nixon's brave family. I am thinking especially of Julie Eisenhower.

Filial devotion is always moving, as is courage, and plain spunk. Ms. Eisenhower's brave combativeness on behalf of her father provided the nation with something valuable, an example of strong and noble character.

Her ordeal, like the republic's, is over and this year autumn, the season of mists and mellow fruitfulness, will be spring, the season of rebirth and renewal. Mr. Nixon, by resigning, has struck the Watergate fetters from

Uncle Sam's wrists. And President Ford, like a healing zephyr, arrives, his decency and goodwill settling like a balm on our lacerated feelings.

Now, at last, there is a stillness. The angry drumbeat of contention dies away "and silence, like a poultice, comes to heal the blows of sound."

The Washington Post, Friday, August 9, 1974

HIGH DRAMA AND FLAWED CHARACTER IN A THEATER TOO ACCUSTOMED TO TRAGEDY
By William Greider

Our King [w]as ruled by troubled sleep, undone by the ghosts of his secret self.

The nation trembles at this awesome drama which is now complete, the fall of Richard Nixon. It was an ancient epic retold in the brutal poetry of modern life, more gripping than the classics because the stage was real, the theater was our own democracy.

He seemed so bold and powerful in the sunlight days of his presidency, capable of great moments. Yet, in his private darkness, he was merely weak, nursing old wounds and fears, feeding the stale resentments which wiser men put aside. Americans and the world knew the first, the public leader of commanding stature. The unfolding drama taught them about the second man and his fatal flaws.

"Let's make the next four years the best four years in American history," the President proclaimed in his hour of triumph. He was surrounded by affectionate crowds, saluted by drums and the flourish of trumpets. No one could pull down a leader endorsed so overwhelmingly by the people, supported by 61 per cent of the voters and 49 of the states.

But Richard Nixon's unprecedented victory did not heal his dark wounds or completely satisfy his need for vengeance and vindication. In the privacy of his Oval Office with his re-election assured, he talked of getting even. "I think we are going to fix the son-of-a-bitch," the President told his applauding courtiers, referring to Edward Bennett Williams. "Believe me, we are going to."

At the inaugural podium, he spoke of higher ambitions, a pious vision of his public purpose. "We shall answer to God, to history and to our conscience for the way in which we use these years," he promised the cheering masses before him.

Yet his whispered thoughts in private were of revenge, a battle to be fought and won, no quarter given. "We are all in it together," he reassured his lieutenants. "This is war. We take a few shots and it will be over. We will give them a few shots and it will be over. Don't worry, I wouldn't want to be on the other side right now, would you?"

And so the stage of American political life was set for high tragedy. Power blinded by pride, unable to confront weaknesses.

His [l]oyal [f]riends, a shrinking circle of the faithful, saw Richard Nixon as a modern-day King Lear who raged magnificently at the storm around him. But Nixon lacked Lear's grandeur. Nixon's enemies cast him as Richard the Third, the King who was crippled by his own malevolence. But Nixon did not have the eloquence of that other Richard or his purity of evil purpose. Nixon was confused. Like Macbeth, who listened to the witches' prophecies and found comfort in their riddles. He was both brave in facing his peril but doomed by his blindness to it.

Shakespeare wrote the curse:

> He shall spurn fate, scorn death, and bear
> His hopes 'bove wisdom, grace and fear;
> And, you all know, security
> Is mortal's chiefest enemy.

For Richard Nixon, the false security was that "mandate of '72." He carried it with him like a shield, as though its magic powers would protect him from any attack by his enemies. As in the tale of that ancient Scottish king, it persuaded Richard Nixon that his throne was safe.

"People who did not accept the mandate of '72," he declared confidently, "who do not want the strong America that I want to build, who do not want the foreign policy leadership that I want to give, who do not want to cut down the size of this government bureaucracy . . . people who do not want these things naturally would exploit any issue, if it weren't Watergate, anything else, in order to keep the President from doing his job."

Lady Macbeth said it more succinctly: "What need we fear who knows it, when none can call our power to account?"

Now, that his flaws are so evident, some in the audience indulge a certain self-righteousness at his fall. It seems just and satisfying and such good theater. But in this drama the spectators are victims too. The tragic awareness has settled not just upon the man, but upon the nation and its own sense of itself.

He was, as he liked to remind everyone, chosen overwhelmingly by all of us. And he won that remarkable election victory by espousing the popular values so common to our nation and its past. Hard work and ambition. Civil piety. A pugnacious sense of patriotism. A zest for rugged endeavors. Winning. He used public friends as emblems of what he believed—Billy Graham and the Washington Redskins, Bob Hope and John Wayne and General Patton. His lovely family, a perfect expression of virtuous striving.

And, of course, Richard Nixon was himself the ultimate example of how the tough-minded and talented can struggle upward in America, from the humblest home to positions of wealth and fame. He talked about that often in public and the familiar story of hard work rewarded became part of what we knew about the man.

Then suddenly it seemed he was saying different things about himself, denials which sounded like unintended confessions.

"I made my mistakes," he said as fortune soured for him, "but in all of my years in public life, I have never profited, never profited from public service. I have earned every cent. And in all of my years in public life, I have never obstructed justice. And I think too that I could say that in my years of public life, that I welcome this kind of examination because people have got to know whether or not their President is a crook. Well, I am not a crook."

People listened to the quavering voice and the feeling spread that, of course, he was.

Now [t]hat [i]t is over the climax seems so natural and inevitable. But it never looked that way as the drama unfolded. On the contrary, at a dozen different junctures it seemed that the President might save himself. Again and again, he was challenged by his enemies and begged by his allies to clear up the matter, to provide the complete factual explanations which would put it to rest. It was the one stroke which was beyond his vast power. . . .

Belatedly, he came forward in the spring of 1973 to announce that there was a stench in the White House—weeks after it was already obvious to the world. His disclosure was too late and not enough. In the fall, he arranged what he thought would be a final gesture of compromise turning over the tape-recorded evidence to his own selected arbiter. When that scheme ended in the dismissal of Special Prosecutor Archibald Cox, the move to impeach began in earnest. . . .

In [p]ublic, he spoke of his ordeal as a fine period of testing, the crisis decision-making, which he relished throughout his turbulent political career. . . .

But in private this man of steel turned out to be malleable and tarnished. He did not sleep well during this period. He made late-night telephone calls to his two trusted mastiffs, [H. R.] Haldeman and [John] Ehrlichman, seeking their reassurances. His family heard him playing the piano, alone, past midnight. His closest pal, [Charles "Bebe"] Rebozo, took him on high-speed drives along California thruways for diversion.

"I'm so sick of this thing," the President confessed in a private moment of torment. "I want to get it done with and over. And I don't want to hear about it again."

While destiny closed on the king, his tragedy was enriched by the cast of minor characters around him who also fell. . . .

Beyond the inner circle, the sub-plots unraveled in a medley of personal disasters, muted moments of self-awareness for glib and purposeful young men whose opaque sense of values was shredded by Watergate.

As it happened, these minor players described their leader's flaws more clearly than he could himself. His last flourish was brave. Even his enemies conceded that. But it did not illuminate a character who had come to self-realization.

"They have tied me to a stake. I cannot fly," Macbeth roared as Macduff closed in with death. "But, bear-like, I must fight the course." So Nixon said stoutly: "I did an awful lot. I cut off one arm, then the other arm . . ." And he fought on.

Might he have saved himself, at one point or the other, simply by telling the whole truth? Early on, the public might have been forgiving, but his character would not allow it. His harshest critics insist that he could never afford to tell the truth because he was always guilty.

But Nixon's character dilemma rested on a more subtle problem than that. To tell the truth meant to reveal his weaknesses, to confess the White House fears and insecurities, to cut away the petty hatreds and tribal loyalties which led him deeper and deeper into the muck. How can a strong king confess that he is so frail? Indeed, each time the President showed a larger glimpse of his private self, it only made matters worse. People were repelled by what Nixon's men had done, but people were horrified when they saw the private man whom those men worked for.

"The [t]hing that is completely misunderstood about Watergate," said Charles Colson, "is that everybody thinks the people surrounding the President were drunk with power. . . . But it wasn't arrogance at all. It was insecurity. That insecurity began to breed a form of paranoia. We overreacted to the attacks against us and to a lot of things."

A tale of small men who did not belong in high places, who perhaps knew down deep that they did not belong, who wanted desperately to prove that their secret insecurities were wrong.

So the high tragedy is done, but only insensitive partisans can be self-righteous about the outcome. There was no moment of catharsis for the hero, no climactic scene when his rage dissolved into self-awareness.

His final disgrace was self-inflicted, a confession delivered two years too late to win any forgiveness from the political process. When he announced this week that he had indeed lied about it all, that he had in fact approved the crime, his belated candor produced an instant consensus across the spectrum of public opinion. He must go, whether by trial and conviction or by resignation. The most powerful of all leaders resisted that collective verdict briefly, then yielded to it, one final reflection of his insecure grasp of reality.

That moment of truth is for the nation itself, the audience which learned so painfully about its leader and, thus, about itself. If Richard Nixon was so evil, after all, can the rest of us be so good? If he was a mean-spirited leader, then who chose him?

Nixon's tragedy asks the most serious questions of democracy. If Nixon reflected authentic popular values, then perhaps he showed Americans a coarse picture of ourselves, one we would rather not face. Or, if he misled us and deceived us in his climb to power, then our democratic process failed at the most serious level.

"I think our country sinks beneath the yoke," Malcolm said of Macbeth's reign. "It weeps, it bleeds, and each new day a gash is added to her wounds."

What do we really know about the leader whom we choose? What do we truly know about ourselves? The spectators depart with complicated feelings, a troubled mixture of satisfaction and self-doubt. They are hopeful that Richard Nixon's disgraced presidency had defined a new standard of public honor, but none can be entirely convinced.

The Washington Post, Friday, August 9, 1974

QUESTIONS FOR WRITTEN AND ORAL DISCUSSION

1. In the article about the FBI discoveries, consider the phrases "intelligence work" and "offensive security." What do they mean? Do they clarify, distort, or simply deny the truth? What role does language play in corruption?

2. Does the public attitude toward power play a part in its abuse? Consider the relationship between trust and betrayal in this scandal. Could the president today succeed as Nixon did in the 1970s in his quest for power without outraging the public?

3. In a coverup, what people say is often as important as what they do not say. In Nixon's resignation speech, what does he say about his reasons for leaving office, and about his part in Watergate? Does he equivocate? Does he appear noble? How does he appeal to the sympathies of the American people and to the honor of holding elected office?

4. Write an imaginary diary entry for Nixon the night before he resigns from office. How do you think his private thoughts compared to his public speech?

5. Three themes appear in George Will's editorial: ambition, blame, and healing. How does he apply them to the Watergate scandal? What connection does he make between character motivation and crime?

6. According to Will, what is the relationship between power and friendship? Using your observation, write a short essay about friendship in *Macbeth*.

7. George Will speaks of Nixon's consuming quest for power; William Greider's article also mentions insecurity. Explain how both motivators played a part in Watergate and *Macbeth*. Does one influence seem more apparent than the other in either case?

8. Both Will and Greider apply the term "tragedy" to Nixon's rise and fall. Do they feel that the term is appropriate? Why or why not? What is the tragedy, as they see it? How do you see it?

9. Compare Watergate and *Macbeth* as tragedies, considering how the tragedy of abused power is different in a democratic system than in a monarchical system.

10. Compare the role of ambition in Nixon's scandal and in Macbeth's tragedy.

11. Greider includes several quotations from *Macbeth* in his editorial. Explain how and why those quotations are appropriate. Find several

other quotations from the play that might be equally applicable and explain how they could be effective.

12. Identify some of the themes Greider focuses on in his comparison of Macbeth and Nixon.

13. An editorial cartoon accompanying Greider's article depicts a series of men in suits standing in a line. They are falling over like a row of dominoes, with Nixon being the last to go. Discuss what statement you think the cartoonist is making about Watergate, and then draw your own cartoon either to accompany Greider's comparison of Nixon and Macbeth or to illustrate the play itself. How will your drawing or drawings capture some of the themes in the play or in Watergate?

14. Consider ways in which both Nixon and Macbeth were blind to circumstances of their own plotting, misinformation, and pride.

SUGGESTED READINGS

Bernstein, Carl, and Bob Woodward. *All the President's Men*. New York: Simon and Schuster, 1974.

Shannon, William V., Stanley Tretick, and Barbara Tuchman. *They Could Not Trust the King: Nixon, Watergate, and the American People*. New York: Macmillan, 1974. Includes photographs and short descriptions of the key players in the Watergate scandal.

The Olympic Games: An Athlete's Dream

Fair is foul and foul is fair.

Macbeth 1.1.11

Competing in the Olympic Games is an athlete's dream. Winning the gold medal marks the pinnacle of success. Thousands of athletes dedicate years of their lives toward seeking that goal. At its best, the challenge develops discipline and rewards sportsmanship, talent, and determination. At its worst, the desire to be number one can turn competitors into cheaters and tempt even those with the best intentions to choose winning at all costs. Some participants are willing to compromise their principles and even break laws for a better chance of rising to the top. Their choices expose the dark side of ambition that is goaded into action by the temptations of fame and fortune and by the power and exhilaration of being recognized as the best performer in a particular field.

Given the high stakes in the world of sports, the level of competition and the intensity of ambition can easily match the potential for tragedy or disaster found in political power struggles. In Shakespeare's play, Macbeth's passionate desire to wear the crown overcomes his principles and ultimately destroys him; at the White House, Nixon's obsession with presidential power and security compromised the integrity of an entire nation. In sports, two recent examples of scandals surrounding Olympic competitors indicate what can happen to fair play when winning becomes more important than the game itself. These stories share patterns with *Macbeth*, for like the play they reveal connections between private ambition and public temptation. They expose the consequences of guilt judged not only by the justice system but by a national and international court of public opinion that responds according to written rules and unwritten standards of acceptable behavior.

In the 1988 Summer Olympics at Seoul, Korea, Ben Johnson, the Canadian sprinter, won the gold medal by breaking a world record with his 9.79-second run in the 100-meter dash. Shortly after that, his gold medal was confiscated because he tested positive for banned steroids. Fans were horrified to discover that the fastest man in the world turned out to be a fraud. In the succeeding year, Ben Johnson became the center of an inquiry by the Canadian government investigating the extent of drug use by Canadian athletes. Initially, Johnson, his doctor, and his trainer tried to cover up their guilt. Eventually, evidence proved to be too strong against them. On June 12, 1989, Johnson confessed. He received a two-year ban from national and international competitions in track and field events. Although Johnson's scandal was not an isolated event, it raised public consciousness, awareness, and concern about the use of illegal drugs in a number of sports activities.

A second scandal that received international attention occurred in American figure skating prior to and during the 1994 Winter Olympics in Lillehammer, Norway. On January 4, 1994, American figure skater Nancy Kerrigan was attacked, assaulted, and injured on her leg just prior to the national figure skating competition and had to withdraw from that event. Evidence soon pointed fingers of suspicion at Kerrigan's American rival, Tonya Harding, and her former husband, Jeff Gillooly. The media sensationalized the story to such an extent that it became difficult to see the assault as anything more than a tabloid version of good against evil, but the underlying motivation for the crime was similar to that of Ben Johnson. Ambition and the overwhelming desire to win appeared to inspire the violent conspiracy.

Harding won the American figure skating championship and qualified for the Olympics, but because Kerrigan's injury was not serious enough to cause long-term damage, the American Figure Skating Association selected her to fill the second American position at the Winter Olympics in Lillehammer. Although Harding was a serious suspect in the assault investigation, there was insufficient evidence to charge her prior to the Olympic competition. Both she and Kerrigan skated. Kerrigan, the favorite, received the silver medal. Harding placed eighth. Following the competition, on March 16, 1994, Harding pleaded guilty to conspiracy charges, although she did not confess to instigating the assault herself. She was given a three-year probation and a $100,000 fine and compelled to withdraw from the United States Figure Skating Association.

BEN JOHNSON AND TONYA HARDING BREAK THE RULES

Several newspaper excerpts below provide the details of the Johnson drug scandal and the Kerrigan-Harding story. The two Johnson articles summarize the judicial inquiry to expose how the sprinter's denial turned to confession. Coverage of both Olympic scandals quotes the two athletes themselves, inviting readers to consider what their words reveal about their ambition, conscience, and sense of remorse. Comments from Judge Dubin in the first Johnson article and references to other sports heroes with criminal records in the last Harding story also probe the complex issue of how to weigh public expectations of sports against the inappropriate behavior of individual athletes.

CANADA BEGINS PROBE OF DRUG USE IN SPORTS
Johnson Scandal Only One Facet of Investigation
By Herbert H. Denton

TORONTO, Jan. 11—Sparked by the Olympic steroid scandal involving sprinter Ben Johnson, a wide-ranging judicial inquiry into drug abuse in Canadian amateur sport began here today.

Johnson, 27 and a native of Jamaica, was forced to return his Olympic gold medal and had his 9.79-second world record wiped from the books after he tested positive for the banned muscle-building anabolic steroid Stanozolol at the Summer Olympics in Seoul. He is not expected to be called for testimony until late February or in March.

In his first public comments after returning home to Toronto from South Korea in disgrace, Johnson flatly denied ever having taken a banned substance. Later, after he retained a lawyer, Johnson changed his declaration to say that he had never "knowingly" used one.

Ontario Justice Charles Dubin, who was granted subpoena power and unlimited staff by the federal government to conduct the investigation and make recommendations to the federal cabinet, made it clear he wants the probe to go far beyond the Johnson episode.

In a statement today, he laid out plans for a sweeping examination of drugs in sports, a situation that, he said, "threatens the very integrity of sports competition and, if unchecked, could destroy it.

"Cheating is the antithesis of sport competition," he said in a crowded hearing room in a downtown building. "It encourages a lack of moral value."

At a news conference a few weeks ago, Dubin set the tone for the probe by asking, "Have we, as Canadians, lost track of what athletic competition is all about? Is there too much emphasis by the public and by the media on the winning of a gold medal in Olympic competition as the only achievement worthy of recognition?"

The Washington Post, Thursday, January 12, 1989

JOHNSON SAYS HE LIED ABOUT STEROID USE AFTER OLYMPICS
By Christine Brennan

TORONTO, June 13—Ben Johnson today said he lied about his steroid use after the 1988 Olympics because he was "ashamed" of what his family, friends and young fans thought of him, but in an impassioned appeal said he hopes to get another chance to run for Canada.

Johnson, the sprinter who was stripped of his 100-meter gold medal and world record after testing positive for the steroid stanozolol in Seoul, finished his testimony before a Canadian inquiry today with an emotional—although not particularly enlightening—flurry of answers to the questions of five attorneys.

While he never was asked point-blank why he tested positive in his drug test in Seoul, Johnson was able to paint a telling picture of a steroid plan gone wrong. By admitting his guilt for the first time Monday and doing so again today, he also seemed to be trying to win the sympathy and support of the Canadian public.

"I lied and I was ashamed for my family and friends [and for] kids who look up to me as a Canadian athlete, who want to be in my position," he said. "I was just in a mess."

"If I get a chance to compete again, I want to say that drugs don't make you run fast and Ben Johnson can beat anybody in the world, if I get a chance to run again."

Johnson, 27, is banned from track events by the International Amateur Athletic Federation (IAAF) for two years, until late September 1990. Canadian sports minister Jean Charest banned Johnson from competing for Canada for life but said he would reconsider the suspension based on the recommendations of Justice Charles Dubin, who is conducting the inquiry. It probably will be several months before the inquiry is complete and the recommendations are made. . . .

In 1988 Johnson's preparation for Seoul was fraught with injuries. On

May 13 he suffered a hamstring injury in Tokyo and went to St. Kitts in the Caribbean with his doctor, Jamie Astaphan, to recover. There, Johnson said, he was receiving pills, "blue, green, red, white, different pills," from his doctor.

He also was receiving injections. "He mixed up different kinds of stuff in the needle," Johnson said.

He returned to Toronto at the end of June, went to Europe in August and performed poorly there, finishing third in two consecutive races little more than a month before the Seoul Games. He cut short his trip and came home Aug. 23. Soon Astaphan was prescribing a special program for Johnson and a few other athletes. It included two banned substances—the so-called estrogol, the milky substance the commission believes to be stanozolol, and human growth hormone—and a vitamin mixture.

It is uncertain why this program was prescribed for Johnson and his teammates so soon before the Olympics.

The Washington Post, Wednesday, June 14, 1989

BODYGUARD: HARDING KNEW OF PLOT
Skater Doesn't Talk on Newspaper Report
By Christine Brennan

PORTLAND, Ore., Jan. 20—Olympic figure skater Tonya Harding knew about the plot to injure rival Nancy Kerrigan and grew impatient when the attack did not occur in the Boston area prior to the Olympic trials, her bodyguard said in an interview published this morning.

Shawn Eric Eckardt said Harding told him "you need to stop screwing around with this and get it done," according to a story in the Oregonian newspaper.

At a practice today, Harding refused to respond to the comment made by Eckardt, whose credibility repeatedly has been questioned by acquaintances. However, it was Eckardt's testimony to authorities that provided the basis for Wednesday's warrant and arrest of Harding's ex-husband, Jeff Gillooly. Eckardt has admitted to his participation in the alleged plot.

Harding continually has denied any involvement in the Jan. 6 attack on Kerrigan, which forced her to withdraw from the trials in Detroit because of a severely bruised right knee. Kerrigan was later named to the Olympic team. . . .

According to the Oregonian interview, Harding spoke about the plot in a conversation with Eckardt at one of her practices last month while [Shane] Stant [the assaulter] was in Massachusetts trying to find an opportunity to attack Kerrigan.

Eckardt suggested she call Stant, but Harding replied, "No, I want you to do it," the bodyguard was quoted as saying.

Eckardt also told the newspaper in a three-hour session that Gillooly offered a $10,000 USFSA check as a bonus if the attack on Kerrigan was carried out immediately.

Eckardt's new allegations expanded on statements in an affidavit, filed by a Multnomah County sheriff's deputy, that led to Gillooly's arrest. According to the affidavit, Harding made two phone calls to Kerrigan's rink in South Dennis, Mass., to try to find out her practice schedule so Stant could attack her there. The affidavit mentioned a record of phone calls from the home Harding and Gillooly shared to the Tony Kent Arena where Kerrigan practices.

Robert C. Weaver, Harding's attorney, told the Associated Press that Harding denied Eckardt's allegations in the Oregonian interview. . . .

As these bizarre allegations swirled around her, Harding sought refuge on the ice. "I felt better today than I have in a few days. I'm sleeping better," Harding told reporters after her first public workout since Jan. 8, the day she won the national title.

She said she will not withdraw from the U.S. Olympic team.

"My skating is my life," she said. "I go out there, and it's an out for me. I love it. That's the only time I'm getting any enjoyment right now. I have bad days where I can't think and concentrate. I hope it can get back to normal soon."

The Washington Post, Friday, January 21, 1994

PLEA ASIDE, HARDING ALREADY CASHES IN
Skater Signs Movie Deal; Her Career Could Resume on Pro
Circuit
By Johnette Howard

Prosecutors in Portland, Ore., and Detroit tried to put the best spin on the plea agreement they struck with figure skater Tonya Harding Wednesday, insisting the fact that she'll do no prison time was offset by the profound damage to her skating career and her personal reputation. But even as prosecutors spoke, the ink was drying on a movie deal Harding signed this week with [a] Hollywood production company. . . .

Harding pleaded guilty Wednesday to a felony charge of hindering the investigation into the kneecapping of rival skater Nancy Kerrigan. Under the agreement, Harding received a lengthy list of penalties requiring her to perform community service, pay a total of $160,000 in fines and costs, submit to three years of supervised probation and undergo a psychiatric evaluation and court-ordered therapy, if necessary.

She was also forced to resign her membership from the U.S. Figure Skating Association, which picks teams for national, Olympic and world amateur competitions.

Harding's resignation prevents her from competing at world or Olympic competitions—for now. But, as USFSA rules stand, she could petition reinstatement. Even if Harding doesn't, some agents and promoters don't rule out her participation in traditional touring ice shows or, especially, the pro competitions that offer as much as $30,000 in prize money to winners and $15,000 to runners-up. . . .

As sports anti-heroes from Pete Rose to Mike Tyson, Denny McLain to George Steinbrenner already have proved, there can be life after jail or self-destruction. And it can pay pretty well.

Especially if Harding's handlers think creatively. . . .

Like Harding, Rose and Tyson and McLain and Steinbrenner all have been in trouble with the law. And all four men have salvaged careers. Tyson—who reiterated in this month's issue of Esquire magazine he'll definitely fight again when his rape sentence concludes—is likely to produce the highest-grossing boxing event in history with his first bout. McLain—the former Detroit Tigers pitcher who served prison time for racketeering—is a popular, general-interest talk show host in Detroit now. New York Yankees owner Steinbrenner was reinstated by baseball and former player Rose, who hopes for the same, maintained in a 1993 Sports Illustrated interview that it's not all that surprising that today's pariah becomes tomorrow's forgiven star.

"See, I got the idea if I took the high road and tried to do things right, I'd be all right because I'm not the first athlete that's ever got into trouble that took the high road and who's gotten back," Rose, banned from baseball for his alleged gambling on the sport, told SI. "America is known for giving guys a second chance."

But Harding never achieved the status in her sport that Tyson and Rose did in theirs.

"She's a footnote in history, everyone will remember her name," said Leslie Van Busker, senior features editor at US magazine. "But it will be because she was notorious, not because of her skating."

Then again, being notorious might be enough.

The Washington Post, Friday, March 18, 1994

Conclusion

In the world of sports, games are serious business. Hockey players are high-paid entertainers, and even in amateur sports events like the Olympics, fame, or the promise of advertising endorsements means that there is a lot more to winning than the satisfaction of receiving a gold medal. Shakespeare's play asks us to consider what motivates Macbeth to climb to the top and to let nothing, not even his initial reservations about murder, stand in his way. Do the evil whisperings of the witches compel him to act? Do the temptations of Lady Macbeth convince him? Or is Macbeth driven by his own private ambitions? In our own time, we can ask similar questions about the atmosphere that surrounds amateur and professional sports. Do the same forces that condemn cheating also encourage it? Who bears the burden of guilt? Do fans love fair players or simply winners? What impels athletes to break the rules? How do games reflect larger social patterns and values?

QUESTIONS FOR WRITTEN AND ORAL DISCUSSION

1. What does it mean to win? Who in the eyes of public sports fans is a winner? Is the athlete alone guilty when he or she breaks the rules? Does public expectation play any part? Address these questions in a written assignment or hold a classroom debate with one side arguing that the dishonest athlete alone is responsible for his or her actions, and the other side contesting that blame is shared by others, such as fans, spectators, coaches, parents, the media, advertisers, or governments.

2. Address the question posed by Charles Dubin in the first *Washington Post* article on Ben Johnson, which asks, "Have we . . . lost track of what athletic competition is all about? Is there too much emphasis by public and by the media on the winning of a gold medal in Olympic competition as the only achievement worthy of recognition?" Answer yes or no and defend your position.

3. Compare Ben Johnson and Tonya Harding as criminals and as cheaters. Is there a difference between breaking the law and breaking the rules of a game? What does either athlete have in common with Macbeth?

4. Discuss heroism in sports. The last article on Tonya Harding refers to sports antiheroes, those who break the law, those who commit crimes, those who fall from greatness and are judged for their behavior. Are Johnson and Harding tragic heroes or antiheroes? Is Kerrigan a hero or simply a victim? What standards of conduct are implied in these labels?

5. Do you see Macbeth as a hero or an antihero? What evidence in the play can you find to support your position?

6. Compose two diary entries for either Johnson or Harding, one that expresses the dreams and ambitions initiating their crimes and one that responds to the subsequent public exposure of their guilt. Consult Macbeth's early soliloquies and later asides to guide your imaginary inquiry into the minds of these two modern seekers of power and glory.

7. Compare the Watergate scandal and the Olympic scandals of Johnson and Harding. What similarities are there between political ambitions and athletic ambitions?

8. Referring to William Grieder's editorial on Watergate, write your own editorial about one of the Olympic scandals, using appropriate quotations or examples from the play to comment on the athlete's guilt or ambition.

9. Construct an imaginative scenario, perhaps one of your own fantasies of success. How do you aspire to be a winner, and what would you be willing to sacrifice or compromise in order to achieve that end? Is ambition merely a negative word to you or can it have positive connotations? What line distinguishes the positive from the negative in your scenario?

10. Almost everyone wants to succeed, but where does one draw the line? Is the hero who is willing to sacrifice everything to win more admirable than the participant who merely plays along? In the violent world of a feudal power struggle where many extreme actions are politically acceptable, where does Macbeth cross over the line?

11. The great football coach Vince Lombardi was fond of saying that "winning isn't everything—it's the *only* thing." In what ways does Macbeth live by this dictum? Is he to be admired for doing so? If so, in what ways? If not, why not?

Haiti: A Terrorist Regime

> Bleed, bleed, poor country!
>
> *Macbeth* 4.3.32

In 1936, when Orson Welles transplanted his stage production of *Macbeth* to a setting he described as "a mythical place . . . anywhere in the West Indies," everyone else assumed it was Haiti. The voodooism representing witchcraft may have been the most obvious connection, but as the *New York Times* review of the play suggested (see Chapter 3), Haiti's civil turbulence in its late-nineteenth-century efforts to sever ties with colonial France paralleled the violence and unrest in Shakespeare's portrayal of *Macbeth* in Scotland. Audiences saw the validity of Welles's original adaptation.

Decades later the similarities still invite consideration and provoke reflection. Haiti seems trapped in a history of political oppression and unrest that has cultivated dictators willing to perpetuate terror for their own ends. Such abuse of power accustoms a population to corruption and violence so that it appears unable to break the cycle of civil war. This story of political instability not only shares *Macbeth*'s pattern of violence and brutality but also raises similar questions about morality and the nature of evil. The witches in Shakespeare's play and the voodoo dolls in

Haiti's culture are simply external signs of evil forces that appear just as compellingly real in the hearts of the power-hungry, unprincipled national leaders who advocate or accept supernatural beliefs. Developments in Haiti over the last half of the twentieth century generate debate about standards of good and evil, and about the influence of morality on international responses and intervention. If *Macbeth* has sometimes been called one of Shakespeare's most moral plays, then the parallels between it and modern Third World politics draw drama and history together to address some timeless conflicts that plague the human condition.

From 1957 to 1986, François Duvalier and his son, Jean-Claude, ruled successively as presidents of Haiti with uncompromising control. This era, known as "Duvalierism," was characterized by military corruption, bloodshed, and a devastating legacy of poverty among the Haitian people. François Duvalier, otherwise known as "Papa Doc," was elected as president in 1957, but in 1964 he abolished the constitution and declared himself "president for life," guaranteeing his support for this role by establishing a police state and manipulating the fears of the public based on their beliefs in the power of voodooism. Members of Duvalier's secret police force, known as the Ton-Tons Macoutes, were licensed in terror, torture, and murder. With their assistance, Papa Doc imprisoned thousands of Haitians, subjecting them to brutality and even death often without solid evidence of their guilt.

In 1971, as Papa Doc became terminally ill, he continued to ignore the constitutional rights of the Haitian people by making plans to install his son as his successor. When Papa Doc died, Jean-Claude, otherwise known as "Baby Doc," assumed his father's power as "president for life." Jean-Claude continued the oppression, injustice, and violence initiated by his father. He maintained a lavish lifestyle while his people lived in desperate poverty. In 1985 a rigged election gave him 99 percent of the vote, but anti-government protests followed. The civil revolt against Duvalier became so intense that it forced him to flee the country in 1986 and give up his dictatorship. The Duvalier powerlock had ended, but the next four years were marked with continued strife and unrest. Legally planned elections were obstructed. Then in January 1988 a president was elected, but by June an army general took the office by force, only to be supplanted, too, within a few months.

Finally, in 1990 Jean-Bertrand Aristide became the first freely elected president with a high percentage of popular support. But his parliament lasted less than a year before the military overthrew him, once again shaking the Haitian people's hopes for a legitimate government. More violence followed. Then in 1994 the military regime crumbled, the leaders fled, and Aristide returned to try to restore peace and democracy. If history ends with this chapter, it concludes with a sense of promise. However, more than a century of turbulence, terrorism, inherited corruption, and poverty leaves the fate of Haiti's future open to question. Can the cycle of repression and terror be broken? As Macduff says, "O nation miserable! / When shalt thou see thy wholesome days again . . . ?" (*Macbeth* 4.3.103–105).

The remainder of this section includes a brief chronology of Haiti's history since Duvalierism began and several newspaper articles that depict the violence characterizing the rise and fall of the Duvaliers and Aristide since 1957.

BRIEF CHRONOLOGY OF HAITI'S POLITICAL HISTORY

1957	François Duvalier is elected president.
1964	Duvalier declares himself president for life.
1971, Apr. 22	Papa Doc dies; Jean-Claude Duvalier, his son, becomes president.
1985	A rigged election gives Jean-Claude Duvalier majority support of the Haitian people.
1986	A violent uprising occurs; Baby Doc flees the country.
1987, Nov. 23	"Bloody Sunday," another violent uprising.
1988, Jan. 17	Elections are held, and a president is chosen.
1990	Jean-Bertrand Aristide is elected.
1991	Aristide is overthrown by the military.
1994	Aristide returns to Haiti as president.

THE DUVALIER REGIME

The following story provides an analysis of the Duvalier era the day after Jean-Claude fled the country in 1986. This summary presents a character sketch of father and son, explains the escalating unrest that precipitated Jean-Claude's exile, and suggests the important influence of two opposing powers, the Ton-Tons Macoutes and the Catholic Church. Consider how the journalist's account portrays dictatorship as a force that ultimately becomes larger and more powerful than the dictators themselves.

DUVALIER'S FLIGHT ENDS FAMILY RULE, BUT NOT HAITIAN
TURBULENCE
By Edward Cody

MIAMI, Feb. 7—Jean-Claude Duvalier's flight to exile has ended a dictatorship founded by his father 29 years ago. But if history is a valid guide, it has not ended the political turbulence that has tormented Haiti almost without letup since rebellious slaves won independence there in 1804.

About 25 dictators have established their rule over Haiti since then, interspersed with military coups d'etat and unsuccessful attempts at representative democracy. When the 34-year-old Duvalier climbed aboard a U.S. Air Force plane in the dark of night, therefore, he was following historical tradition as well as closing an era.

The most recent dictatorship began in 1957 when François (Papa Doc) Duvalier, Jean-Claude's father, emerged as president after a political struggle so chaotic that six governments had held power in the preceding year. Although he took over as the result of elections, Duvalier swiftly asserted himself as one of the most brutal and repressive despots in a Haitian history already rich with blood.

Francois Duvalier, a short, bespectacled physician widely rumored to dabble in voodoo, carried out what he called a revolution in Haitian life. It was based mostly on his pledge to increase the influence of poor blacks over a mixed-race elite that had dominated economic and political life since the end of French colonial rule.

This goal struck a chord among the descendants of African slaves who make up 95 percent of the country's 6 million inhabitants and form a peasantry scratching out a sparse living from a land largely drained of natural wealth by overpopulation. But at the same time, the elder Duvalier established a repressive security apparatus and corrupt economic management that left Haiti the poorest country in the Western Hemisphere and one of the most downtrodden in the world.

Graham Greene, who captured the darkness of Haiti under Duvalier in the novel "The Comedians," wrote in his introduction: "Poor Haiti itself and the character of Dr. Duvalier's rule are not invented, the latter not even blackened for dramatic effect. Impossible to deepen that night."

To enforce his rule, Duvalier created the Ton-Tons Macoutes, described by longtime residents as a cross between a militia and an armed political party. In addition, these thousands of armed followers provided a loyal counterweight to the military, which Duvalier feared might overthrow him and install a mixed-race officer in his place.

Duvalier, perhaps by design in dealing with a people steeped in voodoo, also created a mystique about his person. While it sometimes seemed madcap to foreigners, the aura bestowed on Duvalier unusual powers in enforcing his authority with an iron hand.

When sickness attacked in 1971, therefore, Haitians did not laugh as Duvalier prepared the way for his 19-year-old son's takeover by comparing him to Caesar Augustus, who Duvalier noted was also 19 when "he took into his hands the destinies of Rome." In a referendum that yielded 2,391,916 "yes" votes and not a single "no," the Haitian people approved Jean-Claude as his father's successor as "president-for-life."

Overweight, untraveled and known principally as a lover of fast cars, the young Jean-Claude seemed an unlikely candidate for dictator. But he was his father's only son. As Duvalier's health faded, Jean-Claude swiftly became the object of a government campaign to prepare the way.

Bernard Diederich, in the book "Papa Doc," reported that one poster showed the dictator with a hand resting on Jean-Claude's shoulder and the caption: "I have chosen him."

François Duvalier collapsed during dinner April 21, 1971, and was pronounced dead that night at the age of 50. His son was installed the next day. The fat teen-ager who had been off the island only once and never graduated from college suddenly became president-for-life with absolute powers.

In one of his first public statements, Jean-Claude issued an amnesty for all his father's exiled opponents "except Communists and troublemakers." But Luckner Cambronne, who became minister of interior, national defense and police, was quick to clear up any confusion about life under the new ruler.

"There has been no change," he told reporters then. "President Duvalier's mission was to allow the black people to raise up their faces to the sun. That was the aim of his revolution and we will continue his path."

In fact, there has been change. The young Duvalier never seemed to have the stomach for his father's brutality. In addition, U.S. aid had resumed, and with it came pressure for relaxation of some of the most obviously repressive aspects of the family dictatorship.

The Haitian Catholic Church also changed, abandoning a long tradition of getting along with the government for an activist Gospel attuned to the needs of the poor. This attitude sharpened after Pope John Paul II visited in March 1983. Responding to a request from the Haitian bishops who met him then, the pontiff negotiated an end to an 1860 concordat that had given the government veto power over papal nominations of bishops.

Prodded from several sides, Duvalier relaxed political repression and censorship in what he called "democratization." He authorized long-banned political activity, but insisted that any political leaders vow allegiance to his status as president-for-life.

At the same time, political police and Ton-Tons Macoutes frequently violated civil liberties laws proclaimed as part of the much-heralded liberalization. Duvalier's zig-zag course seemed to illustrate the difficulty of attempting "democratization" within the framework of absolute dictatorship.

Perhaps inevitably, the smell of freedom appeared to give Haitians an appetite for more. In addition, thousands of Haitians had lived for a time in New York or Miami and returned with a new determination to assert their rights.

Their determination was heightened by increasing economic misery in the countryside. African swine fever wiped out the pig population on which peasants had depended as an investment and nest egg. Tourists, frightened off by reports of acquired immune deficiency syndrome (AIDS), largely stopped their contribution to the economy.

Against this backdrop, the opulent life led by Jean-Claude and his circle of family and friends became less tolerable. For example, reports that the president's wife, Michele, had gone on a Paris shopping spree aboard the Concorde while most Haitians suffered from a gasoline shortage contributed to the outrage.

Jean-Claude's marriage to the beautiful Michele also had caused discontent. She was light-skinned and of mixed race, the kind of person François Duvalier had vowed to help blacks combat. In addition, her father, Ernest Bennett, was one of the wealthiest businessmen in Haiti and the epitome of the economic elite resented by poor blacks.

The first sparks flew two years ago in Gonaives, the poorest of Haitian cities. Food riots there turned political, with crowds daring to shout for the first time, "Down with Duvalier." The unrest renewed last fall, building until the young dictator seemed on the verge of falling last Friday.

By then, diplomats, Haitians and almost anyone interested were saying it was only a matter of time until he did.

The Washington Post, Saturday, February 8, 1986

ARISTIDE'S STRUGGLE FOR DEMOCRACY

The two following articles portray life under military rule after Aristide was forced into exile in 1991. These accounts also describe the many forces perpetuating violence and instability after the collapse of the Duvalier regime. Try to identify some of these forces and influences, as well as consider the relationships between violence and fear, between the social and economic costs of civil war, and between international intervention and national self-determination.

ARMY TRIES USUAL WAYS AGAINST UNUSUAL LEADER
Aristide's Support Puts Textbook Coup to Test
By Lee Hockstader

MIAMI, Oct. 1—When Haitian President Jean-Bertrand Aristide departed into exile on a Venezuelan airplane bound for Caracas at 3:10 A.M. today, his wrenchingly poor country's hopes for a better future disappeared over the southern horizon with him—at least for now.

Surrounded at the airport by more than 100 heavily armed troops, some of whom reportedly jeered and taunted him as he waited for the plane to take him away, Aristide had been ousted by the same brutally repressive military that has been Haiti's bane since the end of the Duvalier family dynasty in 1986.

He is hardly the first Haitian president to be seized in a violent coup attempt—not even the first this year. But unlike the many leaders he follows into exile, Aristide, a Roman Catholic priest, carried with him the overwhelming support, even adulation, of the nation he was forced to flee.

"The people flexed their muscles successfully in electing Aristide, and it should be expected that they'll find a way to restore Aristide by themselves, a la Moscow," said Robert I. Rotberg, president of Lafayette College in Pennsylvania and a longtime student of Haitian politics. "I don't think the people will stand for it."

Indeed, Aristide exhorted Haitians today from Caracas to "hold on; don't let go. I have confidence the people will continue on the road to democracy." And outrage voiced by the United States, France and other countries indicated that international pressure will be exerted on Haiti's new rulers to reverse the coup.

If Aristide's ouster stands—which seems unlikely—it will be the most dismal chapter in Haiti's long sad history. He was elected last December in a landslide, winning 67 per cent of the vote against a field of candidates in the first free, fair and competent elections in the nation's 200-year history.

Yet his vote-getting ability is dwarfed by his near-mythic stature in Haiti. He has survived at least three assassination attempts. Some Haitians believe that he eluded gunmen on one occasion in 1988 by turning himself into a dog and bounding out the window of his church.

His eight-month presidency has been marked by some travails and missteps, and perhaps by some modest erosion in his support. Haiti's economy, the most anemic in the hemisphere, has not yet responded to his ministrations.

But the soldiers who rose up against Aristide on Monday represent virtually no interests in Haiti but their own. Their uprising had nothing to do with ideology, because there was no ideological chasm between them and the president.

Rather, Haiti's army is driven by what always drove Haitian politics before Aristide's whirlwind entrance into politics a year ago: greed, corruption and lust for the stature conferred on whoever occupies the gleaming white presidential palace that stands, like a dream amid the squalor of downtown Port-au-Prince.

True to form, the mutineers did what leaders of Haitian coups have always done: They promised elections, pledging their commitment to the democracy they had just violated.

And in the improbable event that they hold power long enough to actually hold elections, the near-certain result will be the installation of a puppet president who in turn will be deposed should he ever question the military's writ.

In his inauguration speech in February, Aristide spoke of a marriage between the Haitian army and the people. But it was never a healthy relationship—more a marriage of convenience.

The army had played a part in propping up the 29-year Duvalier family dynasty until it decayed and finally crumbled in 1986 with the flight of Jean-Claude "Baby Doc" Duvalier, who had proclaimed himself president for life. But even after Duvalier's departure, the army held sway through a succession of unpopular, corrupt and repressive regimes until early 1990, when an interim civilian government took office pledging free elections.

The Washington Post, Wednesday, October 2, 1991

HAITIAN ARMED FORCES REPRESSING AID GROUPS
Rights Workers Say Poorest Are Suffering
By Douglas Farah

PETITE RIVIERE DE L'ARTIBONITE, Haiti—Across rural Haiti, where peasants for decades have eked out a subsistence living, the military is systematically crushing communal, religious and humanitarian organizations that have provided the only help to the poorest regions of the poorest nation in the hemisphere, according to international human rights and relief workers.

While the trade and financial embargo imposed a year ago by the Organization of American States following the military's ouster of president Jean-Bertrand Aristide primarily has hurt urban areas, political repression by the military has devastated the countryside, where most of the people live and where most are outside the cash economy.

Aristide, 38, a Roman Catholic priest who espouses liberation theology, won more than 75 per cent of the vote in rural areas when he was elected in December 1990.

"Even more devastating than the embargo is the repression," said a religious worker driven out of his home. "People are poor and were poor before the elections. But after [Aristide's] election, they had hope for a better future and could express themselves. Now, we cannot even say we are poor or look at the causes of our poverty."

The services offered by the humanitarian organizations, often linked to the Catholic Church and mostly begun after the 1986 downfall of "president for life" Jean-Claude Duvalier, include primary medical attention, literacy classes and small-scale development projects. These efforts are vital in a nation where 90 percent of the people earn an average of $120 a year and 1 percent own 90 percent of the arable land.

The groups largely are disbanded now, according to sources who work in the area, because they are viewed as a threat to the control of the military in the countryside.

"The organizations have been destroyed and leaders forced into exile," said William G. O'Neill, deputy director of the Lawyers Committee for Human Rights, which last month issued a report titled "Haiti: A Human Rights Nightmare." "The offices have been literally destroyed, seeds destroyed, pigs killed, computers and typewriters stolen to destroy the grass-roots organizations. The activity has been beheaded and groups destroyed on purpose."

The committee estimates there have been at least 1,000 extrajudicial executions since the coup, including about 500 selective assassinations in rural areas.

Residents in this central Haitian river valley, where rough brown hills are completely deforested and dust swirls constantly, said the human rights situation is the most repressive in memory, including the years under Duvalier.

Sources, who asked for security reasons that their names not be used, said that "section chiefs," or rural military commanders in the valley, who were disbanded by Aristide in his nine months in office because of widespread abuses, have returned—as have the organizations of the feared paramilitary Ton-Tons Macoutes, who terrorized the countryside during the Duvalier era.

The Lawyers Committee report called Aristide's disbanding of the section chiefs "perhaps the most important step taken to improve respect of law," saying the chiefs "have been at the heart of human rights abuses in Haiti. Their unfettered authority over the lives of the peasants in the communities under their control had led to systematic disregard for individual liberties."

"People are waiting impatiently for Aristide to return," said a deputy mayor who has lived in hiding since the 1991 coup. He is one of the few elected officials who has not fled to another section of the country. "We have lost our freedom of expression, many have fled, but we want him back, even if it means more suffering."

As the man spoke beside a dirt road close to a field he was cultivating, a small crowd gathered and, in an extraordinary act of defiance, some openly agreed with what he said.

"I know the police and army may have spies here," he said, raising his voice and pointing to two men standing on the other side of the irrigation canal, who shifted uneasily, "They will report this to the police, and they will look for us, and if they find us they will beat us. But if it helps bring back Aristide, we do not care if some die along the way."

The Rev. Max Leroy Mesidor, the parish priest here, found pamphlets distributed across town last May telling him that "we, the army and Macoutes, are ordering you to leave town" within 24 hours. Four days later, another tract appeared attacking the priest and nuns of the Sisters of Charity of St. Louis, who run the local school.

The church workers still did not leave, and on May 24 the lights and power to the rectory and convent were cut, and shots were fired at the buildings. Mesidor's and the nuns' rooms were stoned and windows broken for about 30 minutes, although police headquarters is less than 50 yards away.

The following day the priest and three nuns fled, forcing the town's school to close and construction of a clinic to halt. All parish work ended because there was no one left to carry on, and remaining villagers were too frightened to try to organize again.

According to residents, the elected mayor already had fled, the justice of the peace was in exile, and leaders of a Catholic food program had been arrested and beaten.

"Everything is paralyzed, and people are suffering greatly," said a religious worker now assigned to a different parish. "The army comes with arrests and beatings, and you spend a few days in jail. Then you have to pay money to be released. Then you have to go to the hospital because you do not come out in one piece, and that means more money. How can we ask people to face those risks?"

The Washington Post, Saturday, October 10, 1992

Conclusion

Dictatorship can perhaps be seen as a modern version of tyranny. Both are extreme examples of corrupt power. Both exact a high human cost. Both are characterized by fear, for not only do tyrants and dictators often rely on intimidation to maintain control but they are also often guided by fear themselves as they face a constant threat of retaliation. "Blood will have blood," as Macbeth says (3.4.121). A nation raised on violence learns to respond in kind; unbearable oppression encourages civil unrest.

This dark picture of Haiti's history reflects the violence enacted in *Macbeth*. Orson Welles's 1936 production of the play offers connections that have continued to be valid for most of this century. Haiti's recent past offers not only a study of the effects of brutality but also an inquiry into standards of morality and the question of evil. Much of the Western world is prepared to denounce the inhumanity perpetuated by Haiti's governments and give financial assistance in order to restore peace and prosperity: the United States played a significant role in returning Aristide to power. But "evil" is a strong judgment that reaches beyond political questions about just rule and stable government. The parallels between Haiti and *Macbeth* open up the debate about whether interpretations of evil have changed from the seventeenth to the twentieth century, whether there are moral absolutes of good and evil or simply cultural standards, and what kind of responsibility our understanding requires from us as audiences, as foreign observers, and as actively concerned citizens.

QUESTIONS FOR WRITTEN AND ORAL DISCUSSION

1. Discuss the issue of political legitimacy in Haiti and in *Macbeth*. Is there a difference between power and authority? Explain and give examples.

2. The *Washington Post* article of February 8, 1986, describes "the difficulty of attempting 'democratization' within the framework of absolute dictatorship" in the reign of Jean-Claude Duvalier. Explain the clash between democracy and dictatorship and discuss both the problems and the possibilities of achieving freedom or democracy within an oppressive regime.

3. Can you offer a moral interpretation of Haiti's political history? Is evil an appropriate word? Why or why not?

4. Consider the relationship between fear and insecurity in the Haitian experience, beginning with Macbeth's statement "To be thus is nothing, but to be safely thus" (3.1.47). Expand your discussion by comparing Haiti's politics to Watergate, or by considering the applicability of Machiavelli's philosophy to Haiti's tyranny (see Chapter 2).

5. Where history begins and ends depends on the choices of historians. Furthermore, the political winners usually tell the past from their own perspective. Referring to the historical background in Chapter 1, discuss where Shakespeare chooses to start and finish his play and why. What view of Scottish and English history do his choices reflect?

6. How would you select a beginning and an end if you were to tell the story of Haiti's politics? Would you choose a positive or a negative conclusion? Given that most of the news stories about Haiti come from foreigners, how do they reflect an outsider's perspective? Consider, for example, the tone of Edward Cody's or Lee Hockstader's article in *The Washington Post*. What attitude or bias do the journalists express?

7. Try to imagine a period in Haiti's recent history from an insider's perspective and write your view of the experience. Perhaps compose a dialogue between two citizens the night after Papa Doc died, after Baby Doc fled, or after Aristide was ousted the first time. It might help to re-read the conversation between the old man and Ross in Act 2.4 of *Macbeth*, as well as the comments of Haitian people quoted in Douglas Farah's newspaper article.

8. Alternatively, imagine a period in Haiti's history from the perspective of the tyrants themselves. Shakespeare accepts the challenge of inviting us to identify with a corrupt ruler at the same time as we condemn his actions. Can you compose a soliloquy for one of the

Duvaliers that might generate some sympathy or understanding for them?

9. Trace the recent history of Haiti in newspapers and magazines. Has democracy survived? Has the direction of history been changed since Aristide resumed power?

10. In *Macbeth*, the English intervene to assist the rebels in the uprising against Macbeth. In Haiti, Americans offered their assistance to allow Aristide's return. Research the U.S. involvement during this period and discuss the role of foreign intervention against corrupt governments. What limitations should national borders provide? When is it just or right to intervene?

11. Haiti is only one of many modern states plagued by political corruption and injustice. Can you think of other current examples from the news? Discuss how *Macbeth*'s metaphor of the diseased commonwealth might apply.

SUGGESTED READINGS

Abbott, Elizabeth. *Haiti: The Duvaliers and Their Legacy*. New York: Mc-Graw-Hill, 1988.

Ferguson, James. *Papa Doc, Baby Doc: Haiti and the Duvaliers*. New York: Basil Blackwell, 1987.

Greene, Graham. *The Comedians*. New York: Viking, 1966.

BEYOND THE COURTROOM: THE SOCIAL AND PSYCHOLOGICAL IMPACT

Macbeth is not only about political corruption, violent crimes, and their consequences. It is not simply a plot-driven action-drama. It is also very much a psychological play about private motivations and tortured minds, about the power of emotions and conscience to determine actions and reactions. Tragedy, after all, moves toward the fallen hero's increasing awareness, understanding, or insight. Inner conflict is balanced with outer conflict. The escalating violence in *Macbeth* provokes terrors of the mind as well as of the flesh, and those who die rest more peacefully than those who live. As Macbeth says,

> Better be with the dead,
> Whom we, to gain our peace, have sent to peace,

Than on the torture of the mind to lie
In restless ecstasy. (3.2.19–22)

This last section of "Contemporary Applications" suggests some of
the connections between the inner conflicts in Shakespeare's tragedy and similar psychological struggles appearing in other stories,
both in fact and in fiction. These stories ask us to consider the
impact of crime beyond the courtroom by reflecting two of the
driving psychological forces in *Macbeth*: fear and guilt.

The Oklahoma City Bombing: The Aftermath of Fear

It will have blood, they say: blood will have blood.

Macbeth 3.4.121

When Shakespeare incorporated a sense of foreboding and uncertainty into *Macbeth*, he was undoubtedly reflecting or addressing the atmosphere of dread following the Gunpowder Plot of
1605. Fear and insecurity penetrate the heart of Macbeth himself,
as well as those around him who suffer the effects of his tyranny.
If the play's emotional and psychological intensity makes sense
within its immediate historical context, it also generates interest in
the nature of fear itself, a reaction which is no less powerful or
legitimate within social and political experience today than it was
in the seventeenth century. Dictatorships continue to prosper, but
even in the relatively stable countries of the Western world, random acts of violence or terrorism can instantly unsettle the solid
foundations of peace and order. The national shock following the
Oklahoma City bombing in 1995 provides a recent example of the
precarious balance between fear and security that produced such
tragic personal, social, and political consequences in *Macbeth*.
     On April 19, 1995, one hundred and sixty-eight people were
killed when a bomb exploded in the Alfred P. Murrah federal building in Oklahoma City. Nineteen of the dead were children attending a day care center in the office building. Over 400 other people
were injured from the impact of the explosion. Less than two
hours after the blast, Timothy McVeigh, coincidentally arrested on
traffic charges, was soon connected to the bombing. Within several

days the FBI took another suspect, Terry Nichols, into custody. Initially, authorities thought that the suspects may have been "Middle Eastern types," but these two men were American right-wing extremists, members of a private militia strongly opposed to the federal government. The explosion was apparently an act of revenge or retaliation against the government on the second anniversary of a federal raid that resulted in the death of eighty Branch Davidian cult members in Waco, Texas, in 1993.

The bombing was violent, shocking, and completely unexpected. It dealt a psychological blow to the entire nation, triggering a universal response of fear. Nobody felt safe; everybody felt vulnerable. Authorities at every level of government denounced the crime. President Clinton called it "an act of evil." Oklahoma governor Frank Keating said, "Whoever did this was an animal." Some people called for the death penalty, even public hangings in the street. As a series of bomb threats followed a few days after the explosion, several buildings were evacuated and the president ordered heightened security at thousands of federal buildings across the country. In this time of crisis and potential danger, people reacted instinctually and emotionally, using harsh language that matched the extremism of the action itself.

The Oklahoma City bombing is reminiscent of the Gunpowder Plot so much on the mind of the English public in 1606 when Shakespeare wrote *Macbeth*. Many of the circumstances are similar: the motive, antigovernment reaction; the means, heavy explosives; and the opportunity to make a political statement by destroying a federal building and the people within it. The difference is that whereas the Gunpowder Plot was aborted, the Oklahoma City bombing succeeded. Consequently, the victory that mitigated some of the fear in England in 1606 was missing in the aftermath of the explosion in Oklahoma in 1995.

In both circumstances, however, there was an overwhelming temptation to ignore what Macbeth called "the pauser, reason," and to react almost at a level of hysteria and paranoia. Like *The Black Year*, a title of a book describing the current events in 1606, the Oklahoma bombing cast a black, chilling darkness across the United States. Some of the reactions are captured in newspaper articles and editorials that follow.

IMMEDIATE REACTION TO THE BOMBING

The two ensuing articles summarize details of the Oklahoma City bombing and reactions to it. They describe the initial response of horror and the subsequent official action to increase security. Pay attention to how the immediacy of the experience—without the historical benefit of "hindsight"—fosters speculation and affects the presentation of the "facts." Consider how this perspective might help you to understand the position of Shakespeare and his contemporaries after the Gunpowder Plot at a time when news sources were slow and unreliable.

OKLAHOMA SHOCK SENT FEAR THROUGHOUT U.S.
By Reuter
New York

For the second time in two years in the United States, a car bomb has killed innocent people, injured many and thrown a city into panic.

And for a second time it is apparent how vulnerable the United States, with its traditions of an open society and freedom even to buy a gun, can be to anyone committed to an act of violence.

The destruction of a federal building in Oklahoma City sends the same message that the bombers of New York City's World Trade Centre did in 1993—no one is safe anywhere.

"A terrorist gains by creating a climate of fear—they want us to think that they can get us anytime, anywhere," said Steven Emerson, a leading expert on Islamic extremists. And they can, he said.

That bloody message explodes in a city where no one expects such a thing to happen.

One might anticipate an act of terrorism in New York, the U.S. media capital, especially after the Trade Center blast and a plot to blow up the United Nations and the city's bridges and tunnels and its federal office building.

But Oklahoma City, a city of half a million in the heart of Middle America, is supposed to be more synonymous with the musical *Oklahoma* than with terror.

Terrorism experts say that could be the reason for the explosion that destroyed the building.

"Whoever did it picked an easy target, certainly easier than the World

Trade Center is today," said Ira Lipman, president of Guardsmark Inc., one of the largest security firms in the U.S. "Terrorists always pick targets where they are going to succeed."

The Oklahoma bomb was perhaps 1,000 to 1,200 pounds, about the [same] size as the one that shook the World Trade Center, said John Magaw, director of the federal Bureau of Alcohol, Tobacco and Fire-arms.

No group has come forward. Attorney General Janet Reno said it was too early to speculate, and some terrorism experts agreed with her.

"It could be a contractor who has access to explosives, a farmer who has access to fertilizer, it could be a wacko, it could be a professional trying to cover his tracks by using a simple device," expert Jack Kingston told CNN.

"There are also about 10,000 pounds of explosives that are stolen and recovered each year and 10,000 detonators so these devices are available. You don't have to be a rocket scientist to create this kind of bomb. You do have to be very, very careful and very, very determined."

Emerson agreed to a point. "There is no smoking gun. But the modus operandi and circumstantial evidence leads in the direction of Islamic terrorism."

He said Oklahoma City has been for the past decade a centre for radical Islamic activity, a place where radicals established homes and networks.

It has also been the site of various Islamic conventions including one in 1992 where 6,000 people cheered calls for killing Jews and infidels, Emerson said.

But Wednesday was also the second anniversary of the storming of Branch Davidian headquarters in nearby Waco, Tex., and some experts wondered if the blast was linked to the cult.

But a gasp went up from a crowd in Waco marking the anniversary when they heard about the Oklahoma explosion. "We offer our sympathy to the families that have lost loved ones or are injured," said Clive Doyle, a survivor of the Waco disaster.

Appearing in *The Edmonton Journal*, Thursday, April 20, 1995

BOTTOM LINE . . .

Unsafe address: Washington, D.C., has always had its unsafe neighbor-hoods, but the White House itself is not usually regarded as one. That, however, is what it has become. In the wake of the Oklahoma City bomb-ing, security officials decided the home of the president constituted a primary target for many Americans. Pennsylvania Avenue has been closed to road traffic because of fear of car bombs. A number of recent attempts by individuals to get into the grounds have produced an even higher degree of security consciousness—if that is possible.

Everywhere the president goes, he is surrounded by secret service staff. It is a symbol of the time, and no one doubts its necessity. But Americans, along with the citizens of every other country with a well-guarded head of government, should ponder the repercussions. What is the effect on government thinking of itself when the leader spends his entire term in a state of siege against elements of his own population?

The Edmonton Journal, Monday, May 29, 1995

RESPONSE TO VIOLENCE

The following two articles offer a commentary or analytical perspective on the Oklahoma City bombing. The editorial about terrorism raises concerns about fear itself, suggesting that an emotional response to violence can be as potentially threatening as the unexpected terrorism. The movie review by Marc Horton addresses the standard debate about violence in movies but shifts the focus by asking not how violent movies affect behavior but, rather, how real violence influences appreciation of its entertainment value. Both the editorial and the movie review refer to another recent act of terrorism, a gas attack in a Tokyo subway station that affected thousands of people on March 20, 1995. Consider how each writer defines the problem and whether their observations are convincing. Do they suggest viable solutions or challenge you to find your own?

TERRORIST CHALLENGE IS BIGGER THAN BOMBS

The greater challenge to democratic societies—like the United States, like Japan—is to counter the growing threats of terrorists and lunatics without compromising the freedoms of society itself. Peoples' sense of security must be restored, but not at the expense of their liberty. It may turn out, for democratic countries, to be the most difficult challenge of our times.

The United States today is in a suspended state of shock over the bombing of the federal building in Oklahoma City, a community of 400,000 people in the very heart of the American heartland. An office building with its daily rituals and its day care—blown up. The death toll, including small babies, is rising as the rubble is searched. All of America, but especially middle America, identifies with the victims and is shocked to its foundations. And rightly so, because blind and cruel terrorism has intruded where, it was thought, it never does.

Japan, too, is attempting to deal at present with an act of terror that shocked not only the sensibilities of an orderly nation, but also its psyche. On March 20, a nerve gas attack in a Tokyo subway killed 12 people and sickened another 5,000. The attackers are still being sought. A religious cult is suspected—and searches of its properties have produced a chilling amount of potentially lethal chemicals—but there have been no charges yet. Much of Japan is in a state approaching hysteria.

The threat posed by terrorists to a free society is two-fold. The first is the murderous intent—to kill people for whatever fanatical motive. The second is more insidious. It is to shake the society to its foundations, to bring distrust and instability and eventually breakdown.

Enhanced security—greater vigilance in the name of society—is the only means of countering the first threat. In an age of rapid travel, vanishing borders and high explosives, the various security forces must have the means to police airports, to monitor fanatical groups, to track and control the enemies of a society. Not all the groups and individuals in a democratic society accept its rules. Some would destroy them. They must be watched. And there may come a time when they must be apprehended.

But a country like the United States or Japan, or Canada too, has to be just as vigilant in another direction. We do not want a police state. It is our very freedoms that make it easier for a terrorist or a lunatic to travel, buy explosives, hatch murderous schemes. It is also those freedoms that make life meaningful in democratic societies. To sacrifice them in a fight against terrorists would be to surrender to their intents.

Understandably, the Japanese government is considering new means of dealing with a new terrorist threat. Car bombs are one thing. The mix of fuel and fertilizer that destroyed the office building in Oklahoma City is essentially a variant. But nerve gas? The potential for disaster in the Tokyo subway was mind-boggling. An entire city, and a society, can feel itself suddenly to be permanently held hostage. The police, with the support of that society, are seeking new powers. They may get them.

Americans, with the sickening images of Oklahoma City's dead bodies in their minds, will demand action from their government too. And understandably. The day care at the destroyed office building could have been a day care anywhere. On Friday, parents in Omaha were keeping their children home. Middle America will seek protection.

Much of the world has grown used to terror. European capitals have kept their guard up for years, combating the attempts of their own terrorist cells and the exported ones from the world's trouble spots. In some parts of the world, terror is daily fare. All the evidence is that it will grow. We are in an age of fanatical causes and doomsday cults.

The democratic countries can afford neither to bow to fear nor to surrender their precious liberties in the name of security. The terrorist groups, the whole fanatic rainbow, are seeking both. If fear grows, they win. If democracies weaken and turn away from their own democratic bases, they also win.

The only true stability of free societies in a terrorist world lies in solidarity around the democratic values. Hunt down the terrorists by every legal means. Bring them to trial. Beyond that, include as many as possible of society's individuals and groups in the democratic enterprise, because alienation is a breeding ground for fanaticism. Freedoms only seem to make a society an easier prey for its enemies. In fact they are the society's best protection against the spread of terrorism and its hand-maiden, which is fear.

The Edmonton Journal, Saturday, April 22, 1995

TIMING COULDN'T BE WORSE FOR LATEST *DIE HARD* SEQUEL
Oklahoma Bombing Takes a Lot of the Fun out of One of the Most Spectacular Action Movies Ever Made
By Marc Horton

For a movie which depends so much on split-second planning—a subway train explosion, a hair-raising chase through the strollers of Central Park, hair's breadth escapes from ticking time bombs—the timing really couldn't be worse.

While *Die Hard with a Vengeance* was in the movie pipeline for months, any movie where wackos blow up public buildings has a special chill these days. There's no escaping the pall of Oklahoma City as we watch New York's Bonwit Teller explode, or see a bomb disposal expert tinker away at a two-tonne monster in the basement of a New York public school.

And while director John McTiernan, returning to the *Die Hard* series after passing on the second segment, tries hard to make all the violence as serious as a cartoon, the laughs have a hollow ring. This all may be a joke on the screen, but Oklahoma City reminds us all just how close we could all be to evil.

Nevertheless, the stunts are beyond compare. *Die Hard with a Vengeance* tries hard to be the most spectacular action movie ever made— fans will be asked to take a quantum leap from the likes of *Speed, Lethal Weapon* and *Blown Away*—and it just might succeed.

Everything here is bigger, brighter and louder. . . .

Moviegoers, however, might wonder where the genre of action films all might end. These moves [*sic*] are like an addiction, demanding more and more outrageous stunts, more money, bigger booms, louder crashes, crazier villains.

But, hey, here's an idea.

How about a movie where some nutbar cult figure launches a poison gas attack on the subway of a major city, say, Tokyo? Maybe we could play that one for laughs too.

The Edmonton Journal, Friday, May 19, 1995

Conclusion

The last line of Marc Horton's movie review attempts to inject a degree of satirical humor into his reflections about violence. The remark raises several questions. By pointing quite directly to the relationship between fear and laughter, Horton indirectly provokes interest in the boundaries of tragedy and comedy. Are they mutually exclusive or complementary? Second, the comment on modern violence asks about our ability to cope in a world where danger is a daily reality for some people and a potential threat for many. Under such circumstances, when is fear appropriate and when is it irrational or out of control? Which actions of governments and individuals stem from perceived or imagined sources of fear rather than real personal threats? What constitutes a courageous response? These are the very questions that draw us back to Shakespeare's play. Is Macbeth inspired by fear or courage? Is his desire for security understandable? Is it realistic or attainable? Does it explain or justify his behavior? By seeing the world through his eyes, we begin to suspect that the psychological aspect of his experience cannot be dismissed as simply an illusion or a distortion of reality; it becomes the controlling vision that determines not only his destiny but also the fate of those around him.

QUESTIONS FOR WRITTEN AND ORAL DISCUSSION

1. According to the editorial "Terrorist Challenge Is Bigger than Bombs," what is the danger of using fear as a guide to action? What would be a more balanced approach?

2. After watching a production of *Macbeth* and reading the review of the *Die Hard* movie, discuss the role of violence in entertainment. Why is it appealing? Why do we enjoy the stimulation of fear? Does our reaction depend upon our own environment and sense of safety? Does the technology of special effects make the danger more or less convincing and appealing?

3. Bloody babes are a constant image in Macbeth's mind, as are various configurations of blood, destruction, and sickening violence. What do they add to the play? Relate the effect of *Macbeth* to the effect of a particularly terrifying or shocking movie that you have seen.

4. Discuss the relationship between laughter and fear. Why do people laugh when they are afraid? Why does Shakespeare include the humor of the Porter scene in *Macbeth*? Do you think it is appropriate to mix tragedy and comedy or to turn a tragic scenario into comedy? Why or why not?

5. Compare reactions to the Gunpowder Plot (see Chapter 2) with reactions to the Oklahoma City bombing. Is it appropriate to respond to extremist threats with equally extreme measures? Why or why not?

6. Write two imaginary accounts, one by an English subject who has just heard about the Gunpowder Plot and one by an American citizen who has just seen news footage of the Oklahoma City bombing. How does fear enter into your response?

7. Discuss how fear relates to both security and ambition. Is the fear that motivates crime different from the fear that reacts to crime? For example, to what extent is Macbeth driven by fear as opposed to ambition? How does Macbeth's fear compare to the fear of his subjects once he becomes their tyrant-king? Consider similar examples from Watergate, the Gunpowder Plot, and Oklahoma City.

8. Consider the moral implications of President Clinton's declaration that the bombing was an act of evil. What makes an action evil as opposed to simply criminal? Discuss the appropriateness of applying the term "evil" to the terrorism in Haiti and Oklahoma City.

9. Research a recent national or international incident motivated by violence or terrorism and, using both facts and your imagination, compose a psychological profile of the perpetrator. Consider motives and feelings both before and after the crime.

10. Do you feel safe in your own community? How can you as an individual take steps to ensure your own sense of security and the protection of others? What would constitute sensible behavior? What would be a paranoic response?

The Voice of Conscience: Stories of Guilt

These deeds must not be thought
After these ways: so, it will make us mad.

Macbeth 2.2.32–33

We can trace the patterns of inner conflict appearing in *Macbeth* not only through events in the world around us, in our nations, and in our neighborhoods but also through our stories. Myth, drama, and literature reflect and shape our culture and can reach beyond cultural limits to explore our understanding of what it means to be human. In part we are influenced by the age and society in which we live, but we also share experiences that transcend our surroundings. Fear, for example, is universal, although what triggers the response in our modern, urban communities may differ from the causes of fear in an African tribal village or in a Scottish medieval castle. Similarly, guilt is an experience without cultural or temporal limits, although our responses to it will be influenced by the laws we keep, the religion we practice, and the moral expectations we have learned to accept.

The debate about absolute and relative moral standards opens broadly onto the subject of guilt and its relationship to crime, sin, and immorality. Shakespeare explores this voice of conscience in Macbeth's tormented soliloquies, in the widening chasm between him and Lady Macbeth as they carry the weight of their crimes, and in Lady Macbeth's own sleepwalking madness in the last act of the play. Theirs is a story of guilt that raises some timeless questions. Beyond the courtroom, what psychological and social impact does guilt have? How deep and wide does the experience reach? What are the consequences of choice and responsibility? The stories referred to and included in this last section address these questions and encourage us to consider, if not to answer, the relationship between thought and action, between what we want to believe and what our consciences will not let us ignore.

Oedipus the King. Stories of guilt come to us from the classical and Judeo-Christian traditions, from ancient and modern societies. They permeate our culture and exemplify truths of human existence. The Greek legend of Oedipus, which is most familiar through Sophocles' play *Oedipus the King*, is a tragic tale about self-discovery, fate, and the personal and social consequences of guilt. Prior to the play's beginning King Laius, Oedipus's father, receives a promise from the Oracle of Apollo that he will be killed by his own son for committing a crime. To avoid that punishment Laius maims his infant son, Oedipus, and sends him out to the mountains to die. But a shepherd spares Oedipus's life, and the young boy is raised by a royal couple in Corinth, whom he believes to be his own parents. Hearing the Oracle again foretell that he is destined to kill his father and marry his mother, Oedipus flees from Corinth, hoping to avoid that fate. On his way to Thebes, however, he kills King Laius in a roadside confrontation, thus fulfilling the first part of the prophecy. Oedipus then solves the riddle of the sphinx, which has troubled the people of Thebes, and he subsequently becomes their king. He marries Laius's widow, Jocasta, thus fulfilling the second part of the prophecy by unknowingly becoming his mother's husband. This is the background to the play.

When *Oedipus the King* begins, Thebes is plagued with war, infertility, and damaged crops. Oedipus vows to discover the source of the city's curse and to cleanse it. As the drama unfolds, Oedipus realizes the crimes he has committed—incest and patricide, or parent-killing—and learns too late that the Oracle of Apollo's prediction became true. When he and Jocasta discover that Oedipus has killed his father and married his mother, they are mortified and overcome with guilt. At the play's conclusion, Oedipus is widowed, blinded, and banished as he leaves his children behind to go out to the mountains and live his grief and misery. Near the end of the play, a messenger appears on the stage to recount the violence that the king and queen have inflicted on themselves under the burden of their guilt. The following excerpt is his speech, reporting first Queen Jocasta's suicide and then Oedipus's act of self-mutilation as he blinds himself to shut out the horrors of the world around him.

SOPHOCLES, *OEDIPUS, KING OF THEBES*, TRANS. GILBERT
MURRAY
(London: George Unwin, 1911) ll. 1237–1285

MESSENGER:
By her own hand. . . . Oh, of what passed in there
Ye have been spared the worst. Ye cannot see.
Howbeit, with that which still is left in me
Of mind and memory, ye shall hear her fate.
      Like one entranced with passion, through the gate
She passed, the white hands flashing o'er her head,
Like blades that tear, and fled, unswerving fled,
Toward her old bridal room, and disappeared
And the doors crashed behind her. But we heard
Her voice within, crying to him of old,
Her Laius, long dead; and things untold
Of the old kiss unforgotten, that should bring
The lover's death and leave the loved a thing
Of horror, yea, a field beneath the plough
For sire and son: then wailing bitter-low
Across the bed of births unreconciled,
Husband from husband born and child from child.
And, after that, I know not how her death
Found her. For sudden, with a roar of wrath,
Burst Oedipus upon us. Then, I ween,
We marked no more what passion held the Queen,
But him, as in the fury of his stride,
"A sword! A sword! And show me here," he cried,
"That wife, no wife, that field of bloodstained earth
Where husband, father, sin on sin, had birth,
Polluted generations!" While he thus
Raged on, some god—for sure 'twas none of us—
Showed where she was; and with a shout away,
As though some hand had pointed to the prey,
He dashed him on the chamber door. The straight
Door-bar of oak, it bent beneath his weight,
Shook from its sockets free, and in he burst
To the dark chamber.
      There we saw her first

Hanged, swinging from a noose, like a dead bird.
He fell back when he saw her. Then we heard
A miserable groan, and straight he found
And loosed the strangling knot, and on the ground
Laid her.—Ah, then the sight of horror came!
The pin of gold, broad-beaten like a flame,
He tore from off her breast, and, left and right,
Down on the shuddering orbits of his sight
Dashed it: "Out! Out! Ye never more shall see
Me nor the anguish nor the sins of me.
Ye looked on lives whose like earth never bore,
Ye knew not those my spirit thirsted for:
Therefore be dark for ever!"
          Like a song
His voice rose, and again, again, the strong
And stabbing hand fell, and the massacred
And bleeding eyeballs streamed upon his beard,
Wild rain, and gouts of hail amid the rain.
          Behold affliction, yea, afflictions twain
From man and woman broken, now made one
In downfall. All the riches yester sun
Saw in this house were rich in verity.
What call ye now our riches? Agony,
Delusion, Death, Shame, all that eye or ear
Hath ever dreamed of misery, is here.

Oedipus the King raises many questions about the relationship of guilt to responsibility, choice, and fate. Oedipus's tragedy derives largely from his own ignorance. But he is also blinded by his self-righteousness and pride as he strives for the truth, committed to being the savior of his people. Because his virtues and failings derive from a similar source, he inspires both fear and pity, the two responses that Aristotle identifies as fundamental in his definition of tragedy. Oedipus's hands, like Macbeth's, are stained with blood. Like Macbeth, the Theban ruler learns—much to his horror—that the fulfillment of prophecy means nothing more or less than discovering his *real* origins and motivations. Although blindness and growing self-denial are understandable responses, nothing can change the inevitable course of destiny shaped by Oedipus's decisions, and ultimately, as in *Macbeth*, nothing can be done in the king's favor or in reparation for his crime. Because both men have such prominent and powerful roles in society, their guilt is not only psychologically damaging but also socially devastating. The king's people share his curse. Society's health can be restored only when the community is released from the influence of the diseased individual.

Sophocles' version of this Greek legend not only exemplifies the classical dramatic tradition that preceded and influenced the theatrical renaissance of Shakespeare's time; it has also entered the twentieth century through the psychological theories of Sigmund Freud. This story, which has transcended its own culture and been reinterpreted by others, is a story about a tormented character who cannot escape the condemnation of his own conscience.

The Betrayal of Judas. A similar but briefer example of self-recrimination comes through the Judeo-Christian tradition in the story of Judas's betrayal of Jesus. For a price, Judas agrees to identify Jesus for the Jewish authorities and chief priests so that they may arrest Jesus and take him away to be tried and put to death. Even before Jesus' final trial, however, Judas is overcome by guilt and remorse for his betrayal. When he finds that it is too late to undo his actions, he succumbs to despair and hangs himself, as is recorded in the following passage from Matthew's gospel.

MATTHEW 26:14–16; 26:47–49; 27:1–8
(New International Version)

Then one of the Twelve—the one called Judas Iscariot—went to the chief priests and asked, "What are you willing to give me if I hand him over to you?" So they counted out for him thirty silver coins. From then on Judas watched for an opportunity to hand him over. . . .

While he [Jesus] was still speaking, Judas, one of the Twelve, arrived. With him was a large crowd armed with swords and clubs, sent from the chief priests and the elders of the people. Now the betrayer had arranged a signal with them: "The one I kiss is the man; arrest him." Going at once to Jesus, Judas said, "Greetings, Rabbi!" and kissed him. . . .

Early in the morning, all the chief priests and the elders of the people came to the decision to put Jesus to death. They bound him, led him away and handed him over to Pilate, the governor.

When Judas, who had betrayed him, saw that Jesus was condemned, he was seized with remorse and returned the thirty silver coins to the chief priests and the elders. "I have sinned," he said, "for I have betrayed innocent blood."

"What is that to us?" they replied. "That's your responsibility."

So Judas threw the money into the temple and left. Then he went away and hanged himself.

The chief priests picked up the coins and said, "It is against the law to put this into the treasury, since it is blood money." So they decided to use the money to buy the potter's field as a burial place for foreigners. That is why it has been called The Field of Blood to this day.

Although the name Judas is still synonymous with betrayal, his suicide, the consequence of his choice, may be less familiar. Judas did not anticipate the cost of his bargain, just as Macbeth did not anticipate the weight of a borrowed crown upon his head or the desperate blood-letting necessary to consolidate his position. Neither did the ever-practical Lady Macbeth expect that her part in the crime would drive her to sleepwalking confessions and madness. These betrayers are ultimately betrayed by their own consciences, and the guilt of their sins costs them their lives.

"The Tell-Tale Heart." A third story of guilt comes from the master of psychological horror and one of the earlier writers of mysteries and crime fiction, Edgar Allan Poe. His short story "The Tell-Tale Heart" is a riveting account of a man who meticulously plots and murders another in cold blood while the victim lies in his bed. We as readers are drawn in by suspense as the narrator bides his time in the dark room, waiting for the precise moment to attack. We are horrified as he ultimately kills the old man, dismembers him, and hides the body. The climax, however, depends on an unexpected psychological twist in the story as the narrator willingly entertains officers of the law in the bedroom, while assuming that he has committed the perfect crime. As Poe's narrator recounts the torment that ultimately exposes him, we as readers enter into his consciousness and are subtly implicated in his crime, just as we are complicit with Macbeth by sharing his perceptions, strategies, and private agony.

Guilt is the predator that overwhelms Poe's murderer. His conscience condemns him when his intellect and reason would have guaranteed his success. As the doctor in *Macbeth* observes during Lady Macbeth's sleepwalking, "Unnatural deeds / Do breed unnatural troubles: infected minds / To their deaf pillows will discharge their secrets" (5.1.68–70).

EDGAR ALLAN POE, "THE TELL-TALE HEART," IN *THE WORKS OF THE LATE EDGAR ALLAN POE*, VOL. 1 *(New York: JS Redfield, Clinton Hall, 1850) 386–387*

The officers were satisfied. My *manner* had convinced them. I was singularly at ease. They sat, and while I answered cheerily, they chatted of familiar things. But, ere long, I felt myself getting pale and wished them gone. My head ached, and I fancied a ringing in my ears: but still they sat and still chatted. The ringing became more distinct:—it continued and became more distinct: I talked more freely to get rid of the feeling: but it continued and gained definitiveness—until, at length, I found that the noise was *not* within my ears.

No doubt I now grew *very* pale;—but I talked fluently, and with a heightened voice. Yet the sound increased—and what could I do? It was a *low, dull, quick sound—much such a sound as a watch makes when enveloped in cotton*. I gasped for breath—and yet the officers heard it not. I talked more quickly—more vehemently; but the noise steadily increased. I arose and argued about trifles, in a high key and with violent gesticulations; but the noise steadily increased. Why *would* they not be gone? I paced the floor to and fro with heavy strides, as if excited to fury by the observations of the men—but the noise steadily increased. Oh God! what *could* I do? I foamed—I raved—I swore! I swung the chair upon which I had been sitting, and grated it upon the boards, but the noise arose over all and continually increased. It grew louder—louder—*louder!* And still the men chatted pleasantly, and smiled. Was it possible they heard not? Almighty God!—no, no! They heard!—they suspected!—they *knew!*—they were making a mockery of my horror!—this I thought, and this I think. But anything was better than this agony! Anything was more tolerable than this derision! I could bear those hypocritical smiles no longer! I felt that I must scream or die!—and now—again!—hark! louder! louder! louder! *louder!*—

"Villains!" I shrieked, "dissemble no more! I admit the deed!—tear up the planks!—here, here!—it is the beating of his hideous heart!"

Conclusion

Stories have a universal, timeless appeal. They direct us through imagination, legend, myth, and religion to the truth about who we are. Guilt is an inherent part of the human condition that stems from an understanding of good and evil, right and wrong, justice and injustice. Conscience is a guide, yet the conflict between idealism and real circumstances can inhibit the clarity of the inner voice. Guilt is therefore often the subject of tragedy, of human folly and limitation, by reflecting the need for order, the consequences of events that lead to disorder, and the ultimate desire for restoration or redemption. Choices have a moral outcome because we are moral creatures, sometimes, as Macbeth, Oedipus, Judas, and Poe's protagonist learn, in spite of our deepest desires, our unwitting blindness, and our strongest denials. Literature abounds with other examples of the power of conscience and the devastation of guilt: Fyodor Dostoyevsky's *Crime and Punishment*, William Faulkner's *Absalom, Absalom!*, Nathaniel Hawthorne's *The Scarlet Letter*, and Franz Kafka's short stories. In struggling with human limitation, with questions about absolute and relative standards of morality, we find a cultural connection in myths and stories that serve as windows through which we see the world around us and as mirrors in which we strive to see and know ourselves.

QUESTIONS FOR WRITTEN AND ORAL DISCUSSION

1. Read Sophocles' *Oedipus the King*. Discuss the contribution of fate and responsibility to the guilt of Jocasta and Oedipus. To what extent are they to blame? To what extent are they victims?

2. Compare Oedipus and Macbeth. Both commit regicide and become kings. Are they equally guilty? Why or why not?

3. Discuss the responses to guilt by Judas and Poe's character. Are they different? Do their reactions fit their crimes? Does the psychological impact of guilt include a desire to be punished? Why does there seem to be a need to revisit misdoings, balancing moral accounts privately and with others?

4. Trace the development of Lady Macbeth's guilt. Compare it with Macbeth's discontent. Is Lady Macbeth's response similar to the reaction of any of the characters in the other three stories? How is madness related to guilt?

5. When does Macbeth feel guilty? Does guilt play a different role before and after he kills Duncan? Give examples.

6. Hold a classroom debate about whether guilt stems from relative or absolute standards of morality. What, for example, is the distinction between crime and sin? Are laws arbitrary or an inherent expression of human conscience? Why, for example, might you be tempted to break the speed limit but not to commit murder? Why is Macbeth commended for killing enemies on the battlefield but condemned for killing his king? Are there absolute or relative standards for our views of right and wrong?

7. Find a newspaper article about a court case. Construct an imaginative account of the social and psychological impact that the conviction will have on the person being tried, on that person's family, on the victim, or the victim's family, and on the community. Apart from the penalties imposed by the court, what are the costs of crime?

8. Recall an experience that has made you feel guilty. Try to explain the reason for the guilt. Was it fear of punishment or regret about hurting someone else? Did remorse or a confession free you from the guilt? Is punishment necessary for the cleansing of guilt?

9. One of the greatest crimes of the twentieth century was the extermination of Jews during the Holocaust. Write a research paper on the role of guilt in the aftermath of that experience. Is there national as well as personal guilt? Is the guilt of one generation visited on the next? How do we explain and understand war criminals such as Adolph Eichmann, who professed no guilt, demonstrated no re-

morse, and left Germany to begin a completely new life after the war was over?

SUGGESTED READINGS

Poe, Edgar Allan. "The Tell-Tale Heart." Found in numerous anthologies or collections of Poe's fiction.

Sophocles. *Oedipus, King of Thebes*. Available in numerous translations and anthologies.

Index

About the Author

FAITH NOSTBAKKEN teaches literature at the University of Alberta, Canada. Her research focuses on Shakespeare and Renaissance drama, and she has a particular interest in connections between the theater and its political and social context. She has published and presented papers on English history plays and critical theory.